'Fascinating'
Bryony Gordon

'An icon of the Quit Lit movement'
Condé Nast Traveller

'The first half of the book describes in graphic detail Gray's misadventures as a borderline alcoholic…but the second half jauntily and convincingly argues that sobriety can be just as enjoyable as intoxication.'
Jake Kerridge, *The Sunday Telegraph*

'She wants us to us question our reliance on drink and the way society pushes it on us. Mainly, though, without being remotely preachy, she wants to convince anyone who'll listen that a booze-free life isn't just worth living, it's better.'
Hilary Rose, *The Times*

'The appealing pitch of Gray's book is that sober life is not just good for you, it's actually better fun, too. Sobriety has had a bad rap, being equated since time immemorial with seriousness and dull, muted colours. In fact, sober life offers you the whole rainbow…She writes about her addiction with admirable honesty, and in a tone that is light, bubbly and remarkably rarely annoying.'

Alice O'Keefe, *The Guardian*

'Hard to put down! This book combines a riveting, raw yet humorous memoir with actionable and well researched advice for anyone looking for the joy of a sober lifestyle. Catherine Gray combines storytelling and science, creating a throughly readable and unexpectedly educational read. Her contribution to this genre is truly unique. Not only entertaining; it holds a universe of hope for the reader. I highly recommend this wonderful book.'

Annie Grace, author of *This Naked Mind: Control Alcohol. Find Freedom, Discover Happiness & Change Your Life*

'Like listening to your best friend teach you to be sober. Light-hearted but serious, it's packed with ideas, tools, tips and, most importantly, reasons for living a sober life. This book is excellent.'

Eric Zimmer, host of podcast *The One You Feed*

'Catherine's writing style and voice captivate me. She has a way of translating her story into an experience I don't want to end. I want to drink every drop she produces.'

Holly Whitaker, founder of Hip Sobriety School and co-presenter of *Home* podcast

'This book is great. A balanced, informative and entertaining mélange of memoir, sociology and psychology. I identified very strongly with huge sections of it.'

Jon Stewart, guitarist of Sleeper and *Leaving AA, Staying Sober* blogger

'Sober is too often equated with "sombre" in our culture. Gray's book turns that idea on its head. Her experience of sobriety is joyful and life-affirming. A must-read for anyone who has a nagging suspicion that alcohol may be taking away more than it's giving.'
Hilda Burke, psychotherapist and couples counsellor

'Catherine Gray really captures the FUN we can have in sobriety. This book challenges the status quo; sobriety sounds as liberating as taking a trip to the jungle. Fun and inspirational. What an important book for our time! A joy to read.'
Samantha Moyo, founder of Morning Gloryville

'This book is a gamechanger. Everyone deserves to have Catherine hold their hand as they navigate the new world of not drinking – whether exploring alcohol-free periods or going for full on sobriety – and this book enables just that. Wise, funny and so relatable, *The Unexpected Joy of Being Sober* adds colour to the "dull" presumption that often comes with not drinking. A book for the times as sobriety continues to be the "wellness trend to watch". Keep it in your bag as you navigate the world of not drinking, and let Catherine lead the way for you as she re-defines sobriety in the 21st century.'
Laurie, *Girl & Tonic* blogger

'Brave, witty and brilliantly written. It'll make you look at life through sharper eyes. What a revelation.'
Tracy Ramsden, features editor, *Marie Claire*

'Gray's fizzy writing succeeds in making this potentially boring-as-hell subject both engaging and highly seductive'
The Bookseller

'Haunting, admirable and enlightening'
The Pool

the

unexpected

joy of

being

sober

the
unexpected
joy of
being
sober

aster

catherine gray

*To my kindred spirits who always
want to go to one more bar.*

This is for you.

An Hachette UK Company

www.hachette.co.uk

First published in Great Britain in 2017
by Aster, an imprint of

Octopus Publishing Group Ltd
Carmelite House
50 Victoria Embankment
London EC4Y 0DZ

www.octopusbooks.co.uk
www.octopusbooksusa.com

Text copyright © Catherine Gray 2017

Design and layout copyright
© Octopus Publishing Group 2017

Distributed in the US by
Hachette Book Group
1290 Avenue of the Americas
4th and 5th Floors
New York, NY 10104

Distributed in Canada by
Canadian Manda Group
664 Annette St.
Toronto, Ontario, Canada M6S 2C8

ISBN 978-1-91202-338-7

A CIP catalogue record for this book
is available from the British Library.

Printed and bound in the UK

16 15 14 13 12

Some names and identities have been
changed to protect people's identity.

Publishing director Stephanie Jackson
Senior editor Pauline Bache
Art director Yasia Williams-Leedham
Designer Nicky Collings
Production Beata Kibil

CONTENTS

PREFACE

Joan Didion, the super-cool American essayist, said, 'I don't know what I think until I write it down.' And that's how I was. I didn't know what I thought about drinking and sobriety, until I started writing about it.

I didn't intend to write a book. At all. If I time travelled right now back to 2013 and said, 'you're going to write a book about this one day' to the Drinking Me who was desperately trying to hide her empty bottles, shaking hands and shattered soul, she would have been horrified. She would have howled with shame.

The me of 2013 wanted to shrink into the wallpaper like a nifty chameleon, not step out and hang a sign around her neck saying 'sober!' It's absolutely the pinnacle of irony that I have fulfilled the lifelong dream of publishing a book, by revealing the very secret I spent years trying to conceal. But, I like irony.

I started out by writing long posts and comments on secret sober groups on Facebook. I noticed how that straightened out my conflicted desires (Drink! Don't drink. Drink! Don't drink). After writing I felt a lot less like drinking. Writing felt like tipping the jumbled contents of my head onto a table and slotting them neatly together, like a jigsaw puzzle. Pictures formed. So, I started writing privately too. I remember sitting down at two weeks sober and finding that 3,000 words flowed out of me like water from a finally-turned-on hosepipe. Phew. I felt unburdened. So, I did it again, and again, and again, until I had 200,000 words of…total nonsense. Which I then began to slowly shape into a book.

This book took three years of a-bit-here, a-bit-there, to write. For the first two years of that, I absolutely intended to don the cloak of a pseudonym. I said to people, 'I can't talk about the shakes, about morning drinking, about promiscuity, about the wind-chime tinkle of tiny bottles in my bag, under my real name. HELL NO.'

But then I slowly realized that the people I admired the most in the sober-sphere are those who have chosen to step away from the shadows. Those who are fully 'out'. I was inspired by the 'I am not anonymous' movement*, a series of beautiful portraits of sober people. I realized that if I hid behind a fake name, I would effectively be saying that growing

*Check out www.iamnotanonymous.org. It's ace.

addicted to booze, or getting sober, are things to be ashamed of. Which they're really not. I am no longer remotely ashamed. Unveiling some of these personal details puts me well out of my comfort zone, it's true. But nothing truly great ever happens in your comfort zone.

Stigmas grow in the shadowlands. So, let's floodlight the sober movement. Alcohol is an addictive drug. There's no shame in not being able to use it moderately. You are not unusual if you can't stop at one or two. You're not broken. Or weak. You're actually the norm. Two-thirds of Brits are drinking more than they intend to.

We should be able to drop 'I don't drink' or 'I'm teetotal' or 'I'm taking a break from drinking' into conversation just as smoothly as we say 'I don't eat meat' or 'I'm a non-smoker' or 'I'm taking a break from dairy'. There shouldn't be any cringe around choosing to do something positive for your body and well-being.

Our thinking about drinking, as a society, is wonky. Drinking is not inevitable. Or compulsory. We don't need to have a doctor's note to excuse us from swan-diving into wine. We don't have to be driving to say 'no ta'. And it's not just recovering alcoholics, like me, who can choose not to drink.

We have a collective shame around feeling like we're 'failing' at alcohol. We've been conditioned into that hangdog shame. We've been taught to hide away our struggles with alcohol. It's high time that changed. It's a moonshot goal, but I'm hoping this book will help re-brand and re-align how people see sobriety. I hope this will start the 'I'm-drinking-too-much-and-I-don't-know-how-to-stop' conversation. Instead of sobriety being something a clutch of 'failed drinkers' have to do, it's something we all get to do. If we choose it.

I could say that I wrote this book purely for Britain's boozehounds, as a selfless exercise. I could say I martyred myself and bared my questionable past, to show other people how rad sobriety is. But, I did it as much for myself, as I did for you. Writing this helped me immeasurably. So, thank you for having me. For buying these pages that got me, and keep me, joyfully sober.

Catherine

INTRODUCTION

Sober

Adjective

1 Not affected by alcohol
2 Serious, sensible and solemn
3 Muted in colour

Synonyms: not intoxicated, grave, staid, businesslike, strict, puritanical, no-nonsense, plain, severe, austere, conservative, unadventurous, quiet, drab, plain.

Antonyms: drunk, light-hearted, frivolous, sensational, emotional, flamboyant.*

This is what I thought for twenty years:

'Sod that. Being sober sounds so *dull*. I do not want to live in that grey, businesslike, cold and unadventurous place. I want to live in the technicolour, sensational, opposite-of-sober instead. Let's open another bottle!'

As a teenager, I had a handmade photo frame above my bed. Inside it, there was a picture of my friends and me, curled around each other like cross-eyed kittens, batfaced after having smuggled ourselves aged 13 into a club after an Elastica gig. I'd dotted neon star stickers around it and had written, 'Reality is a hallucination brought on by lack of alcohol' with my curly, dramatic calligraphy pen. Why be sober, when you could be drunk?!

Alcohol has long been up on a throne. Anointed as the fun-king, the joy-giver, the golden gateway of social connection. Whenever anything good happens, we automatically associate celebration with the pop, fizz and glug of champagne. Meanwhile, being sober has been forever yawned at, shunned and marked as 'deprivation'. Memes smirk, 'There's a reason why "sober" and "so bored" sound almost exactly the same.' Greeting cards announce, 'Wine: It's like a hug from the inside.' Pub clapboards go viral with jibes like: 'Alcohol. Because no great love story started with eating a salad.'

An abridged version of the definition of 'sober', and synonyms and antonyms for 'sober', listed in the Oxford Living Dictionary.

Great! So, drinking is divine and being sober sucks. Gotcha.

However, if drinking is so tremendous, if it's such a bond creator, if it's such a love-story trigger, then why do so many of us desperately want to do less of it?

> WHY DO **43 PER CENT OF BRITISH WOMEN AND 84 PER CENT OF BRITISH MEN WANT TO DRINK LESS**, IF IT'S SO BRILLIANT? IF ALCOHOL IS SO WONDERFUL, WHY DID **FIVE MILLION PEOPLE SIGN UP TO DRY JANUARY IN 2017**? WEIRD CONTRADICTION, HUH?

The reason the stats don't reflect the 'drinking-is-amazing-let's-do-more-of-it' story, is because it's *not amazing.* As a society, we have a blind spot when it comes to booze. We've been brainwashed into believing it's ace, into following each other like lemmings to the pub, when deep down, we know it's not. We know it's bad for us. It causes soul-crushing hangovers and skin-crawling anxiety. It kills five times more people in Britain than traffic accidents. And yet, we bully each other into it, we drink-push, we even try to talk pregnant women into drinking despite the new 'just don't do it' guidelines.

Why do we do this? Because sobriety has such a bad rep. 'You're not drinking? Don't be boring!' Requests for soft drinks are met with outrage in pubs. Phrases like 'stone-cold sober' and 'sober as a judge' only serve to drive home this message. Nobody wants to be stony and cold; or preachy in a deeply unflattering wig, beating a hammer and shouting 'order, ORDER'.

BEING SOBER SUCKS, RIGHT?

Back in 2013, I realized that I was hopelessly addicted to alcohol. I realized that if I continued drinking, I was going to wind up drinking three-for-two wine in a bedsit, having alienated my beloved friends and family, with no career to speak of, essentially committing a very slow suicide through paint-stripper alcohol. I had an epiphany that unless I quit drinking, I was *not* going to get the life I wanted.

But, giving up drinking felt like an enormous loss. A bereavement. I was convinced it brought fun and laughter to my life. I thought, 'I will never date, dance, party or feel truly relaxed ever again.'

To my astonishment, I discovered that the actual definition of a sober life should read something like this:

Sober
Adjective
1 Not affected by alcohol
2 Bright, joyful and serene
3 Dazzling in colour

Synonyms: not intoxicated, authentic, thoughtful, kind, quick-witted, chilled, clever, adventurous, exciting, capable, reliable, fun.

I found that I was about a million times happier sober than I ever had been while drinking. As were the hundreds of sober pals I picked up along the way. I found myself with dozens more hours in the week, heaps more energy, £23,000 more money over four years, deepened friendships, revived family relationships, better skin, a tighter body, tanned legs for the first time ever (see page 174), the ability to sleep for eight uninterrupted hours, a bone-deep sense of well-being, a totally turned-around positive outlook and an infinitely more successful career. What's not to like?!

I was no longer stuck in the spiral of drink the world, snarf fried chicken, limp through work, repeat. My life had shrunk into that sad little cycle. Sober, I felt free! My world got bigger. I spent all of my newfound money on travelling. I made loads of new friends. I (eventually) stopped dating emotionally unavailable knobheads. I even learned how to dance in public sober.

See, 'stone-cold sober' needs a re-brand. It should be called 'sunshine-warm sober' instead. Because that's what it feels like. The loveliness of daylight, clarity and authentic social connection. Yes, you can no longer drink that magical potion to take social situations from level-two 'insecure' to level-eight 'pogo-ing around a dancefloor'. You need to learn how to chug through levels three to seven for real, rather than using the dark art of an addictive drug. But once you learn the superpower of socializing sober, it never leaves you. And you'll never want to go back.

There are, of course, things that I can't do now I'm sober. Bummer. Those things are: snog people I don't fancy, spend time with people I don't like, do the Macarena in front of 90 people (see page 154), dance to music I hate and laugh at jokes I don't find funny. Hmmm. Not such a great loss, is it?

BRITAIN IS SOBERING UP

Indeed, it's not just me alighting on the unexpected joy of being sober. It's not just me figuring out that it's way easier to have none at all, than to attempt ever-elusive 'moderation'.

Alcohol is a highly addictive drug that is *moreish*, like all addictive drugs. We're told we should be able to 'take it or leave it'. So when we can't stick to the recommended weekly units (I used to be able to sink a bottle-and-a-half of wine in a night, frankly), we feel defective. Fretful. And we bury that worry deep.

A third of regular drinkers are worried that they drink too much; but 51 per cent of them have done nothing about it. They feel paralysed, presumably. Sound familiar? Well, your inability to drink a bottle-and-a-half a week is not unusual, it's actually the norm. Because alcohol *is* addictive. Simple.

A quarter of British women and a fifth of Brits overall are now teetotal. 'Dry bars' are popping up all across the land, while nightclubs close in their droves. Sober raves like Morning Gloryville, are all the rage. Spending on booze, fags and drugs has fallen below £12 a week for the first time ever.

> A RECENT SURVEY FOUND THAT **43 PER CENT OF BRITS WERE TOTALLY TEETOTAL IN THE PAST WEEK**; THE HIGHEST RECORDED PERCENTAGE SINCE 2005.

Goliath brands such as Diageo, owner of Guinness, have responded to this by investing in alcohol-free drinks like Seedlip. Magazines like *Stylist* are saying that 'Being booze- and drug-free is a status symbol' and that 'we can safely assume that alcohol is on the decline.' Meanwhile, *Grazia* is running pieces about the 'sober-curious' movement. *Elle* is quoting doctors on how toxic and dastardly alcohol is to skin, the *Guardian* is printing headlines such as 'Sober is the new drunk', the *Huffington Post* is rolling with, 'Why sober sex is much better than it sounds' and *Men's Health* is saying that 'Under the influence, men are prone to lose their keys, car and dignity.'

Millennials are at the forefront of this sober-curious revolution, with only three per cent of them saying that drinking is an 'essential part of socializing', marking a massive sea change from the generation before. There's been a 40 per cent rise in millennials choosing to be teetotal. Just as it's becoming totally normal to swerve dairy or be mostly vegan, or to choose spinning and brunch rather than pub and club, it's becoming common, cool and even sought after, to be sober.

Once you see the world through sober eyes, it becomes clear that after one drink, most people are indeed looser, quicker to laugh, unclenched. However, at drink three that social alchemy begins to tarnish and rust. The looseness turns to sloppiness, the laughs become too loud, the jokes become muddled, quiet confidence turns to arrogance, mascara starts to smudge, cuddles become inappropriate. You'll wish you could hoover the wine out of their system and return them to being sober. People feel like they're more charming, more sexy, wittier and socially invincible after a few drinks. I know I did. But it's a drug-induced illusion. Just because we *feel* that way, it doesn't mean we *are* that way.

THE DRUNK-TO-SOBER RIDE

So, what's this book all about? I'm going to take you through my boozehound-to-sober journey. It's going to be pretty gnarly at the beginning, so strap in and hold tight, as we descend the white-water rapids of jail cells and morning drinking. We're then going to plummet down a log flume at the speed of a bullet train, into a pool of suicidal thoughts.

But then, we're going to do what most boozy memoirs (nicknamed 'quit lit') spectacularly fail to do. We're going to leave the fearsome waters of 'why drinking is frightful', dry off and bob happily in a boat down a Disneyland-esque lazy river, to have a look at 'why sober is better'. The bulk of this book will be about the happy-ever-after.

We'll look at why moderation is so bloody difficult to achieve and why most of us find it impossible to stick to one or two. We'll hear from experts on how putting booze into your brain and body is like filling a petrol engine up with diesel. We'll muse on how common it is for introverts to drink their way into acting like extroverts, rather than embracing their quieter, more thoughtful selves.

We'll marvel at how drink-pushy society is; delving into messages buried in alcohol advertising and hard-drinking role models on TV. We'll look at why 'I don't drink' is so much harder to say than 'I don't smoke' or 'I don't snort coke'. We'll talk about how you should be unapologetic about making the decision not to drink, rather than feeling like a buzzkill. We'll revel in the wonder of a totally hangover-free life. I'll tell you exactly what it's like to go to a wedding, deal with a job loss and kiss someone for the first time sober.

But, it's entirely up to you, what you choose to do with the alternative reality that I unroll at your feet. I'm well aware that many people reading this book have no interest in shooting for 100 per cent sobriety. I get it. I tried to keep alcohol in my life for about five years after it was definitely time to kick it out. Like a relationship I just couldn't disentangle myself from.

Just as people read a vegan book and decide to be 80 per cent vegan, that might be your choice – to shoot for eight sober days out of ten. It might be that all you want to commit to is three months off. It may be that the only consequences from your drinking are the odd horrific hangover. You may be a four on the addicted-to-alcohol spectrum, whereas I was a nine. It's not my job to convince you to quit drinking.

What is my job, however, is to show you what life would be like if you did quit. To say: why not give it a whirl? Try being sober for a while (I recommend at least 90 days). Then, you decide. But, I personally believe that totally sober is the right call. Because why bother taking a drug, when you can feel, look and be so much better without it?

I have so much to tell you. Let's begin.

I: THE NIGHTCRAWLING NETHERWORLD

I WAKE UP BEHIND BARS

SUMMER 2007

I wake up shivering. On a wafer-thin mattress. My head against a naked concrete wall. A bare bulb above me. I squint against the unforgiving light, like a vampire shrinking from the sunrise. Where the fuck am I? I struggle to sit up, hold my head in my hands for a while. Oof, that hurts. If I was in a cartoon, stars would circle my head.

I see bars blocking the windows. A brick wall beyond. It looks like I'm in a jail cell. That can't be right.

'Excuse me,' I shout, through a foot-thick door.

No answer.

'EXCUSE ME', in an imperious tone, as if I'm not being served in a restaurant.

A police officer swooshes a partition open with a snap and peers in at me, through a porthole.

'Where am I?' I demand.

'Brixton police station,' he replies, patiently.

'Why?'

'You were arrested last night for being drunk and disorderly. A police officer was trying to help you get home. You told her to eff off.'

I pause, as the blood-freezing horror of my predicament chills me. I recall snatches of talking to a nice but weary doctor, who asked me how much I'd drunk, asked me to walk in a straight line. I have zero memory of a police officer.

'Well, can I leave now?'

'Nope. Doctor says you'll be sober enough to leave at 9am.'

'But I have to be at work at 9.30am! I have to be getting on the train at 8.30!'

'Sorry, that's just how it is…You seem like a nice enough girl, why did you drink so much?'

I have no response. The truth is, I don't know how to answer his 'why?' I never really feel like I have a choice. Once I start drinking, I finish. And 99.9 per cent of the time, I get trashed. Hammered. Wasted. Lifting the wine once seems to lead to me lifting it until I can no longer lift it, because I've run out of money, or my friend is making me go home, or all the bars have shut, or indeed, because I'm unconscious in a jail cell.

I'm outraged. How dare they incarcerate me for simply swearing? Whatever happened to freedom of speech? Or is that an American thing? I desperately need the loo, but the only option is a very non-private one in the corner, and they could slide the partition back open at any time. I feel like a caged animal.

It's a work day! I need to be at work. I should be showering now. Trying to firefight last night's damage to my hair and face. At 9am they finally release me. I have to pay a £90 fine, but I won't be charged, or have to go to court. I've been let off lightly. I should be grateful. Instead, I'm fuming.

'I'll just get your belongings,' an officer says.

He seems to be amused about something. He seems like he's trying not to laugh.

I harumph and sigh deeply at his delay. Well, at least I still have my handbag. Small mercies.

He hands me a plastic evidence bag. Inside, there's a tiny, watermelon-pink, glittery child's hairbrush. A TINY PINK HAIRBRUSH. That's it. I've never seen this hairbrush before. No handbag, no keys, no phone, no money, no cards, no nothing. I redden with shame and further outrage, stomping out of the police station, muttering about filing a complaint.

I manage to get into my flat because my freelance flatmate hasn't left for his meeting yet. 'Jeez, what happened to you?' he says, stepping back with alarm when he claps eyes on me.

I crawl into bed and call my boyfriend from the house phone to tell him what happened. (He is the only person I ever, ever tell, until six years later, when I get sober.) He tells work he has a family emergency and comes around to cuddle me while I cry. About how unfair it all is. Of course I got hammered at the free-drinks work party, doesn't everyone?! If only that stupid do-gooder police officer hadn't tried to help me, I'm sure I would have found my own way home.

I roll into work four hours late. My lovely boss called me at 10.30am on my landline saying that she'd heard I was in a state last night, and to sleep a little more, have some tea and recover, before coming in. Talk about forgiving! But judging by the long-suffering look on her face when I walk into the office, I don't think she meant for me to take half of the day off. (I later get told in a kindly, gentle performance review that she was 'very disappointed' in me that day. Understatement of the century.)

Last night was the work summer party, so everyone knows why I'm so late, everyone knows I'm hungover as hell, and everyone is crazily unimpressed. 'We managed to get to work on time, and we're hungover too, why couldn't you?' one workmate says. I keep my head down and long for home time.

I try to pinpoint where my memory starts skipping and fuzzing, like an illegal DVD. Around 9pm, when it was still light. Apparently, we went from the pub on to Beach Blanket Babylon, a fantastically opulent bar that looks like a Greek god's palace, and where the golden-heeled Chelsea set hang. I have no memory of being in there. Apparently, I got kicked out, for being off my face.

Then, I was told I got into a cab around midnight with some colleagues back to Brixton, where my fairly new flat share is. But I couldn't remember my address. Nope. No idea where I lived. So they dropped me on Brixton Hill, a five-minute walk away, because I knew it was somewhere near there. And then I must have encountered the police officer while trying to lurch home. Who arrested me for being drunk and disorderly, as well she should.

In Brixton, no less. For those of you who don't know this part of South London, it's really, really difficult to get arrested for being drunk and disorderly in Brixton. Back in 2007, it was the kind of place where you got offered drugs by 'psssst'-dealers when you exited the tube at 6pm. Post 9pm, it was utter bedlam.

This was well before Brixton started to become hipster-gentrified and rolled in chia seeds, this was way before the vintage market and the polished noodle bars, years before the cocktails in jam jars and the overpriced vinyl and the Reformer Pilates studios, yonks before the bearded elite of London drove their MGs in and began driving the prices up.

This was when Brixton was still *grimy*. When the residents were still as poor as church mice. It was where you went when you couldn't get in anywhere else. The end of the night, the end of the road, the end of the world. You could get into my favourite pubs there, the Dogstar, Mango Landing and Hootananny, even if you were blackout drunk and could barely stand. Which was probably why they were my favourite pubs.

I once saw a woman get off a bus in Brixton at 2am, have a poo on the side of the street, and then get back onto the bus like 'what?', as if she'd just popped off to pick up a forgotten shopping bag. Drinking excessively was child's play in Brixton back then; I saw people shoot up in the park. It was the Babylonian corner of London where you could be a total maniac and blend into the maniac wallpaper, because there was always someone drunker or more aggressive or more nuts than you.

So, it's almost impressive that I managed to outshine the motley crew of other drunks that night and bag a place in one of the scarce cells. I must have been a real piece o' work.

I don't drink that Friday night, after waking up in the cell. But on Saturday, I get back on it. Of course I do. I think I deserve to. I think it's still fun, despite the horrifying experience I have had a mere 32 hours previous.

My life has become a zoetrope. Those spinning toys where you look through the slats and see a sketched figure doing the same thing over and over. Just like that figure, I feel stuck in a pre-destined sequence, a rut of kismet. Drink, hangover, squirm from beneath the consequences, recover, drink, hangover, squirm…

It seems inevitable, this hellish whirligig. How do I get off? How do I emancipate myself from this repetitive sequence? Draw a new one? The enormity of it hurts my brain. I don't know how. So I drink more instead.

GETTING SMASHED IN SUBTERRANEAN SOHO

'Drinking steals happiness from tomorrow'

– UNKNOWN

The first time I got drunk I felt like I'd finally unzipped my 'wrong' skin and slipped into a slinky new one. One that felt ridiculously right. One without the spiky inhibitions. It was like taking off chainmail and slipping into a heavenly silk gown.

More than four in ten people who start drinking before the age of 15 will eventually become addicted to alcohol. I was 12 when I started. As an incredibly nervous kid, I began to believe that relief resided in bottles. That great stories were at the bottom of glasses. That booze was anaesthetic for my ever-present anxiety.

Before drinking, my life had felt terribly dull. I started out with the classy combo of drinking White Lightning cider in the car park of McDonald's. By the age of 13, I was clubbing up to three times a week. My best mate and I fell in with a crowd of 17-year-olds who dressed us up in their clothes, helped us with our make-up and snuck us into The Venue and The Dorchester in Wolverhampton.

I was an indie kid, a grebo, who burned incense until my room stank of sandalwood, pierced my nose with a tiny silver stud, hennaed my hair and completed the effect with Doc Marten's and tiny flowery dresses. I pored over *Melody Maker* and the *NME*, and waited outside HMV the day the new Weezer album was out. I basically wanted to be Angela Chase in *My So-Called Life*.

Magazines were my obsession; an escape from my humdrum existence. Every Wednesday I would hotfoot it to the newsagents with 70p in my hand, to buy *Just Seventeen*, and then trip over myself as I walked to the bus-stop reading it. Later, I became obsessed with *Minx*, *19*, *Glamour* and *Cosmopolitan*. I read about Justine *Elastica* and Sonya *Echobelly* and Marijne *Salad* and Louise *Sleeper* running around Soho and Camden. I wanted to go join them but I lived in Dudley, a running joke of a backwater Black Country town. People literally laughed in my face when I said I lived in Dudley.

Life was too sharp, too painful, too real and too loud when I was sober. Drinking softened the edges and blurred the clarity. It turned an intimidating Andy Warhol pop-art world into a misty Monet watercolour. Sober, nightclub dancefloors were about as appealing as the Mad Max Thunderdome. Drunk, they were my domain. It made me party-ready when I was party-meh. But, it wasn't real. That me was not *me*.

Blackouts were commonplace right from the get-go. I thought everyone experienced lost hours of nights out – turns out they don't. I thought everyone felt jangly-nerved and ill-fitting until they'd had a drink – turns out they don't. I'd always felt like I was on the outside, looking into social situations, never quite able to fully shed my inhibitions and engage. Booze opened the door, beckoned me in from the cold and thrust me into the thick of the party.

I only attended about a quarter of my lectures at university and yet, I managed to somehow scrape a 2:1, like a magician summoning coins from their sleeve. I thought I was addicted to going out with my mates, but the truth was, when all of my uni friends vacated the town for the summer and I stayed on to work my bar job, I still drank just as hard. With any company I could find, including the dubious regulars at the pub. Are you a big drinker? Great! Let's get blitzed.

I wrote dozens of letters begging for work experience on magazines. I spent a year doing a dull job in marketing to save money. I finally got my toe through the door and after a year of hardscrabble interning at *Glamour* and *Cosmopolitan*, I was offered a junior role at the latter.

I LAND IN SOHO

I loved my job and worked dang hard. But, my job came with a catch. A catch that I regarded as a boon. My job gave me access to nightly parties. I could drink most nights for free, if I wanted to. I wanted to.

I made the louche underbelly of Soho my home, chasing the night right until the end. I learned where the secret subterranean speakeasy bar was, Trisha's, hidden behind a gleaming cornflower-blue residential door, and learned the code word to get in. Trisha's was cluttered with tat, it reeked of fags, the wallpaper was peeling and the wine was warm. It never closed though, so it was my nirvana.

I watched Amy Winehouse perform an impromptu gig in a scruffy cubby-hole of a jazz bar on Greek Street. As she sang, 'They tried to make me go to rehab, I said no, no, no' I sang along. 'She can barely stand,' my mate whispered to me. I shrugged. I thought she was cool.

I blagged my way into the VIP room of a spangled casino hotel by saying I was Delta Goodrem (if you squinted, and it was very dark, I could have been back then, just). My mate and I (he was supposedly Brian McFadden, her boyfriend at the time) shared the living-room-sized space of the VIP with Victoria Beckham and Gordon Ramsay. We danced with them to Britney. Until the barman kindly escorted us out. VB sent us a bottle of champagne as a consolation prize.

I hung out in a handsome '50s mahogany-panelled, cigar-scented member's bar, with a Mafia-esque vibe, where men with magnificent moustaches would have cradled brandy and struck business deals. As I was leaving one night, I saw Christian Slater. I bounced over and told him I'd loved him in *Pump Up the Volume*. He said, 'Hang on, don't go' and invited me to join him for a drink. He said he liked my name, and rolled it around on his tongue like a butter candy. Cath-er-ine Graaaay.

I stayed out until 6am doing karaoke with Johnny Vegas. That night, rather than going home, which was pointless, I napped in the ladies' toilet at the *Cosmopolitan* offices, where I worked, and tried to wash myself in the sink.

I wangled backstage tickets to Live 8 and met Madonna, Sting, Snoop Dogg, Paris Hilton, the Kaiser Chiefs, Richard Ashcroft and the Stereophonics, collecting celebrity handshakes like I was collecting face cards during a game of poker. After the concert I drank with Jo Whiley and Fearne Cotton, pow-wowing about who was the best act. Sunshiny Fearne and I hit it off. She invited me to an after-show party with Razorlight. 'Please come. I need a wingwoman.'

I smoked weed with Finley Quaye. Stephen Dorff invited me to a Girls Aloud gig. Marco Pierre White told me he loved me at the end of our interview and invited me to dine anytime at his restaurant for free, which I never got around to doing, because, well, drinking got in the way. Eating was cheating. I always went for drinks, not dinner, even a free Michelin-starred dinner. I judged people who left wine on the table as harshly as I judge people who leave dogs in hot cars.

I was flown to Washington, DC first class when I worked at *Glamour*, and put up in an elegant five-star hotel to interview Reese Witherspoon. The moment the interview was in the bag, I went to a pavement cafe amid the rainbow townhouses of Georgetown and sank wine after wine, telling myself I was 'experiencing' DC. (It makes me want to cry that I didn't actually explore that great city.) I was invited to the White House to meet Michelle Obama the next day (along with about 100 other people). Even though I was scrubbed and coiffed for my trip to The White House, my hangover was bone-deep. When Michelle looked at me, shook my hand and said 'hello', her forehead furrowed with concern. (Smart woman, Michelle.)

This was the dream, no? This was the kind of life everyone wanted. My friends kept telling me how jealous they were of my job. I worked my tail off during the day and shook my tailfeather at night. I took the odd night off and pounded my urge to drink into submission at the gym.

But inside, cracks were beginning to show. I lived in a state of perpetual alarm that I would be busted, for lying about fictitious food poisoning, or that my blackout tryst with my male co-worker would be revealed. Fear ate away at me like invisible termites inside the walls of a house. My very structure and foundations were beginning to falter.

THE PARTY ROAD TOLL
The partying took its physical toll. Calling in sick to work became a regular occurrence. I told myself that because I never phoned in sick when I was actually ill (instead I would inflict my infections upon my co-workers, which was nice of me) I deserved a few hangover sickies. I used to note them in my calendar so that I knew how many I'd taken that year. Why did I deserve days off when my other hard-working colleagues didn't take them? Dunno. I felt like the world owed me a favour somehow.

The hangovers that I saved my sick days for were the paralyzing ones. The times when I felt I literally could not move from my bed for the entire day. Or the times when I woke up wearing last night's clothes, on the other side of London from my flat, at 10am (which was often).

I was often cautioned about having too many sick days in work reviews by my managers. They would make embarrassed jokes about me perhaps needing to take more vitamins, or gently temper the criticism with praise on how great my work ethic was the rest of the time. In the big picture, I was getting away with it. I was promoted again and again. I won an award for being Best Editorial Newcomer, and was shortlisted for another.

Nonetheless, the words 'can I have a word with you?' or a jokey 'I have a bone to pick with you' could send me into a terrified spin. My post-spin strategy? Patching up my hungover face and charging out into London to do it all over again.

I suffered from Wishful Drinking. Tonight would be the night I cracked it. The night I would have two drinks in the pub, laugh with my friends and go home, rosy-faced and aglow with wine, to make a stir-fry and have an early night. Tomorrow would be the morning I would actually get up and go for the 7am run before work, rather than groaning and stabbing at the alarm to make it stop. Like the desert spring the dying man crawls towards endlessly, but never reaches, I was never able to locate that oasis.

My ideal 'tonight' and 'tomorrow' remained shimmering in the distance. The vegetables for the stir-fry always lost their will to live in my fridge. It was always the same last-orders outcome. The same dejected night bus, the same urgent scrabbling in the morning, standing in the shower willing the water to wash off my shame, the same bacon sandwich at my desk with a full-fat Coke.

I was scared to sit still. To stay in. To take a long hard look at myself. If I kept going out, kept drinking, kept running this-a-way and that-a-way, I wouldn't have to actually confront what I'd become. A fraud, beneath the sequined dress and make-up. A liar who didn't actually want to lie but kept finding herself in situations where the options were: a) get dumped by your boyfriend, b) lie. Or, a) get sacked, b) lie. Or, a) get kicked out of your house by your flatmate, b) lie.

Lying was simply something I had to do to survive.

Sometimes I had to write down the lies to remember them accurately. I would rehearse them in a soft voice in my room before seeing the unfortunate recipient of the lie, like an actor running lines. The thing with lying to everyone, to varying degrees? No one ever truly knows you. Which is a really lonely place to live.

But I also felt indignant. Why did the universe keep curve-balling these impossible dilemmas and predicaments my way?! It wasn't fair. I truly could not see that booze was a villain, rather than a hero. I thought it was the pain-remover, rather than the source of the pain. And I couldn't see that I was complicit. I was happening to life; life wasn't just happening to hapless me. I was the architect of my own destruction every single time, along with my trusty sidekick, wine.

An unnamed dread spread inside me like an ink blot. My fear that something Godawful was about to happen became more and more urgent. The 'watched' feeling grew. I was convinced people were starting to notice. I felt like cornered quarry. The only thing that drowned the dread, that pulverized the paranoia, was more wine.

FAKE BONDS

At any given party, my real friends would leave at a semi-sensible time. They could drink (otherwise they wouldn't have been my friends at all, frankly) but they couldn't drink like me. Hell no. So, come 1am, when I was just getting warmed up, I would find myself short of a wingwoman.

No matter, though. I would generally have spotted and already started grooming a BBF (Boozy Best Friend) for the night. As Sacha Z. Scoblic writes in the brilliant *Unwasted: My Lush Sobriety*, 'Already living life underwater, I grabbed at other people's legs as they swam by and tried to pull them down with me.'

I would cozy up to her and, with the help of several glasses of intimacy-accelerator, we would bond. Only, it was a totally fake bond. A 'fond', as I like to call it. We would stumble around a dancefloor together and then find a lock-in and shout at each other until dawn. Disclose relationship woes, bitch about mutual friends/work colleagues, recount dark episodes from our childhood. Y'know, the secret stuff that you really only tell people after you've known them for, oh, around three solid years. All of that would come tumbling out, on the wine waterslide.

The next time I saw my BBF, it would be excruciatingly awkward. Willing-a-meteor-to-hit-you awkward. Scanning-the-street-for-a-car-to-throw-yourself-under awkward. We would be crawling into work late. Or bump into each other in the supermarket. And the cringe would begin. 'So, last night/week was crazy, huh? Errr…' The vestiges of our newfound affection nowhere to be found.

I reasoned that the *lack* of alcohol was the problem. The fact we were both now sober was the reason these encounters were butt-clenchingly bad. My addictive voice said that wine was the fairy dust new friendships needed. That without it, things weren't as magical, like a snow globe before you shake it. We just needed to get drunk together again, and then the shimmer would start to dust us once more.

The truth was actually the polar opposite. We had accelerated to levels of intimacy that it takes years to build. And in the sober light of day, our 'fond' became exposed for what it actually was: a sham.

I START TO LOSE MORE THAN MY BAG

Alcohol unlocked my true self, I thought. I was willing to pay for that luxury. Sober, I just felt *wrong*.

What I didn't know was how terribly high the price was going to be. It was going to cost me friends, familial love, many boyfriends, the respect of my colleagues and all of my self-esteem. It was going to place me in dangerous situations – scenarios in which it was amazing I wasn't killed.

The pace was glacial, over the next 21 years. The scary times were one in a hundred. Then they were one in ten. Then every other time. Then just every single time. But I'd long forgotten there was an alternative.

Addiction has an imperceptible grip, that tightens ever-so-gradually. Nobody wakes up one day and suddenly can't stop drinking. The progression is apparent to others perhaps, but mostly dismissed with quizzical glances. However, the person themselves is usually totally oblivious, because they are shrouded deep in denial. Deep, deep, deep in denial.

For me, addiction manifested itself in the breaking of hundreds of tiny rules. Tiny threads that tethered me to the ground snapped, one by one. The rules of Normal Drinking. I never thought I'd use my last grocery money to buy wine; until I did. I never thought I'd drink in the morning; until I did. And once you've broken a rule once, it becomes very easy to break it again. And again.

FAILED MODERATION ATTEMPTS

'Trying to have "just one drink of alcohol" is like trying to knock just one domino down in a huge line of them.'
– CRAIG BECK, ALCOHOL LIED TO ME

In 2009, it became clear to me that I did not have a grip on my drinking. At all.

Now that I wasn't in my early 20s, when you're 'supposed' to be a hellraiser, I was starting to worry. I had noticed that my friends' drinking was slowing down, as mine sped up. They were decreasing their intake as the demands of their jobs increased. I wasn't. They could drink one or two on a week night and go home. I…couldn't.

My drinking had previously proffered cute, funny stories. Like the time I tried to open the door to my flat, that I shared with a girl called Nat. My key wouldn't work. WTF? A man opened the door. 'Who are you?!' I asked, outraged. 'What have you done with Nat?' I peered behind him, willing to fight if I saw a gagged-and-bound Nat. Of course, I was trying to get into the wrong flat. He patiently explained this to me, several times, before I stopped trying to rescue Nat from this flat-hijacker. The next day I left them a bottle of wine (what other present could they possibly want) as a gift with an apology note.

So. There were less funny stories these days. And more scary stories that I kept secret. Like a wet gremlin fed after midnight, my drinking had mutated from fluffy to frightening. It'd grown teeth and claws. I would go out, totally intending to be home by 10.30pm to watch *Lost* before bed and get a solid eight hours' sleep; I would end up getting home at 2am, steaming, on a school night, having spent the last £20 in my bank account on the cab.

It was so demoralizing, never being able to live up to my best intentions. What I wanted to do, and what I ended up doing, never matched. My friends turned my name into a verb that was shorthand for getting obliterated and rolling home in the wee hours – 'I got "Cathed" last night.' People frequently called me 'trouble'. They did so affectionately. But I was. I was trouble.

At 8am, the morning after a big night, I would lay down a cast-iron rule that I would not. drink. that. night. Definitely not. No drinking tonight.

No way! But my mind would slowly dismantle it, as the day rolled on. By 3pm, the rule had been chucked out of the window, and I was sending out a blanket text to ten friends saying 'drink tonight?' I didn't care who I went out with, really: as long as I went out.

The dark side of my drinking had become horror-show scary. I was terrified that I was going to lose my lovely job at *Glamour*, my lovely flat with my best mate from university and my lovely boyfriend, if I continued. So, I decided to take control of booze (ha). I bought a beautiful golden notebook and started a 'drink less' project within it. I would outfox alcohol! I wrote curly, thoughtful notes in it about how much my life would improve if I stopped getting wankered all the time.

In the golden book that was going to help me drink less (yes it was), I wrote 'our secrets make us sick' and underlined it three times. Drew stars either side of it. I felt like my secrets were making me sick. I didn't know where I'd heard that phrase but it had snuck into my brain and rattled around in there for years. Like a coin that finds its way into the lining of a jacket.

And so, with the advent of the golden 'drink less' book, began my many, many failed moderation attempts:

1. NOT KEEPING 'SPARE' ALCOHOL IN THE HOUSE
It was becoming indisputable that if I bought a bottle of wine, I drank a bottle of wine. So, I decided that I would manage my consumption at home by only buying those teeny tiny 250ml bottles. It worked, for a while. Until it didn't.

2. GOING TO THE GYM DIRECTLY AFTER WORK
I figured out that after a good, hard work-out and a cleansing sauna, I felt less like sitting on my roof terrace and mainlining wine while smoking and staring at the sky. Hallelujah! So, I started taking my gym bag to work and going directly to the gym from the train station. My house was a four-minute walk from the station, but I lugged the gym bag around all day regardless, because I knew if I went home, I'd end up saying 'fuck it' and going to get a bottle.

The gym strategy worked for a good long while – a year maybe. Until I started telling myself that I needed a 'treat' for going to the gym, and that treat was, of course, wine.

3. 'FREE DRINKS PARTIES' BAN

Eureka! I had it. There appeared to be a direct correlation between my disgrace-filled 'what did I doooo?' blackouts and free drinks parties. I wrote in my little gold book that clearly free drinks parties were bad news, and that I should avoid them from now on. What happened as a result? I stopped going to free drinks parties. And started spending way more money on drinking.

4. THE 'FOUR DAYS A WEEK DRY' STUNT

At the start of the week, I would write in my diary which days I could drink, and which days I couldn't. The plan was to keep drinking to three nights a week. Easy, right?

Except, it didn't work. I never managed it. Not even once. My record was three nights off. I could white-knuckle my way through dry nights, but I felt thoroughly deprived. A thought-loop circled around my brain. 'I am not drinking. I am not drinking. I can't drink tonight. I am not drinking.'

I wasn't drinking, but all I could think about was not-drinking. I thought it proved I wasn't addicted, but actually, it proved that I was.

5. A UNIT TALLY RECORD

Then, I started a unit diary in the golden book, whereby I would count how many units I had consumed. The aim was to try, desperately, to keep it under 30 per week, or three bottles of wine. I'd written a health piece for *Glamour*, in which an expert had said that 30 units a week was probably safe-ish. However, I kept clearing 50 units, or even 60, and having to write notes to myself in it. Like a furious teacher on a disappointing essay. Angry, spiky notes saying things like, 'Why are you so bad at this?!' Or, 'This has to stop!!' Or, 'This amount can kill you long-term!!!' So, yeah, the unit diary was a bust. I stopped keeping it. It became too depressing. It was like a numerical catalogue of my downward spiral.

6. THE DRINK-SWITCH FIX

Another bright idea. 'It's white wine! That's my problem. It's just too strong and too easy to down. I'll switch to red.'
Still drinks four or five big glasses.

'Er, OK, um. It's wine! Wine is the problem. I need to try more voluminous drinks with less alcoholic content.'
Switches to cider. Still gets trollied each and every time.

'I need to order a pint of tap water with every drink! That'll do it. There'll be so much water sloshing around in my belly, that I won't want as much cider.'
Ends up being a drunk girl who needs to pee every ten minutes.

7. POST-IT NOTES IN PURSE FORAY

I started writing notes to myself and putting them in my wallet; tangible reminders of how much I intended to drink, before I started drinking. The notes said things like, 'three beers and no more!' Every morning I would look at the Post-it in defeat, screw it up and bin it. 'Next time. Next time I will nail this moderate-drinking thing.' I remember telling a similarly heavy-drinking friend about the notes I wrote to myself, before a night out. She looked at me like I was a basketcase. I thought she'd get it. She didn't.

My life was just a string of 'next time' moderation attempts.

Nobody had the foggiest, not a notion, that I was engaged in this relentless struggle. This eternal quest: the three-drinks-and-then-home quest. Or the 'don't-go-back-out-to-the-off-licence-tonight-after-you've-finished-this-bottle' mission. Regardless of my best intentions, I would always stagger home after five drinks, or sneak back out to the shop for 'just one can of cider'.

I would tell myself that the 11pm cider was a night-cap. Like in black-and-white movies. Very civilized. Like Audrey, or Greta, or any of the celluloid icons. I would think this as I was stumbling down the street in my trackie bottoms and a ignominy-covering cap; the irony was completely lost on me.

I once passed my suave banker neighbour and his friend while on a trackie-bottom mission for 'just one more'. When they saw me they burst out laughing. I must have been weaving across the pavement. The shame literally stung me. I stopped in the street and fought back tears. My solution? To drink the shame-sting away. I drank on the humiliation of having been drunk so, so many times.

My friends, my boyfriend, my family: none of them knew about my moderation battle. Because I didn't tell them. I kept it locked down and secret. Because I knew, somewhere at my very core, that this was not 'normal'. That other people didn't put this much time and energy into trying to only drink three drinks.

WHY MODERATE DRINKING IS SO DANG HARD

I was only perhaps a six on the addictive spectrum when I was cycling through these failed moderation attempts. I would find success short-term, and then my drinking would always slalom out of control again. Why is moderate drinking so hard to achieve, even before you're a seven, eight or nine on the addictive scale?

'Alcohol is a disinhibitor,' says psychotherapist Hilda Burke.* It causes us to behave more impulsively. 'Someone can go out intending to "have a couple", but after the first drink that resolve has lessened, and by the end of the second, it's been drowned out.'

> 'ALSO, THE DRINKER'S SELF-IMAGE IS AT PLAY.
> MANY CLIENTS I'VE WORKED WITH HAVE AN
> **IDENTITY THAT IS BOUND UP WITH ALCOHOL.'**

'They see themselves as bubbly, wild or spontaneous,' continues Burke. 'Often those labels are treasured. It's something they've been rewarded for; people find them entertaining and they get invited to every party. If they feel those "likeable" qualities are dependent upon alcohol, it can be very scary to imagine living without it. It could be a cover for shyness and social unease. Whipping that comfort blanket away could unearth a raft of anxieties.'

I relate, massively. I was always the 'party girl'. I didn't know who I would be without drinking, and that scared me. What about you?

For me, I found that zero drinks were a lot easier than the ever-elusive one or two. 'If you're failing to moderate, then abstinence is the best option. It's easier to be abstinent than moderate,' says neuroscientist Alex Korb.

'The chains of habit are too light to be felt until they are too strong to be broken.'
– SAMUEL JOHNSON

*Check out www.hildaburke.co.uk.

I WALK DRUNK PEOPLE HOME
DECEMBER 2009

Myself, Suzy and Kate are drinking in Balham. We're nearing kicking-out time. I can't take my eyes off a girl slumped alone in the corner, wearing a lopsided paper crown. She's clearly been at her work Christmas party.

It's not just me watching her. There are a couple of lone men at the bar whose eyes linger on her. Sizing her up like hungry coyotes. I insist to my friends that we walk her home. I've been her. All too often, lately. Which is why I want to look after her.

A FEW DAYS LATER
I am changing tubes at Stockwell when I see a woman in her late 30s, wearing a party dress, collapsed on a bench, vomiting. People are walking past her, cracking jokes, gazes sliding off her with disgust. The Underground staff are ignoring her.

I give her a tissue, some water, ask where she lives and get the tube with her. I help her walk home and open her door. All she's saying is, 'Thank you, thank you, thank you.'

I've done both of these women a good turn, but it's not entirely selfless. I hope that I've just put some money into the karmic piggybank. That I can withdraw the next time I am smashed and unable to get myself home. Before the hungry coyotes descend.

THE SHAKES SET IN
JULY 2010: I GET THE SHAKES FOR THE FIRST TIME
Having drunk my usual bottle of wine the night before, I'm on the train to work, trying to apply mascara. My hand's trembling. And the train is stationary, so I can't blame it. I shake it, bemused, clench and unclench my fingers, then try again. Nope. It flutters in front of my eyes, useless.

A guy sitting opposite me has clocked what's going on, and looks mildly amused. I pack my make-up away and resolve to do it later, in private. Fear flashes through me like an electrical surge. I've always reasoned that since I never get the shakes, I can't be an alcoholic. 'Look', I would say smugly to dejected, hungover friends, the morning after. *Holds out steady-as-a-surgeon hands*

I eat a full English breakfast and it goes away. An anomaly, I reason. Low blood sugar. Must remember to eat breakfast. That's all it is.

PITY PARTY FOR ONE

'I tried to drown my sorrows, but the bastards learned how to swim.'

– FRIDA KAHLO

In June 2010, a couple of months after my 30th birthday, I was dumped by my beloved boyfriend of three years, Seb. 'I know we'll get married if we stay together, because I do love you,' he said, sitting on the edge of my bed, staring at the floor. 'But I don't think we'll be happy.'

I didn't know it at the time, but he was absolutely right. 'It's like you *look* for things to be unhappy about,' he would say. And I did. Because they were great excuses to drink.

He took me to Paris for my 30th. The day before my actual birthday, I had a 50-person-strong party planned, in a posh rooftop bar in Soho. When he presented me with the tickets and I saw that our Eurostar to Paris was leaving at 8am the next morning, I was furious with him. 'We'll need to get up at 6am!' I wailed to my friends. 'AFTER MY PARTY.' I thought he was so selfish, and I told him so.

The Paris episode was just one in a long line of times I acted like a selfish brat, a controlling shrew, or a manipulative wretch. In retrospect, Seb was very wise to dump me. Good call, Seb.

I was utterly heartbroken. In the wake of the break-up, I started hosting my very own pity parties. Invited: me and alcohol. I didn't know it at the time, but I was starting to isolate. Staying home, turning down invitations to go out, in order to be able to drink as hard and as fast as I liked, without outside interference.

Going out had lost its allure. I told myself I was too tired, I couldn't be bothered, maybe I was growing up and 'nesting'. But the reality was, I didn't want to have to socialize in order to get smashed any more.

Going out presented irksome drinking-delays. People taking far too ruddy long to get their round in, despite my looking pointedly at my forlorn, empty wine glass. People wanting to eat, which was unnecessary, in my view, when there was serious drinking to be done.

My indignation was also laced with fear. That step into the unknown night, which had once filled me with the exhilaration of possibility, had become more like base-jumping. I didn't know if I'd survive it.

So, I would arrive home, breathe a giant sigh of relief, throw my bag and coat on the floor, skip to the kitchen and pour myself a giant glass of Sauvignon Blanc. I would then sit in the garden, 'watch the sunset' and smoke skinny menthols.

I would look at pictures of Seb and me on Facebook, switching the radio station to Magic FM, the saddest love-song station in Britain, in order to enhance my wallowing, like you would enhance a movie by watching it in HD. Think Roxette, 'It must have been love', The Cranberries, 'Linger', Natalie Imbruglia, 'Torn'.

The first time I drank alone on sorrow was eight years previous. I was 22 and I'd just been dumped by a guy I'd been fixated on for about a year. We'd only had about seven dates (love addict! More about this later). He told me via text that it wasn't working for him any more and my response was to listen to sad songs over and over (Daniel Bedingfield, 'If you're not the one', Radiohead, 'Creep'), drink eight beers, cry until my face was double the size and lie on the floor wailing dramatically. I thought I was in love with him, when I didn't even know the dude.

Before the wine was finished, given my visceral fear of the empty bottle, I would go and get a bottle of cider or beer, to top off the wine nicely. I would, of course, go to a different off-licence to the shop where I had purchased the original bottle of wine.

I never, ever, ever bought my sum-total night's alcohol in one shop. Two trips to the off-licence was standard. This was because I always started the night with the intention of consuming a certain amount. And it would always, always end up being more.

I liked the victim costume. It was warm, comfortable, unchallenging. A fleecy onesie I could hide away in. To sort through the shards of my self-smashed love life with honesty would require catching glances of myself. So, I chose to see things through the twisty prism of the wine glass.

I turned Magic FM up, scrolled for sad films and thought some more about how the world had done me wrong. What would you call multiple sorrows, I wondered? A herd? A clutch? A maudlin. That's it.

PHYSICAL ADDICTION

'Shame is a soul eating emotion.'
– CARL JUNG

Shortly after my professional pity parties began, I landed an enormous job as features editor on a million-selling magazine, *Fabulous*. My duties included heading up the features team, managing two full-time staff and two freelancers. Presenting ideas to fifteen people every morning in a boardroom.

I couldn't hack it. The pressure was intense. I just wanted to take the fat pay cheque and hotfoot home at 5.30pm to dive into the wine. This didn't go down well. I was desperately unhappy there, and they were far from happy with me, so I quit to go freelance.

Freelance, I was finally able to drink the way I wanted to. I would start drinking at 3pm, while interviewing people from my sofa. Over the next two years, I gradually slipped into physical addiction.

Here's what it feels like to be physically addicted to alcohol. People describe the booze buzz as a click or a warm glow. And sure, it was like that for a time. Back in the beginning, it was like drinking sunshine; it made me feel brighter, warmer, lazier.

Gradually, the alcohol broke. It stopped giving me the warmth, the click, the buzz. And started to feel as imperative as oxygen. When I wasn't drinking, I felt like I was suffocating. When I got the oxygen, I gulped it hungrily, needily. The hardest bit was, I had to obtain the oxygen, while seeming nonchalant about it. Like I didn't need it.

Sidling into the shop and just-so-happening to buy a bottle of wine. Walking into your friend's kitchen and saying, 'oh, go on then, if you're having one'. Or, 'I haven't had any in three days after all, haha.' (They didn't ask.)

I would breathe in half the amount I actually wanted, and wait for them to offer more. All the while feeling like I just wanted to grab the bottle and pour it into my face, urgently.

Most physically addicted drinkers deserve an Oscar.

THE TYRANNY OF TOO MANY BOTTLES

In 2012, I started hiding bottles. Stuffing the cold, hard evidence into public bins, rather than into my own rubbish. Or, glancing up and down the street shiftily, before slipping them into a neighbour's recycling bin. 'That bottle is their problem now! Ha. Theirs. Not mine.'

As soon as I walked into any house, say if I was staying at a friend's for the weekend, I would subconsciously scout the area for bottles. I became a bottle-spotter, who makes mental notes, just as a train-spotter would. Russian vodka in the freezer: noted. Three bottles of Chardonnay in the fridge: roger that. A cluster of rare and little-seen spirits atop the dresser in the lounge: gotcha.

The location of the fetishized bottles would bleep in my head, on a map located in my brain. I knew exactly where they were, should I need them. It never ceased to amaze me how much alcohol other people had in their houses: I soon drained any bottles that I lived with.

I started regularly plundering my housemate's alcohol. I'd done it before, but this was the year my bottle-pillaging started to run riot. I didn't see it as stealing. Just surviving. Foraging for sustenance.

The levels of their bottles became a fixation. If I drank too much of their rum/vodka/whatever, they might notice; which would not do. No, not at all. So I was careful. Very careful. The problem was, once I'd started drinking, my carefulness would ferment to recklessness. And then I would have to top it up with water. And hope they didn't notice.

> MY FLATMATE'S GIN WOULD BE 80 PER CENT GIN AND **20 PER CENT WATER IN OCTOBER.** THEN 50 PER CENT GIN AND **50 PER CENT WATER COME NOVEMBER.** IN DECEMBER IT WOULD DWINDLE TO 20 PER CENT GIN AND 80 PER CENT WATER.

At which point I would have to admit defeat, and replace the whole thing. Jeez, it was exhausting.

The other problem with too many bottles is: they make a noise. Bottles would jangle together in my bag like an alcoholic alarm. In the small hours, I would cough to cover the snap-hiss-pull of the cider can opening, scared that my sleeping boyfriend would hear it from the other room. Even though he slept like a dead person. I would pull three doors between us to pop a Merlot cork.

Agoraphobia competed with the urgent need for alcohol. I was simultaneously terrified of leaving the house, but desperate for alcohol, I would revisit old bottles and upturn them into my mouth, hoping that some drops clinging to the bottom would take away the pain. Would allow me to exhale.

I would hide bottles inside the wardrobe and slip upstairs for a swig, under the pretence of going to the loo. I would empty the milk into the sink, yell to my boyfriend that we were out of milk and then drink a portable gin and tonic on a dark spot in the street before coming home.

PRIMAL NEED

My shaking episodes became more frequent and savage. My self-diagnosis of low blood sugar held up for a while. Until the shakes stopped going away when I ate.

My desperate 'it's not the alcohol. Anything but the alcohol!' research hunt finally hit upon something called Essential Tremor, believed to be genetic and triggered by caffeine, anxiety or tiredness. Bingo! Best of all, medical resources said that 'many people find that alcohol is useful in reducing their tremor.' A big green light to drink the shakes away.

Deep down, I knew I didn't have Essential Tremor. I knew the real reason. But I couldn't look it in the eye. If I did, it would tell me something I didn't want to know.

Often, the shakes were entirely psychosomatic. I wouldn't have them, until I tried to lift a glass of wine to my lips that evening, and bam, they would strike.

My body needed alcohol, yet it was rebelling, stopping me. Here I was, trying to stop the shakes with a drink, but because I was getting the shakes, I couldn't drink it. If I tried a glass of water, the shakes would invariably stay at bay. I sometimes think my body was trying to rescue me.

I started getting to the restaurant or bar an hour before my friends, in order to get the shake-stopper inside me. Even if my hands hadn't quivered all day, I would want the wine inside me so urgently that my hands couldn't hold it still. Alarmed by this, I would end up downing it. It was as if my body was trying to bust me. 'LOOK! THIS ONE. She's an alchy, everyone. Yoohoo. ALCHY.'

The fear of getting the shakes and them being noticed started to consume my thoughts. It became a thought-loop that must have repeated hundreds of times each day. Inane, everyday tasks became terrifying. Going for a coffee with a friend – scary shit. Signing my name at the post office – nerve-wracking. Punching my pin into a credit card machine – daunting. Giving a ticket to a train conductor – anxiety-inducing. Handing a colleague a sheet of paper – aargh.

It was mental torment, trying to think of strategies to outwit my hands. I remember having to pick up a glass of wine with two hands in order to disguise the tremor, while my boyfriend's mother pretended not to notice. I remember ordering many burgers and sandwiches that I didn't want, in order to have something that I could legitimately eat with my hands, rather than a fork. Eating with a fork was impossible until I had gotten my medicine inside me. Which had become a pint of iced cider, the heaviest drink the bar served, in order to lessen the severity of the shakes. When the heavy-drink-strategy stopped working, I started asking for a straw.

The drama, right?! But it really felt urgent. Like a life-or-death imperative, that I hide this physical manifestation of my addiction because, the terrible words, 'Are you shaking? Why?' could set a chain of events into motion, whereby I would *have to stop drinking*. I felt like I was literally and figuratively losing my grip on my life. And I really believed that if I couldn't drink my wine, life wouldn't be worth living. It would be bleak, joyless, insufferable. No matter what, I had to keep the shakes hidden.

My physical addiction intensified. I hallucinated insects and faces that weren't there, I felt constantly nauseous, I lost all interest in food. My voice shook. Unloading the dishwasher felt like running a marathon. I was exhausted yet I couldn't sleep, and I started finding it difficult to walk even short distances.

All the while, I was somehow managing to hold it together and work as acting celebrity editor on *Woman & Home* magazine. I was still managing to pass as a regular person, sort of. I was producing decent interviews with wholesome celebrities like Emma Bunton, Lulu and Helen McCrory.

I was like a house that looks presentable enough on the outside. But when you open the door, you're engulfed by a cloud of dust, unseen inhabitants scurry around, none of the lights work, and there's unopened mail all over the floor.

Once my three-month freelance stint at *Woman & Home* passed, I started to fall apart. I was totally freelance now, so I had nowhere to be, no reason not to drink.

I progressed to hiding bottles in the bathroom. Tucking a bottle of beer behind the cistern. Or a bottle of vodka behind the claw-foot bath. It made more sense, keeping the bottles in there. After all, that was where I was doing most of my drinking.

ROCK-BOTTOM CONVINCERS

'What has worked for me is to find something I wanted more than I wanted to drink, which was a fuck of a lot... The way to stop drinking is to want sobriety more.'
– AUGUSTEN BURROUGHS, THIS IS HOW

Movie versions of rock bottoms are dramatic. The character nearly kills someone in a car crash. They get caught in bed with someone else. They wake up and find a tiger reclining in their bathroom.

The reality of most drinkers' stories is that the last day drinking is more of a whimper than a bang. It's a slow, insidious undoing.

I would say I have had hundreds of tiny rock bottoms, mostly imperceptible to others. They were the moments when I realized that my actions were not mirroring my values in any way. The night my best friend stormed out of a club and texted, 'when did you become such a bitch?' after I literally just stole the guy she'd been cozying up to. The look on a boyfriend's face when he found out that I'd unceremoniously drunk the wine he'd been ceremoniously awarded with, for starring in a play. I was wrong, and I knew I was wrong, yet I couldn't seem to stop behaving in ways that completely contradicted how I wanted to behave, or expected others to behave.

Some people describe hitting rock bottom as when they decided to stop digging, and decided to hurl their shovel down and start climbing out of their self-made pit.

Bottom looks very different for different people. For one person, it's their first ever blackout. For another, it's losing their job. One person digs until they are just about losing the golden tops of autumnal trees; another digs until they're nearing the earth's core and are surrounded by skin-melting lava.

Personally, I would describe my series of bottoms as a sea floor with shelves. Abrupt shelves, rather than a gently sloping shore. The sea-shelving started out innocently enough, fun even, despite dicey moments. Yabadabbadooo, where am I now, this is some ride!

Then the sea-shelving grew to be ghoulish. Each time I thought I'd hit bottom, and surely I wouldn't dare to go deeper. Deeper couldn't possibly exist, FFS. But then I would pick up a glass of wine and eight hours later, *thud*, I would find myself way deeper than my worst imaginings. Encounter creatures I'd never seen before. What-the-devil-is-that beasts. Malevolent mermaids. Nine-foot-long eels with translucent skin and fearsome teeth.

For me, each rock bottom was what recovery people call a 'convincer'. They added fuel to my desire to get sober. Without them, I would never have stopped drinking. They're pitch-black moments in my life, but they serve a bright purpose in the long-term. It's because of those blood-chilling moments that I finally scraped together the wherewithal to start swimming as fast as I could for the sober shore.

CONVINCER #1

MARCH 2013: A TYPICAL DAY

I wake up at 1pm, drink a cup of tea with a shaky hand and freak out about the ever-worsening shakes. Force some toast down, drag my ass out to walk the dogs, walk past the river and think 'maybe drowning myself is the way to go'.

I swing by my boyfriend's mother's house to do an errand for her and siphon off some of her rum, enough to stop my hand shaking so I can go to the supermarket to buy my wine. Going to the supermarket takes all of my courage: I barely interact with people these days. I pick up a threatening letter from the tax office that mentions jail. I was meant to file my tax return two months back, but I have been shoving the letters beneath the sofa, as if there is a vortex down there that will gobble them up. They are fining me £10 a day and I feel paralyzed.

I try to do some work, but thoughts just slide out of my head, before I can grasp them. Drink wine, smoke, cry, compare myself to people on Facebook. Finish wine. My boyfriend, Ralph, who I live with, is out tonight, so I can drink unchecked. The no-more-booze panic sets in. I pull myself together to go and get just one beer. Maybe two. It's a superhuman effort to act sober in the off-licence. Am I imagining the look of distaste on the shop owner's face or is it really there? It's really there.

Come home, smoke, drink, cry. I realize I haven't showered, but I'm too drunk to do it now. Look at pictures of myself when I was happier. Wonder what I'm doing wrong now. Watch a mindless film. Halfway through: fade to blackout.

CONVINCER #2

APRIL 2013: THE ONE WHERE I WANTED TO KILL MYSELF

On Friday my boyfriend, Ralph, and I hosted a party, at the flat we share. People brought booze; lots of it. I drank to blackout, which is just normal now. I can't remember the last three hours of the party. On Saturday morning we had a furious row; he told me that I'm a pathetic drunk.

I cried and drank the rum left over from the party. I didn't eat anything. He didn't come home that night.

This weekend my suicidal ideation has stepped up a notch. Last night I got into a hot bath with a knife and willed myself to do it. I couldn't do it. I hate myself even more for not having the guts. I don't actually want to die. But I can't endure being alive any more. It's a catch 22.

Today I have been Googling 'painless ways to commit suicide'. Turns out there is no painless way. One post jolted me out of myself. It said: 'There is no painless way to end your life. You'll probably fail. And even if you succeed, you will cause your loved ones endless heartache. Seek help instead.'

It sparks a moment of clarity. I do need help. I need to tell someone. I phone my dad, a recovering alcoholic, and sob unintelligibly down the phone, 'I think I'm an alcoholic.' 'I know,' he says.

He books a flight to London, phones my lovely cousin, who's also in recovery and they both turn up at my door 12 hours later. 'Nice to meet you; the real you,' they say. We talk about the shakes and the suicidal plans. We go for lunch. 'I'll have the penne à la vodka,' I joke, as I survey the menu, trying my damnedest not to tremble as I hold it.

CONVINCER #3

MAY 2013: THE ONE WITH THE PARADISE BAY SPLIT SCREEN

I've been putting together little spells of sobriety. Three days here, five days there. As a treat, my mum has taken me away on holiday to Malta. 'Let's go and relax in the sun.'

I spend the days at this James Bond-esque beach, a dreamy cove called 'Paradise Bay'. Mum hangs out at the pool in the hotel because the walk is too far for her. Every day I swim the kilometre across the bay and back. I lie star-shaped on my back halfway across the bay and float. I'm finally learning to float again.

On the fourth day, I'm sat next to a bunch of university friends, who are all drinking beer and laughing. I feel like I have an arrow over my head saying 'loser'. Every time I show up at the cove the beach attendant good-naturedly shouts, 'Ahhhh, girl who is alone! Alone again, hahaha. Come with me!' I have become the 'girl who is alone'.

Yesterday I thought this was hilarious and posted it on Facebook. Today, I cry silently behind my sunglasses. I know I have lot of work to do to get my friends back on side, most of whom have their foot halfway out of the door.

Today, instead of going for a swim, I order a beer and break my seventh day sober. The beer doesn't taste good. It tastes rancid, in fact, but it smothers some of my psychological pain. I order another. And another.

By the time I am walking back along the clifftop to the bus which will take me back to the hotel, I am slightly tipsy. But it feels dark tipsy, not fun-times tipsy, and it has felt that way for a very long time now. Years, in fact. I am surveying the cliff. I approach the edge and look at the water lapping at jagged rocks 50 feet beneath. Definitely enough to kill me. But then Mum would have to ID my body? Gah. I'll wait until I get home.

Then it strikes me. Yesterday I did this exact same walk, only I was six days sober. I had zero suicidal thoughts. In fact, I was eating a Calippo and singing along to the The Lemonheads' 'It's a Shame about Ray'. I even skipped when I found myself on the road alone. The penny starts to drop. Don't drink = happy. Drink = suicidal.

CONVINCER #4
JULY 2013: THE ONE WHERE I FORGOT TO GO TO WORK
I wake up at midday. Sunlight is stabbing my face like daggers. Where the fuck am I? There is a dog snoring next to me. I remember thinking last night that this dog is my only friend. Aha. The dog.

I am housesitting for people with a dog. And lots of booze. Booze which I started drinking yesterday (or was it the day before?), telling myself I would replace it. My soul and body feel totally broken. I literally feel like I am going to die unless I get a drink inside me.

I hear a clunk downstairs. I peep down the staircase to see the cleaner hoovering. I need a drink right now, right this minute, to stop these *shakes and this all-consuming terror – and she is in the goddamn way. I slip past her and shout that I have flu, so that she doesn't come too close and detect noxious fumes. I shakily pour some gin and orange juice into a coffee mug, go outside, light a cigarette and pour it into myself to start my day. She leaves. Thank fuck.*

> I DRINK, I STARE, I SMOKE. I OPEN A BOTTLE OF WINE. AT ONE POINT THE DOORBELL RINGS AND I PHYSICALLY HIDE BEHIND THE SHED BECAUSE **I AM SO SCARED OF ANOTHER LIVING PERSON SEEING THE DERELICT STATE I AM IN.**

There are spiders crawling over me. I hate spiders. I don't care. I have my wine.

I don't eat lunch; I just smoke, drink and stare. I run out of cigarettes and start smoking half-butts. At around 6pm I remember today is Monday – I was meant to be working today, on a freelance job. I can't even bear to check my emails to see their worried messages. I pour myself another drink instead of thinking about it. I'll lie, which is what I always do to get myself out of these predicaments.

I watch two inane films. I am staring slack-jawed at the TV. I can't even understand the words, they just slither around like fish in a barrel, slippery things I can no longer grab. I finally shovel down some nuts and crisps. I slip into unconsciousness fully dressed on the sofa.

CONVINCER #5
JULY 2013: THE ONE WHEN NOTHING HAPPENED AND EVERYTHING HAPPENED

I broke up with my rakish, casually cruel boyfriend, Ralph. The final straw snapped when I asked him to empty the bin, since I was making dinner, as I always did, and he told me to 'fuck off'. I said, 'I've been at work all day the same as you.' He replied, 'You don't have a real job. You just swan about in short skirts and fanny about with press releases.'

Yep, he quoted Daniel Cleaver from Bridget Jones. He actually did. When your boyfriend starts quoting misogynistic romcom villains without irony, it's probably time to get the eff out of there.

*He knows I've been trying to quit drinking. He hasn't exactly been...
helpful. He started calling my addiction 'dick disease', because it
makes me act like a dick. He would offer me a glass of wine and then
say, 'Oh no, you can't, because you've ruined it for yourself'.*

*To be fair, I am far from blameless in this split; I've been hacking into
his Facebook messages for months, trying to find out if he's cheating
on me with the three exes he is meeting up with. I am melodramatic,
needy and as dependent upon his approval as a parasite. 'How not to
be a healthy couple.'*

*Anyhow, I've been staying with my mum and stepdad for the past
month or so, avoiding him. Now, I've come back to this sleepy
riverside village where we lived together. I need to pack up my stuff
and hammer the final nail in this relationship coffin. The plan is to
move back home to Birmingham, to live with my folks until I find
sustained sobriety.*

*Returning is like stepping back onto the scene of a crime. The cutesy
streets filled with vintage shops and froufrou tea rooms hold nothing
but traumatic memories for me. There's the alley that I skulked down
once to chug a mini bottle of wine, there's the riverbank tree that I
used to sit under drinking, smoking, crying, late at night.*

*I unlock the door with trepidation, as if unlocking Pandora's Box.
During my year living here, I have increasingly become physically
addicted to alcohol and stayed in a relationship about a year longer
than I should have done. Why? Because I didn't respect myself, so
him disrespecting me? I was fine with that. Until I started to string
two, three, four, five days together sober, and started to see him
clearly. 'When people show you who they are, believe them.'
Thanks, Maya Angelou.*

*As I pack, I am arrested by a constant thought-echo. 'You could go
to the shop and get some wine now and nobody would know.
You could go to the shop...' I have a fortnight sober, but it repeats,
over and over.*

> PEOPLE THINK THAT THE HARDEST TIMES IN EARLY SOBRIETY MUST BE AT PARTIES OR PUBS. WHILE THOSE ARE UNDOUBTEDLY TRICKY, **I'M ACTUALLY FINDING THAT THE MOST CHALLENGING TIMES ARE WHEN I'M ALONE.** WHY? BECAUSE I CAN DRINK WITHOUT ANYBODY KNOWING.

I give in. The voice shuts up once I have the wine, silenced, for now. I drink two-thirds of the bottle, as I'm packing.

The results are alarming. My mind turns from a cloudy-but-benign day, into a nasty stormscape. I feel it happen, as I drink. Like watching a sped-up time-lapse of a thunderstorm growling into action. I pour the rest of the bottle down the sink. I've done that plenty of times before, but this time feels different, since it's not the morning after. A sink-pour during the drinking? That doesn't normally happen. Huh.

I lie on the bed and long to be sober again. The lighting has turned from moon-grey to inky-menacing. I wish I had a mighty machine with which to suck the wine out of my system. I don't like this feeling any more.

CONVINCER #6
SEPTEMBER 2013: THE ONE WITH THE SEVEN-DAY BENDER
DAY 1
I'm in Venice! Stylist *magazine have sent me here to write a travel piece.*

It's hard to believe that Venice isn't the result of some sort of majestic Neptunian spell. The creation of a big, beardy god astride a giant seahorse. Who with a swoosh of his trident, magicked a city from the watery depths like some sort of reverse Atlantis.

Who knows what the first Venetian settlers were thinking around AD 811, when they built their huts on this shoal of tiny marshy islands. 'Ah yes! This is where I shall live!' But, I'm glad they did, because they started a thing of head-exploding wonder.

You hear that there are no cars, only boats in Venice; but until you see a family playing a board game with the canal sloshing beneath their window, or witness a leathery, badass Italian man with a bulldog, commuting to work in his chugalong, it's impossible to wrap your head around it.

Titanic-vast ships that are 15 storeys high – carrying 3,000 passengers and featuring swimming pools, basketball courts and 30 restaurants – slice through the Giudecca Canal. The cruisers dwarf the normally majestic Doge's Palace, like galactic spaceships looming over a tiddly house.

I'm in awe of Venice. I'm also 30 days sober and as shaky on my sober legs as a 30-day-old Bambi stumbling about the forest. I didn't think too hard about whether this Venice trip would be a threat to my sobriety, because I didn't want to not go. Venice first, sobriety second.

It will be fine. I'm feeling unbreakable. I've just completed a sprint triathlon, so I'm physically strong. My shaking hands have steadied, my depression has lifted, I'm feeling like I've nailed this sucker. I have plotted with my friend Laura, who is accompanying me, to tell everyone that I'm just about to do the triathlon, so that I can dodge the drink-pushing that always happens on press trips.

Somebody offers me a drink and I garble an overly long reply about the triathlon, blah, blah. They look bored. My friend Laura whispers in my ear afterwards, 'I don't think people are bothered that you're not drinking, love. You don't have to give them a big explanation.'

I go to bed feeling pleased with myself, but I also feel like I've been a dullard without the booze. I was practically gripping the underside of the table with my fingernails. I drift off, listening to the friendly horns of the cruise ships, talking to each other like gigantic whales. It will be fine.

DAY 2
We fight through the swarms of tourists coughed up by the cruise ships in St Mark's Square. We goggle at the wedding-cake ornate Bridge of Sighs, so named because the view from it was the last that convicts saw before lifelong imprisonment. Locals said you could hear a thousand sighs from it as the incarcerated took their last hungry look at Venice.

We shake and cry with laughter, pointing at the spectacularly ugly dolls in the tourist-trap shops. We take a waterbus around the canals heaving with gondoliers trying to save clients from meeting a watery end as they make wobbly descents into bobbing crescent-moon crafts. It's been a good day. A great day, even.

That night the fiery-haired manager at the hotel corners us and asks us if we're excited about the five-course meal we're about to consume, prepared by a famous local chef. 'And we've had a sommelier pair all of the wines, so you must try them all!' she enthuses. 'Ah, I'm not drinking...' I start. 'It would be rude not to!' she replies, wide-eyed with outrage.

I let it get under my skin. I don't drink during the meal, sticking to water, but I feel like a social pariah. 'You're not drinking?!' the owner of the hotel says, who's sitting next to me. 'Awww, you're no fun!' I laugh, awkwardly, but I take it to heart. He turns away from me. I feel frozen out. All knees and elbows and forced smiles and stuttery attempted anecdotes.

When the digestifs come out, I take one. Fuck it. I drink it. I feel the melty warmth. I feel like I'm instantly funnier. I drink another. I feel the thirst for more, starting to grip me. It scares me. I stop drinking. I switch back to cola.

I go to bed and think, 'I did manage to drink only two drinks. I'm tucked up by 11pm. Maybe I'm not an alcoholic.'

DAY 3

We wander through a rabbit warren of boutiques, passing rich people with teacup dogs and shopfronts displaying a kaleidoscope of jewel-bright wine goblets. Wine. I want wine. It's only 10am, I can't have wine.

Laura goes with the Peggy Guggenheim exhibition group, while I head off with the press group that is going to mooch around the humungous Biennale. The Surrealist dollhouses and haunting skeletal sculptures are leaving me cold. I am normally spellbound by art, but I can't concentrate. I only want wine.

We finally leave and I enlist a partner-in-crime to hunker down in a dive bar with me, wallpapered with wine labels and playing French rap. I drink the large wine fast, in five gulps. More. I have another.

That night we whoosh over to Burano in a water taxi. It's an island crowded with candy-coloured houses, painted such so that medieval fishermen could find their way home. I feel itchy, impatient to get there. Enough of this boat ride already.

We sit down at an elegant table festooned with crystal, linen and candles, jutting out over the canal. I snatch at the champagne awaiting us greedily. I barely notice the gourmet food. I am here to drink. I push *my prawn around the plate and take pictures of its beady eyes. 'Are you playing with your food Cath?' somebody asks. I laugh a little too loudly.*

Drink after drink. Edges are starting to blur and I'm starting to slur.

We head back to our Shoreditch-hip hotel for its launch party. I chat to a 24-year-old Italian DJ as he shows me how to work the cigarette machine. I'm drinking, so I smoke. Laura goes to bed, annoyed with me for some reason, but I have no idea why. I dance with the 24-year-old. I kiss him. The tall, elegant barman who congratulated me at the start of the trip for not drinking ('I like that you don't drink. It's rare for the British not to drink') is eyeballing me warily. The warmth I saw in his eyes has turned to steel.

They stop serving. I pull the bewildered 24-year-old up to the bar and demand they give us a bottle of wine to take up to the room. I behave like an entitled child.

DAY 4

I wake up next to the 24-year-old, with all of my clothes on. I feel like I've been hit by a truck. I stagger to the toilet and take a look at my haggard reflection, fake eyelashes crawling down my face like spiders. Fuck. I did it again. Worse still, I brought a boy back to the room I am sharing with Laura, who has sent a much friendlier text than I deserve, saying she decided to 'head out to explore and leave you guys to it'. 'Why are you sad?' the handsome Italian boy asks as he kisses me goodbye. 'I'm not,' I say, faking a smile.

We're heading home today. I am so hungover and hot-cheeked with shame that I skip breakfast with the others.

The horror in my head is back. The unquenchable thirst is back. It never went away. It was waiting for me. I drink as much as they will serve me on the plane without drawing attention.

My group are drinking too, which makes me feel better, but they're doing so while talking and laughing. I'm doing it intently, without talking or laughing. Must not feel this way. The wretchedness. Only solution is to drink. Try to fill the hole. I've started, so I'll finish.

I get a bottle of wine from the supermarket on the way home to Laura's in London. 'Why don't you just get a little one, Cath?' she says, gesturing at the single-serving miniature bottles, 'I'm not drinking tonight.' 'Awww, it'll be fine, I don't have to work tomorrow,' I bluster.

I've run out of places to go. I left Laura's yesterday and went to Dan's, having drunk all day and eaten a bag of crisps. Dan told me I stank of booze and suggested I shower. I cried when he said that.

He made me a cup of tea, slept on the sofa and gave me his bed. I couldn't believe he had been so mean to me. What kind of a friend tells another friend they smell?

Today I am sitting in a park in Notting Hill, wearing a pretty clingy cream dress with a lace trim. It's lunchtime. I have my suitcase. I'm smoking and swigging pink wine from a water bottle; cunning plan, hey? It could be cordial, no one will know.

I see a homeless man emerging from his cardboard bedroom and reaching for his can of super-strength lager. It strikes me that we are the same.

If I go back to my mum's house, where I am currently living, they will not let me drink. I need to drink. This morning I started drinking as soon as I woke up. Who will let me drink? I know. Peter. Peter will let me drink.

By the time I am weaving my way to Peter's flat, I am a bottle of wine in and I have eaten nothing all day. I am having trouble seeing the map on my phone. I stop and ask for directions from a kind-looking man. He hurries past, studiously ignoring me. What's his problem, how bloody rude.

A running woman stops for me, her forehead creasing with…worry? She slowly directs me to my destination. 'Are you sure you will remember that? Are you… OK?' 'I'm fine,' I garble.

DAY 7

Peter did let me drink. He encouraged it, in fact. When I was drunk enough, he made a pass at me. I folded into it in defeat.

He asked me to leave today. I told him I couldn't leave, that I couldn't catch a train in this state. He was firm. I had to leave.

I am sitting in the park outside his flat in North London, drinking wine from a water bottle. I stole the wine from his house before he kicked me out. It doesn't feel like stealing. I need it more than him.

I'm wearing tracksuit bottoms and a stained jumper. I am staring at the lake, smoking, while mothers push Bugaboos past me. A four-year-old points at me and says something to his mum. 'No,' she says urgently, pulling him past me. He turns and stares at me. She stops and talks to another mother; they both turn and look at me, talking in hushed voices.

I can see it. I can see what I look like to them. A bizarre collage of expensive wheelie suitcase, bedraggled clothes and clearly no place to go. I can see that I'm going to end up homeless, begging for shrapnel to buy super-strength cider. I can see this so clearly, as I stare out over the lake.

A thought in my head repeats over and over, like a train announcement tannoy stuck on a loop. 'I need a drink, I need a drink, I need a drink.' I'm drinking, but I still need more to drink.

And then, I suddenly know what I have to do. I am at a fork in the road here. I can either pull myself together to go buy some wine. Bed down in those trees over there, tonight. Or I can phone my mum and ask for someone to come and get me. I weigh the two up. I have no fight left in me. The thought of walking into a shop and trying to persuade them to sell me wine, when I'm clearly already drunk before midday, is just untenable. I can't do it. I have to go home. I don't have the grit to be homeless.

My stepfather picks up after one ring, saying 'Thank God, Cath, are you OK?' I have dozens of missed calls from them on my phone. I was meant to be home two days ago. He drops everything and drives from Birmingham to London to collect me, enclosing me in a big bear hug and not asking any questions about where I've been.

At a service station, he stops and gets me a burger and fries. It's the first thing I've eaten in over 24 hours, but I can barely eat half. My hands are shaking so violently that fries fly all over the floor. My mum runs me a bath when I get home. She's crying. She holds me and doesn't say anything other than 'I'm so glad you're home'.

LATER THAT DAY...
That would be a neat ending to my drinking, wouldn't it? That would tie everything up with a pretty bow. But no. Still, I drank. I made excuse after excuse to go out to the garage and drink the beer there. Once

they realized and locked away the booze, I drank mouthwash.

DAY 8
I am writing up my Venice article and drinking peppermint tea topped up with mouthwash. Clever, eh. They can't tell there's mouthwash in it. My pepperminty breath is totally putting them off the scent.

My stomach starts to twist, painfully. Ouch. What was that? It contorts again. I Google 'is mouthwash dangerous to drink?' I read article after article that says that not only is mouthwash toxic; it can kill you if you drink enough of it. How much have I drunk? I'm not sure. I go into the bathroom and scrutinize the bottle. Probably three shots' worth – 75ml.

I sit there waiting to see if I'm going to die. Maybe this is a good thing, I have now committed suicide by accident. I wanted that, didn't I. Fucccck. I might die today. I sit there and try to absorb that fact into my brain.

And with that, I finally realize. I do not want to die.

I suddenly understand that if I continue drinking, I will die. I will DIE. Maybe it will take decades, but still, drinking will eventually kill me prematurely. And I don't want to die. I want to live.

THE NEXT DAY
I don't drink.

> I AM UNDER NO ILLUSIONS THAT I HIT ACTUAL BOTTOM ON THAT DAY. I KNOW THAT IF I CHOOSE TO GO OUT TO SEA SOME MORE, **I WILL FIND DEEPER BOTTOMS AND MORE MALEVOLENT CREATURES.** I KNOW THERE ARE INKIER DEPTHS STILL. DEPTHS I NEVER, EVER, EVER WANT TO MEET. I NEVER WANT TO SWIM INTO THE COLDER, DARKER WATERS OF THE ABYSS.

What happened with me, and what happens with most dependent drinkers, is that I put more and more time together sober. Four days, seven days, ten days…so on. And spending that time sober, although tremendously hard, was also like being transported from the perilous, deep-sea shelving, to pootling around in a safe, warm, shallow reef with cute clown fish and smiley stingrays.

You start to see that you like the reef a heckofalot better. Each time you go back out, you realize it's a harder, longer swim back to the reef. You begin to realize that next time, you might not make it back.

You choose the reef.

'New beginnings are often disguised as painful endings.'
– Lao Tzu

II: LEARNING TO BE SOBER

30 TOOLS FOR
THE FIRST 30 DAYS

'For a seed to achieve its greatest expression, it must come completely undone. The shell cracks, its insides come out and everything changes. To someone who doesn't understand growth, it would look like complete destruction.'
– CYNTHIA OCCELLI

Don't get me wrong. I didn't want to *not drink*. My day one did not look like that. But I didn't want to drink, either.

For all I knew, this was going to be yet another 30ish-day failed attempt. I'd been running at sobriety, and failing, for five months. I didn't know that this run at it, this day one, this attempt would stick. I didn't know anything, other than I just couldn't stay where I was, and that things needed to change. That I needed to change.

The first few days of sobriety are an almighty slap around the face. It's like waking up in a trashed hotel room, which now happens to be your life. Welcome! You stare around in horror at the torched embers, the ransacked wreckage, the bottles, the fag butts, the mysterious stains. Did I do this myself? Motherfuck. Yes, yes I did.

The urge to slip back into unconsciousness to escape is *almost* irresistible. But, instead of deep-diving into a bottle, you have to roll your sleeves up and set about the lengthy job of clearing up. You have to confront the angry hotel manager hammering down the door. It's nothing short of terrifying.

> THE RECOVERY SAYING, **'THE BEST THING ABOUT RECOVERY IS THAT YOU GET YOUR EMOTIONS BACK. THE WORST THING ABOUT RECOVERY IS THAT YOU GET YOUR EMOTIONS BACK'** IS SCORCHINGLY TRUE.

You'll find yourself hijacked by feelings that you're just not used to feeling, because you're so accustomed to numbing them out.

As Brené Brown sagely says, 'We can't selectively numb out emotion. Numb the dark and you numb the light.' Ergo, when you numbed out the bad stuff, you numbed out the good stuff too. You will now swerve wildly between extremes of euphoria and wretchedness. You'll find yourself floored by shame as a blackout corpse bobs to the surface of your memory, aargh, and you'll frantically try to shove it back into the murky depths with your oar.

An hour later, you'll be all skip-down-the-street sunshiny because you just went to the supermarket and you weren't hungover. You bought peas, whoopdeedoo! High, low, high, low, up, down, up, down. It's madly exhausting. You will need a lot of sleep to deal.

The real world is brighter, louder, rawer and scarier than a carful of hostile clowns. Without your alco-armour you feel utterly naked and vulnerable, awaiting the inevitable attacks from the Big Bad World. Like a de-jacketed prawn, a plucked hedgehog or a cowering snail ripped from its safe-house shell.

But the initial horror will fade, I promise you, as long as, in the wise words of the inimitable Wilson Phillips, you just hold on. 'Hold on for one more day.'

Channel Thomas Edison, the chap who invented motion pictures and the light bulb. In 1914, his lab burned down and his life's work whooshed up in a ball of flame, raining back down upon him as black confetti. Instead of being plunged into depression, Edison saw it as a chance to rebuild. He reportedly said, 'Thank goodness all our mistakes were burned up. Now we can start again fresh.'

This is day one of the rest of your life. A life that you will choose, rather than feeling like you're at the mercy of some sadistic puppeteer.

Here are 30 things that got me through the first 30 days. Your 30 are likely to look different. Perhaps very different. What is a magic bullet for one person, may prove to be a useless straw bullet for another. We are not the same person, even though we share the same barfly habits.

1. I TOOK SLEEPING PILLS
When your body is detoxing from a bender (and let's face it, most sober attempts are inspired by a bender) it finds it very difficult to sleep, yet desperately needs to.

I've already described physical withdrawal above, but let's talk about it again. Withdrawal is gnarly. It can actually be physically painful. Physically addicted alcoholics, like I was, can expect nausea, a total lack of appetite, burning skin, screaming nerves, a piston-pounding headache and absolute constant panic. It will last around five to ten days. I'm sorry.

But let's get one thing straight. This is not life without alcohol. This is not how you feel sober. This is how you feel because of the drinking. This too shall pass, after just ten days. Don't blame being sober; blame the booze. That's the real villain of the piece.

You may require a medical detox; you need to talk to your doctor about that if you have withdrawal symptoms such as the shakes. I didn't need one, which was gobsmacking given how incredibly ghastly I felt, but the doctor did give me sleeping pills. Little blue saviours which proved to be like those ting-a-linging winged gifts they send into the arena of *The Hunger Games*.

I was the most tired I've ever been, yet adrenaline was screeching through my body like an electric shock, meaning I would lie there for hours, eyeballs stinging in defeat. The pills brought me abandon on the pillow. I took them for a fortnight.

2. I LOADED UP ON VITAMIN B AND THIAMINE

The other thing my doctor did was prescribe me a super-strength vitamin B complex and thiamine (B1). He had me on three times the regular daily allowance.

Intrigued, I read up on it, and found that vitamin B is vital for energy, appetite and mood regulation. Drinking leeches your body of this lovely stuff. So, much of the dun-dun-dun (*Jaws* music) doom I was feeling, was simply a vitamin imbalance.

Get your paws on some vitamins.

3. I WATCHED *28 DAYS* OVER AND OVER AND OVER

In the first few days of sobriety, my brain was mush. I couldn't have followed the serpentine plot of *House of Cards* any more than I could have sprouted wings and flown to the moon. So, I just watched kids' films: *Hop, Rio* and *Monsters Inc*. I needed pastel-perfect endings.

After a week, I tracked down recovery-themed films and watched them over and over. I watched *28 Days* literally about 28 times, curling up into the foetal position with cringe as Sandra Bullock's character spectacularly buggers up her sister's wedding, and bawling when she goes home with her little plant. 'I want that,' I thought. 'I want what she has.'

I took in *Flight*, watching through my fingers during *that* scene when Denzel Washington's hand swipes the hotel minibar vodka.

I watched *Rachel Getting Married*, flinching as Rachel's family's despair of her behaviour. A little compassion for my loved ones crept into the room and elbowed aside my self-pity.

I watched *Young Adult* with Charlize Theron, feeling chilling familiarity as she slobs around during daylight hours in tracksuit bottoms, biding her time until she can head back out on the prowl, like the leopards that stalk the streets of nighttime Mumbai. Something clicked in my head.

4. I SAW AN ADDICTION COUNSELLOR

If you live in the UK, you should be able to get free addiction counselling through your GP. I did.

When I showed up for my first session I was so angry with the world and, by extension, with him, that I was practically waving a gun in his face. The layers of denial were thick, like bandages I'd wrapped around an infected wound, when really, what it needed was a good clean and some air.

He asked me some questions during my first session. My replies went like this. 'Have I ever hurt *anyone* through my drinking? Er, no. I have never hurt anyone. Have I ever hurt myself? NO. I mean, unless you count that one time when I chipped my front tooth because I fell into a door.'

What absolute garbage. I was lying, without being aware that I was lying. That's how confusing denial is. Of course I had hurt people. Practically all of my friends and family; not physically, but certainly emotionally. Of course I had hurt myself, several times a week, both mentally *and* physically.

It took a few sessions before I put down the gun and allowed the defensive padding to be unwound, so that he could have a proper look at me, and start to actually treat my pain.

He gave me so many anti-anxiety techniques. Reciting the alphabet backwards if I'm walking to a boozy party and feel my heart start to jackhammer. Tapping along to a song, which does something fancy in the brain. Or holding somebody's hand. I still use these tools to this day. (Thanks, Andrew.)

5. I CARRIED AROUND A MINIATURE MY LITTLE PONY

At around a week sober I saw some teeny tiny My Little Ponies for sale in a shop, and I simply had to have them. Before I knew it, I'd bought them, as if on auto-toy-buying-pilot.

They comforted me. I didn't know why. I didn't need to know why. In retrospect, I think they reminded me of a childlike, innocent, fun time in my life, before everything got sticky and nasty from alcohol. I carried one around with me everywhere, like a purity talisman.

I've since given them to my niece. You can outgrow some tools, just as a child outgrows toys.

6. I USED THE DORY METHOD

Y'know Dory from *Finding Nemo*? The blue tang fish that constantly forgets who she is, and where she is, and what she's doing? I was like that, during the first 30 days.

One minute I would know why I wasn't drinking and be firm in my resolve; eight seconds later, I would have completely forgotten why drinking was a terrible idea. Why am I not drinking right now?! A glass of rosé at a chic pavement cafe sounds lovely. Let's go!

I had to constantly, patiently remind myself why drinking was the worst idea in my world. I had a few grim drinking memories that I would return to again and again whenever I had a Dory moment (incidentally, they're on pages 20, 34, 109, 125 and 157). I had to repeatedly look at them, just as an amnesiac looks at flash cards to remember who they are and how to get home.

7. I EXERCISED DAILY

Oh, exercise. This was probably my most important tool in the first month, for real. I sweated so many resentments out in hot yoga. I pounded so much anger out on the pavement. Swam away from my piranha demons in the pool.

My paranoia, defensiveness and worry went rat-a-tat-tat-tat every waking minute, as if there was a possessed antique typewriter in the attic of my brain.

The only thing that slowed the rat-a-tat-tat was exercise. So, in my first 30 days sober, I discovered a mania for exercise that I have sadly, never located since. I was running 12km for kicks. Swimming 50 lengths for jokes. Doing 90 minutes of hot yoga and wanting more. I have never been more toned. I would head out for a run wanting to rip someone's head off, or hating on myself with the power of a thousand suns, and come back feeling Gandhi serene. A runner called Monte Davis summed it up beautifully in the 1970s, when he said, 'It's hard to run and feel sorry for yourself at the same time.'

In a way, dedicated drinkers have many of the same qualities as athletes. A tolerance for physical pain, a monolithic stubbornness, an all-or-nothing leaning towards the extreme. Once we find an activity that gives us an endorphin rush, maaann, we embrace it. We don't hold back! Which is why so many newly sober people discover a tiny athlete tucked away inside their drunk self.

The phenomenal bonus of all of this, and perhaps the reason our bodies tell us to do it, is that exercise actually helps our brains recover from decades of alcohol abuse. It literally helps rebuild the brain tissue we've lost, restoring the white matter we've ravaged.

A study carried out by the University of Colorado, Boulder concluded that aerobic exercise can actually reverse the brain damage from benders. 'What our data suggests, is that beyond just giving people a different outlet for cravings or urges for alcohol, exercise might also help to repair the damage that may have been done to the brain,' says the study's co-author Angela Bryan, a psychology and neuroscience professor. 'It might even be a more promising treatment approach for alcohol problems, because it is both a behavioural treatment, and a treatment that has the potential to make the brain more healthy. The healthier the brain is, the more likely a person with alcohol issues is to recover.'

On top of that, exercise actually creates new neurons in your brain, the little guys that transmit information. Up until recently, it was thought that our brains got a finite amount of neurons, and that was your lot. But it turns out that new neurons can be created. The only catalyst? Vigorous aerobic activity, according to Dr Karen Postal, a neuropsychologist. 'That's it,' she told *New York Magazine*. 'That's the only trigger we know about.' Best of all, those new neurons crop up in the hippocampus, which is strongly linked with learning and memory. 'If you are exercising so that you sweat – about 30 to 40 minutes – new brain cells are being born,' reveals Postal. 'And it just happens to be in that memory area.'

Mind-bending, huh? Or should I say, brain-mending. So, lace up your trainers or churn up the pool. And even if you don't have the time or inclination for a long run, one study found that just ten minutes of exercise can zap a booze craving.

8. I CRIED MY EYES OUT
For some reason, running often also acts as a crying release valve. In early sobriety I would often stop in the middle of a run and burst into gulpy sobs, as puzzled builders or rabbits looked on, chewing their biscuits or grass. I've read that crying calms us down because tears literally carry the stress hormone, cortisol, out of our systems.

9. I TOOK L-O-N-G BATHS
When I was drinking, I thoroughly despised baths. I rarely drank in them, for a start, so they were time away from my precious wine glass. Secondly, I hated being alone, which is utterly bizarre, since now I love being alone.

Too much time alone meant that I had way too much time hanging out with my latest all-consuming fuck-up. I would lie in the bath and the corpses would bob up in my brain, irrefutable evidence of my wrongdoing.

Thirdly, drinking raises our skin's temperature. I was always too hot. Even in winter. Slipping into a steaming bath was the last thing I wanted to do.

10. I STUDIED TO BE SOBER LIKE I WAS STUDYING FOR A DEGREE

I immersed myself in sober literature. I devoured clickbait articles listing dozens of sober celebs. I must have read at least half a book a day.

Before, I had mooched around the recovery universe half-heartedly. Like a party that I didn't really want to be at. I stood on the edges, not engaging, looking at my watch, eyeing up the door.

I didn't know it, but it was because I wanted to drink again. This time, I threw myself right into the middle of the throng.

I wanted to listen to every interview, learn about every scientific study, read every 'how I got sober' story. I became obsessed; just as obsessed as I had been with drinking.

My top sober reads are: *Unwasted: My Lush Sobriety* by Sacha Z Scoblic, *Blackout* by Sarah Hepola, *This Naked Mind: Control Alcohol* by Annie Grace, *Dry* by Augusten Burroughs and *Kick the Drink...Easily* by Jason Vale.

For podcasts, I love *Home* and *The One You Feed*.

I treated learning about recovery like a full-time job. I would sit down and wade into a weighty technical document about what addiction does to the brain, and come up for air three hours later.

I journaled about my feelings, wins and struggles. Augusten Burroughs has said in interviews that he wrote himself sober; I get it. Some people talk themselves sober in recovery meetings. That wasn't what happened for me. I wrote, furiously.

Writing isn't just emotionally healing; it physically heals too. One study took 120 volunteers and had them write either about a distressing event, or about the bland ins-and-outs of the previous day. They then punched a tiny hole in their upper arm. The group that had done the cathartic writing task were six times more likely to have a wound that had healed within ten days. Amazing, right?

Another study found that those who wrote about their innermost feelings, rather than neutral events, were significantly less likely to need a trip to the doctor.

11. I REDISCOVERED MUSIC

Before drinking became my number-one hobby (and actually, let's face it, my only hobby), I was fixated with music. That all went away when I started devoting all of my time and money to drinking.

Sober, I re-entered the world of music with wide-eyed wonder and hunger, downloading hundreds of songs a month, and finding sober solace.

Lyrics in these songs twanged at my soul-strings. I listened to them on the way to boozy parties and felt fortified by them. I listened to them on the way back from boozy parties and felt affirmed by them. They plumped up my motivation and sang to my frazzled nerves.

I felt like they were written about recovery, even though they most likely weren't. It didn't matter either way, because I interpreted them the way I needed to.

When I dug around in the origin of boozy song lyrics, I found gems of soberspiration. Take 'Oh! Whiskey' by Jimi Goodwin. 'I saw a child with a skipping rope, I said I used to be like that...maybe give up the booze, recover some youth.' He refers to whiskey as a 'false friend' with a 'contractual clause or two'. When interviewed about alcohol, Jimi said, 'The thing that you think is your crutch is actually a shackle. Like if you're in the studio and you can't do a vocal without half a bottle of wine beforehand, something is up. This is my art, I should be able to do this sober, with an open heart, because it's what I dreamed of doing as a kid.' Yes, Jimi. So true.

I listened to almost offensively happy '80s tunes when I was running, such as 'Walking on Sunshine' by Katrina and the Waves, 'Can You Feel It' by The Jacksons and 'The Power of Love' by Huey Lewis and The News. These songs had the power to turn my frown upside down.

I count my Spotify Premium subscription as one of my recovery tools. And it's not my imagination. A study by Missouri University found that music can hike up happiness levels.

12. I JOINED A 100-DAY CHALLENGE

There's a well-known psychological phenomenon called the Hawthorne Effect. Basically, psychologists found that when people are observed, they tend to work harder and perform better.

> FEELING WATCHED AND HAVING ACCOUNTABILITY
> WORKS. WHERE YOU GET IT IS UP TO YOU; SOME
> FIND IT IN RECOVERY MEETINGS, WHILE OTHERS
> LOCATE IT ONLINE, OR GET IT FROM THEIR
> FRIENDS AND FAMILY. **THE KEY IS HONESTY.**

If you drink and don't tell anyone about it, you will find yourself doing it again. And again. Relapses grow in the dark.

A game-changer for me was finding Belle's *Tired of Thinking About Drinking* blog. She runs a 100-day challenge, whereby you commit to 100 alcohol-free days and have to email her every day saying whether you're sober, or whether you've slipped. That simple shift, of having to check in and be honest, was a seismic one for me.

13. ADDICTIVE VOICE RECOGNITION
Another thing that Belle's blog taught me: to separate out the voice in my head that told me, 'it would be a fabulous idea to have a drink', and 'what about now?' That told me that I deserved it. Or that I was entitled to it. Or that I was a piece of crap loser, so I may as well drink.

This tactic is called 'addictive voice recognition'. It's been around for decades, but has not received as much spotlight as it deserves. It's so important that I've devoted a whole chapter to it, on page 84. But in a nutshell, learning to see that voice as not me, but a sinister force within me plotting my downfall, was crucial.

14. I TREATED MYSELF AS I WOULD A TODDLER
They say to protect your newborn sobriety as you would a newborn baby. A simile that helped me many a time.

This led me to the idea of self-parenting. In drinking, I was an abusive parent to myself. I constantly placed myself in situations where I was endangered (the night I stayed after-hours in a dodgy pub in Brixton to play pool with oh, around 20 strange men, alone, springs to mind).

I was often exhausted from being out until 2am on a work night, cold in my teeny man-pleasing clothes, unhappy in my private hangover hell, and hungry because I spent money on wine rather than food. I had completely, utterly and totally forgotten how to look after myself.

When I stopped drinking, my self-care was so crazy wonky and my kamikaze self-destructive streak was so ingrained, that I found it difficult to grasp even the most basic tenets of looking after myself. Making sure I got enough sleep. Drinking litres of water, rather than cola. Not hanging out with people who I didn't like that much.

I had to relearn, ever so slowly, how to become a soothing parent rather than an abusive one. Tired? Nap. Hungry? Eat. Manky hair? Wash it. These sound like eye-rollingly obvious things, but for me, they had become lost.

Toddlers need regularly timed, long sleep, clockwork food, fresh air and exercise, comforting when they're upset and nighttime baths. Now apply that principle to yourself. You deserve it. Yes, you do. And you need to remind yourself that poking your fingers into the fireplace or eating potpourri, is not a wise idea.

Beginning to trust myself to take care of myself has been a really amazing process. I've stopped eyeing myself suspiciously, as a toddler would an unpredictable parent, and started folding into myself with relief.

15. I ATE FIVE TIMES A DAY

This is related to the toddler model. Dependent drinkers tend to forget to eat, and supplant food with booze. At my drinking nadir, I was only eating a round of toast a day.

Because of this relationship of medicating hunger with booze, hunger can be one of the mightiest triggers there is. Hunger makes you feel panicky and incomplete. As if there are frightened fireflies flitting about your head. Thus much more likely to reach for alcohol as a fix.

In the first 30 days, I would often experience sky-caving-in cravings, only to discover that they completely went away when I ate something. Magic! I learned to carry fruit, nuts and some chocolate in my handbag, everywhere.

The newly sober become sugar fiends because there are spoonfuls of sugar in booze. You skip dessert when you're drinking, because your secret sugar fiend is being fed by the wine. When you quit drinking, an unprecedented hankering for sugar hits. I devoured family packs of jelly sweets. Roll with it. You can look at your sugar consumption later. For now, the most important thing is just: don't drink.

16. I CANCELLED DRINKY EVENTS

I remember getting on the tube to go see a musical with some journalist friends in early sobriety. One knew I'd quit drinking, one didn't. As a press event, there would be a lot of cocktail-pushing. I experienced a can't-breathe panic attack on the tube and had to get off before my final destination.

I sat there on the platform, and texted my friends to cancel. If you're freaking out about a boozy event, just don't go. Do. Not. Go.

You don't have to go. For the first 30 days at least, all you have to do is not drink. If you want to stay in all month and watch back-to-back *Scandal* and order takeaways every night, do it. Listen to your instincts and don't force yourself into situations that will trigger you. This may mean that you have to give bars the swerve altogether, or it may mean that you can go to bars, but need to phase out toxic people; only you know what triggers you.

No night out, no party, no *anything* is worth diving back into the bottle. What's that, the cast of *Friends* are going to be there, in character? I'll pass. You're going to present me with my very own flying dragon? No ta. The party is in a magical land that you enter by walking through the shimmering curtain of a waterfall? Sorry, I'm too busy being sober.

It may seem like the end of your social life, the cancelling, the swerving. And you will certainly need to do things differently for a while, perhaps bailing on parties early, seeing friends during the day instead, so on. But soon, after you've pushed through the social awkwardness barrier, you will be able to do everything you used to do, just minus the drinking. Now is not the time to test yourself. Do whatever helps you not to drink.

17. I CREATED A BOOZE-FREE HAVEN

Trying to give up drinking in a house heaving with booze is, in my opinion, like trying to swim the English Channel when you've only just cracked swimming a mile.

I learned from my many, many day ones that my slips were mostly spontaneous, opportunistic reaches. Whenever I placed a simple obstacle between me and alcohol, that of having to go to the shop to purchase it, it made an enormous difference.

Alcohol is pushed on newly sober people everywhere; from supermarkets ('would you like to try this new liqueur, madam?') to restaurants, to picnics, to parties, and even on play dates.

Creating a booze-free nook where you can exhale and not have to worry about drinking, is such a gigantic relief.

18. I TOLD PEOPLE I'D QUIT DRINKING

Another thing that my struggles taught me, was that when I didn't tell people that I'd quit drinking, I was about 1,000 per cent more likely to drink. At first, I kept pockets of people in the dark, telling myself that I didn't want to make them feel awkward, why should I have to tell everyone, this is a private journey, blah blah blah. Actually, my subconscious motivation was that I wanted to have pockets of people that I could still drink with.

This is not true of everyone – I know people who are successfully long-term sober, having only told their husband and sister the full truth, but for me, this was absolutely the case. I had to tell everyone. I had to dynamite-kaboom the bridge back to drinking. They needed to know that it was really, really important that I don't drink.

19. I LEFT THE PAST ALONE

I came into being sober, like many people, having made thousands of bad decisions. Remorseful memories that would stab at my brain, even on the most honest-to-goodness wholesome sober days.

For me, the right decision was to lock it all in a box marked 'Do not open' for the first 30 days. A few months in, I would unlock (most of) the box and let my closest sober confidantes have a look. The chorus of 'is that all?' and 'I've done that' and 'you're human' responses cleared away my fear. The box wasn't so bad, after all.

You might open it in the confidential enclave of a therapist's office, or to your sponsor, or to your best friend. But, do it when you're ready. Don't rush it. And if you're never ready to let anyone see the entire box, that might be the best choice for you. You don't have to do anything. Other than not drink. I didn't show my entire box-o'-secrets to anyone until I was over three years sober.

20. I FOUND A SOBER TRIBE

I'll talk more about this later, but finding my sober tribe was vital.

I honestly don't know how people ever do this alone, without sober buddies to bounce off. I felt so very alone for so very long, and operated in a vacuum where I pretended to be OK when I wasn't, locking away vulnerability. I needed to break that pattern.

Addiction wants us alone; we find safety in numbers. Whether you find your recovery tribe through AA, Rational Recovery, Refuge Recovery, SMART, Soberistas, Meetups or online recovery groups, it really doesn't matter. There is no 'right' way, and you should probably avoid those who tell you there is. Lean on your tribe, whether they're two people or 46, and tell them when you want to drink.

Showing another person your craving removes the power the thought has over you. It's like you're being hypnotized by a swaying snake and telling someone breaks the spell. When I tell other sober people about my desire to drink, I never drink. Fact. The crucial part? Doing it beforehand. It's a sorcery that works.

I've had big twilight chats about hiding bottles while driving along the snaking roads of the Big Sur underneath a crescent moon so sharp you could cut your finger on it. Talks about how to defrost snowballing resentments on a horse and carriage clattering around Bruges. Bonds over drinking peer pressure while supping on virgin mojitos overlooking stick people in London's Trafalgar Square. Without my tribe, I'd be on my way to hell in a handcart.

21. I DEVELOPED A TWILIGHT HAIR-WASHING RITUAL
This was a small, but useful tactic for me in the first couple of weeks. I found that if I washed my hair in the triggery hours of early evening, tossed it up in a towel turban and put on my PJs, I was in for the night.

It put one more obstacle between me and the wine at the shop. I had to dry my hair and put on clothes to go outside. That put a good 20-minute job between me and leaving the house.

22. I USED THE UPSIDE-DOWN-TRIANGLE MODEL
Remember when I put visiting Venice above protecting my newborn sobriety? Yep. That shit had to change.

My day ones started sticking when I made my sobriety the tip of an upside-down triangle. And realized that everything else – my relationships, my career, my health – depended on that one thing staying intact. Without it, the whole thing toppled and fell.

I had to be willing to do anything, rather than drink. I once ran out of a restaurant in tears, just as my friends and I had sat down for a meal. My friends thought I was batshit crazy, and they didn't look too chuffed as we all walked home instead to get a takeaway, but the busy restaurant and the smell of booze had triggered a full-on panic attack.

I had to be willing to leg it out of the party, if I felt I was about to pick up a drink. Willing to risk raised eyebrows, or disgruntled hosts, or annoyed boyfriends, or whatever. It didn't really matter in the grand scheme of things, because: the upside-down triangle. And the people that really matter will understand.

23. I GAVE MYSELF PEP TALKS

People who don't understand addiction think it's self-indulgent. That you inhale that bottle of wine because you are a reckless, selfish, pleasure-chasing lush. It's not like that.

While I undoubtedly chased pleasure at first, there was a point where my use of alcohol mutated from self-indulgent to self-harm. You can see that the person shoving a 15th eclair into their face is no longer having fun. You can tell that the gambler holding their head in their hands at the roulette wheel is not having fun. Why can't people see that the blackout drunk unable to walk is *not having fun?*

There is, of course, a brief burst of relief in the first glass of wine. Just as a cutter finds pleasure in the pain of the razor, or an anorexic finds satisfaction in a 150-calorie day. But those practices – cutting or anorexia – are undoubtedly viewed by society as self-harm. Addicted drinking is the same.

Addiction is all about seeking external relief from mental pain; whether you use cocaine, online poker, shopping, sex, razors, cake or exercise. Addictions are all the same ultimately. You seek to treat an internal pain with an external substance or activity. You pursue a once-pleasurable activity to the point of self-sabotage. Alcoholics often lose their jobs, houses, relationships, friends, everything; how can anyone call that self-indulgent?

A self-indulgent person seeks to hang on to the things that make them happy. A self-harming person finds themselves torpedoing them. Addicted drinking is a very slow suicide.

For me, I had to stop hating myself and start liking myself in order to find sobriety. I had to replace self-loathing with self-soothing. I had to start to believe that I was worth something. That I deserved better than drinking.

So, I started to challenge the 'loser' belief that was stitched into the very fabric of my self-esteem, like a name-tag in a kids' sports kit. I started to give myself pep talks. I would even write myself letters, reminding myself of all the things I was doing right, when the critical voices in my head became deafening.

Self-critical scripts are actually addictive, says neuroscientist Alex Korb, author of *The Upward Spiral: Using Neuroscience to Reverse the Course of Depression, One Small Change at a Time*. 'Guilt, shame and self-pity activate the reward circuitry in the brain. The only way out of this addictive loop is to practice radical self-compassion instead.'

I truly believe that most addicted drinkers, especially women, don't need to shrink to become the 'right size'. They actually need to grow. 'I think dependent drinkers have enough self-loathing anyway,' says Dr Julia Lewis, a consultant addiction psychiatrist for Alcohol Concern. 'Most of them actually need a good dose of compassion.'

Rather than being humbled, I think addicted drinkers need to be bigged up. For me, I needed to find my 'I deserve to be happy. I deserve not to drink' size, and stay there.

24. I CLEANED MY HOUSE

I discovered early on that when I sat still, I was a much easier target. A recovery friend once sent me a message advising me on how to get through cravings: 'Clean the oven. Sort your sock drawer. Go for a walk. It doesn't matter what you do, just MOVE.'

She was absolutely right. And especially with the cleaning. A clean house makes you much less likely to want to drink. It's why some recovering addicts offer free house-cleaning services to those who are still struggling.

25. I COUNTED DAYS WITH AN APP

Day-counting, for me, is imperative. If I wasn't counting days, I likely would have drunk again. The crushing disappointment I would feel about having to go back to day one is a wonderful deterrent. There's a hashtag very popular in recovery circles right now: #fuckthezero.

I discovered an app, called *I'm Done Drinking*, which counts days, drinks not consumed, money saved and calories saved. At the end of my first 30 days, I had not consumed 28 bottles of wine, I had saved £350 and I had not drunk 14,718 calories.

In the description of the app, you find out that it was created by a sober person. 'If I could stop drinking I could do anything, even create an iPhone app.' How cool is that.

26. I TOOK RESPONSIBILITY FOR MY OWN HAPPINESS

I had no idea that my happiness was my own responsibility, until recovery. Not. A. Clue. If you had said this to me while I was still drinking I would have been thoroughly baffled. 'Errrrr OK. Anyway. Shall we get another drink?' I thought happiness was something other people had to give me. That the world owed me. That I was somehow being short-changed. Gimme.

Unless it's a day when a parent dies, or your city is bombed, or some other nuclear event hits your life, most days you wake up and have a choice. To be happy. Or to be unhappy.

I had a day within the first 30 when I chose to be unhappy. I overslept, smoked all day, drank too much coffee, didn't exercise, ate greasy pizza, picked over my faults, allowed the 'loser' voice in my head to win. At the end of that day I had a 'kapow!' moment. 'I made this day wretched. ME.' I wallowed and chose *not* to do the things that make me happy (work, exercise, being kind to people).

When I look to *other people* to fill me up, as if I'm some kind of empty vessel, I make myself helpless. Sitting there and waiting for other people to gift me with happiness; such a waste of time.

I choose what kind of day I have. Good days are next-right-things piled on top of one another. When I have a busy day and do what I intended to do, I get a heart-shaped glow of satisfaction at the close of the day, as opposed to a low thrum of guilt.

27. I MADE MEDICAL APPOINTMENTS

I hadn't been to the dentist in four years when I arrived at sobriety. Four years. Turns out that going to the dentist and getting my wonky wisdom tooth pulled was cathartic. I was thrilled once I'd done it. It felt like a self-care slam dunk. Now I go to the dentist every six months, like an actual grown-up. It's great. And I assume my Adulting Parade will be arriving any day now.

28. I USED SPLIT-SCREENING

When I was two weeks sober, I was jammy enough to go and see Fleetwood Mac live. It was with a bunch of people who are used to me drinking the world, so I was very, very nervous about it.

You've seen *Sliding Doors*, right? If not, the film splits off into two storylines: her life had she caught the tube, and her life had she missed the tube. I apply that principle to my life constantly now, split-screening and imagining 'how would this night be going if I was drinking' when I have wobbly moments.

Anyway, I was at Fleetwood Mac. Handily enough, the last time I'd been at that venue was to see The Black Keys, a few months previous, so I had a good split-screen reference.

I had shown up to The Black Keys early so that I could have a shaky drink to sort out my hangover. At Fleetwood Mac, I felt normal already, albeit nervous normal. Well rested, fed, bright-eyed. At The Black Keys, I didn't really pay attention to the band, all I was concerned about was 'is so-and-so going to the bar, are they going to get me a drink, aargh they bought me a small wine, oh no, the gig's over and the bars are closing, need more drinks'.

Whereas at Fleetwood Mac I felt calm, happy and free from the obsessing. And it was a spectacular show.

I finished the night by slipping into clean sheets, rather than slipping into a blackout.

29. I GAVE MYSELF TREATS

This is how shopping went when I was drinking.

Trudges around behind friends 'Why are we not in the pub? That is where the fun and connection is! Why would I want to spend money on things other than wine? Are we going to the pub later? There's a pub over there! No? WHAT? You want coffee? Oh, for heaven's sake.'

I hated shopping. It seemed so thoroughly pointless when there was drinking to be done. In sobriety, I finally understood what all the fuss is about.

Remember Belle's 100-day challenge? A key part of that is to reward yourself with treats. And remember the app, which calculated that I'd saved £350 in the first month? Well, I spent around half of that amount on treats in my first 30 days – #sorrynotsorry.

> I BOUGHT BOOKS THAT IMPROVED MY BRAIN RATHER THAN ELIMINATED ITS PRECIOUS CELLS. I SPENT EVENINGS AT HOT YOGA. DAYS CANTERING ON A VERY PRETTY CHESTNUT MARE, CALLED MOLLY.

Feasts with friends where I ordered everything I wanted, rather than only ordering a main course to save money and space for wine. Evenings writing (what would eventually become this book) and enjoying the scent of a jasmine candle. I booked myself massages after stressful, boozy events.

Spending some of the money rewarding myself helped. Carrot, rather than stick. Pretty, life-sweetening treats helped me associate sobriety with gladness, rather than denial. I used to think that getting obliterated and chain-smoking ten cigarettes was the only worthwhile way to 'treat myself'.

30. I REMEMBERED THAT A THOUGHT CANNOT MAKE ME DRINK

A very important one, this. No matter how much 'I want a drink, I need a drink, I could have a drink, there's a drink, pick up the drink' echoes in your head, a thought cannot make you pick up that drink and put it into your mouth. Did you know that? I didn't, before sobriety.

I honestly thought that thoughts were faits accomplis. That I was a slave to that tug. But it was just because I gave into it, so often, that it became second nature. I allowed the tug to pull me to the off-licence to buy the wine, I allowed it to lead me to the bottle in the fridge, I followed it into the liquor cabinet and enacted its demands.

Once I realized that only the physical act of picking up a drink and putting it into my mouth, could lead to me drinking, I felt much, much safer. Thoughts don't reign you. Thoughts are locked in your head. They can't move your hand. You can deny thoughts of drinking, argue back, soothe them, laugh at them or stroke them until they fall asleep. How? Personally, I gained a sense of detached mastery over my thoughts through mindfulness-based meditation, which we'll talk about on page 216.

FILLING YOUR TOOLBOX

So, those are my 30. Overall, something you'll notice in the first 30 days is fireworks-style epiphanies. Sudden, gorgeous and awesome. 'Oooooh.' You'll be walking down the street and bam! You'll realize that it's digital self-harm to stay friends with your ex on Facebook, and you'll no longer want to do that to yourself. Your mind will expand on a near-daily basis. As your brain starts to repair and you start to see things clearly for the first time in years.

Early sobriety, for me, was all about filling my toolbox, which used to be crammed with alcohol, cigarettes and the phone numbers of inadvisable men, with healthier alternatives. Swimming, nutritious food, early nights, fascinating books, podcasts, bubble baths, rubbing dogs' bellies, sober friends, milestone treats, counselling, music...learning to turn to those things for comfort and stimulation, as opposed to turning to wine.

The key was getting my tools out and using them *before I drank*. Exercising before going to the restaurant where everyone would be drinking, meditating on the regular, topping myself up with sober study daily. Using my tools in advance was like taking a car in for a check-up every six months. So that they can fix stuff before it breaks. Rather than calling out emergency services once your car has broken down and you're stood on the side of a lonely road, stranded, scared, crying.

The first 30 days were the most savage. Simultaneously, they were exquisite. I never wish to do them again. But they were beautiful *and* brutal. As Glennon Doyle Melton would say (another recovery author I love, especially *Carry on Warrior*) – they're brutiful.

'You say, it's dark. And in truth, I did place a cloud before your sun. But do you not see how the edges of the cloud are already glowing and turning light?'
- NIETZSCHE

I'M DELIGHTED ABOUT
A SMEAR TEST

DAY 61 OF SOBRIETY

Today has been one of those luminous, sunny sober days. I went to the hospital this morning for the smear test I have been procrastinating over for a YEAR. And I was delighted about the whole thing.

The last time I had a smear test, over four years ago, I was heinously hungover and paranoid that I stank of booze. I could barely string a sentence together. Today, I was chatty and happy to be sorting out my healthmin. Like a proper adult. I was beaming throughout. The doctor must have thought I was insane, grinning away in the stirrups. It was so much fun, getting it done!

Maybe my body has finally rid itself of all those toxins? Who knows. But I do know I haven't felt this happy in years. Years! I even enjoyed waiting for the bus. And getting on the bus too.

I feel absolutely mega. Euphoric. Is this what regular people feel like, all the time? I've found out that in recovery circles, this psychological phenomenon is called 'pink clouds'. And boy, does it feel good.

WHY WAS I SO DELIGHTED?

Moving from a life of active addiction to a life of sobriety is a bit like being transported from a *Game of Thrones*-esque winter to a Yosemite summer. Crushing hangovers turn even the simplest tasks – taking a cheque to the bank or buying food for dinner – into arduous nightmares.

I remember trying to sign my name in the bank with a severe case of the shakes. I remember having to turn tail and dash home, having had a vicious panic attack about the terror of: going to the supermarket. Hangovers and the anxiety of active addiction turn molehills into mountains.

So, when you perform these humdrum, everyday chores without a hangover, or free from panic, it can trigger a surge of delicious joy. You feel like hugging the clerk who is taking in your cheque, or skipping through the supermarket scattering rose petals. It's a spectacular feeling.

MY FAVOURITE
SOBER-INSPIRATION BLOGS

TIRED OF THINKING ABOUT DRINKING
Holds a special place in my heart, because it helped me so damn much in the early days. When I found it, I literally spent about five hours reading it compulsively, until I finally put my iPad down at 3am.
www.tiredofthinkingaboutdrinking.com

HIP SOBRIETY
Holly Whitaker, who masterminded this blog, is one of my best friends now. Holly's background is in healthcare; she could see there was a gap in the market for non-AA recovery and created the marvellous Hip Sobriety School. She truly knows more about addiction and the psychology of being sober than anyone I have ever met. Her approach is empowering, intelligent and groundbreaking in the recovery sphere.
www.hipsobriety.com

LAURA MCKOWEN
Laura writes oh-so beautifully. My favourite blog of hers was a pictured/not pictured rundown of her Facebook pictures, revealing the reality behind the smiley showcasing.
www.lauramckowen.com

ONE YEAR NO BEER
Run by a couple of incredibly likeable chaps, this very down-to-earth blog sets members (15K and counting) the challenge of taking a year off booze.
www.oneyearnobeer.com

GIRL & TONIC
Has a lovely, gentle approach to recovery, rooted in her status as a yoga teacher. I particularly love her Not-Drinking Diaries, a regular slot featuring inspirational teetotal women. Very accessible for the sober curious.
www.girlandtonic.co.uk

TEETOTAL POWER PLAYLIST

'SO GOOD AT BEING IN TROUBLE'/*UNKNOWN MORTAL ORCHESTRA*
'So good at being in trouble, so bad at being in love.'
I was SO BAD at relationships while I was drinking.

'DAYS ARE GONE'/*HAIM*
'And I got back up, when I lost control...knew that I couldn't take no more.'

'HOLD ON'/*WILSON PHILLIPS*
'Why do you lock yourself up in these chains? No one can change your life except for you.'

'RECOVERY'/*FRANK TURNER*
'Blacking in and out in a strange flat in East London...And you know your life is heading in a questionable direction.'

'IT'S A SHAME ABOUT RAY'/*THE LEMONHEADS*
'The cellar door was open, I could never stay away.'

'DO YOU STILL LOVE ME LIKE YOU USED TO'/*BEST COAST*
'I wake up to the morning sun, when did my life stop being so fun?...
I don't remember what it means to be me.'

'SHAKE IT OUT'/*FLORENCE + THE MACHINE*
'It's always darkest before the dawn...drinks in the dark at the end of my road...it's hard to dance with the devil on your back, so shake him off.'
YES, Florence.

'HERE COMES THE SUN'/*NINA SIMONE*
This entire song sums up what getting sober feels like.

ALCOHOL-FREE INSTAGRAM HEROES

@off.the.rocks
Weight-lifting, disco-dancing chancer who is laugh-out-loud funny and an unapologetic atheist in recovery. She plucks pearls of wisdom from the likes of Jimi Hendrix and Jeff Buckley, and her roomy-minded motto is 'Respect all ways. Always'.

@motherheart
Nourishing, visually gorgeous, spiritual take on 'high vibe substance-free living', with posts on the ego vs. the soul, and corkers like 'It's about creating a life that feels so good, that I don't feel the need to drink.'

@sasha_tozzi
Big-hearted beauty who has written about addiction in the Huffington Post, is proudly imperfect and shares gold dust like 'In a society that profits from your self doubt, liking yourself is a rebellious act' or 'People say a lot. So, I watch what they do.'

@sillylara
'Sober AF' badass who says things other people daren't, has a pet pig and works in the recovery sphere. Posts subversive gems like 'A couple of days ago I was at the beach and I ordered two virgin Pina Coladas. The bartender said, "That's exciting." As if we need ethanol and booze to have an exciting life. Silly her.'

@thesoberglow
Teetotal broad who shares the 'sweetness of life' sans booze, unedited realities of marriage and stunning panoramas of Utah deserts with thought-provokers like 'Your new life is going to cost you your old one.'

@soberevolution
Run by a dynamic chap who works for a rehab centre, this inspiring feed delivers wisdom such as 'I've got 99 problems, but a hangover ain't one' and 'Emotions are only temporary. Consequences due to our reactions can be permanent.' His before/after pics will blow your mind.

ADDICTIVE VOICE RECOGNITION

To be an addict is to have a disembodied voice in your head. A voice that is constantly chat, chat, chatting at you about why it would be a great idea to have a drink right now. A voice that takes your 'I'm not drinking tonight' sworn promise to yourself and dismantles it piece by piece. The voice is illogical, persistent, relentless, wily. Utterly maddening. It will stoop to any lowdown, dirty, or ludicrous trick to hoodwink you into a drink. It plots and wheedles to push you closer to the bottle.

Here are some examples of what my addictive voice says:

'You are alone with wine! Alone with wine! Give in now. You will give in eventually. You can't resist it.'

'You're broken, you're useless, you're a failure. May as well have a drink.'

'Drinking is fun! Drinking is relaxing! See how those people over there are laughing over wine? You will never laugh like that again. Unless you drink. C'mon. You're boring without booze.'

'Everyone at this party thinks you're weird because you're not drinking. Everyone is staring at your lame sparkling water. This time will be different. This time you will be able to moderate.'

At the end of a meal in an Italian restaurant. 'What's that. Limoncello? Well, it's practically dessert. It really would be rude not to. Noooo, don't give it to your friend. Take it back!'

'I can't believe you didn't get your astronomically unrealistic to-do list done! You may as well drink. It's all fucked.'

'I just realized something. No man has ever told you he loves you in sobriety. It seems you are much more lovable when you drink. Have a drink!'

'The only cure for this growing-thunder-in-your-ears panic attack is alcohol.'

'If you drink tonight, no one will know. You're by yourself. I won't tell them. You deserve it!'

And my absolute favourite. The most laughable of them all:

'You have toothache. Hmmm. Do you know what's great for toothache? VODKA. Yes it is! VODKA. Vodka will kill that red-hot throb stone dead. It's not drinking. It's medicine.'

A game-changer for me was separating this tyrannical voice out. Realizing that this voice was the wannabe architect of my destruction. Understanding that this voice was not me. It was my addiction talking.

I alit upon this concept through Belle's brilliant *Tired of Thinking About Drinking* blog. She calls her addictive voice Wolfie. Grrr. He's the big, bad wolf, trying various crafty tricks to entice Little Red Riding Hood from the path. A monster in a friendly guise. Belle talks about starving and dehydrating the wolf, so that his roar and power dwindle.

This approach to recovery is called 'Addictive Voice Recognition Therapy', or AVRT. It was first developed by the founder of *Rational Recovery*, Jack Trimpey, in 1986. He defines the Addictive Voice (what he calls the AV) as 'any thinking that supports or suggests the possible future use of alcohol or other drugs'. Trimpey carried out a study of 250 people and found that AVRT had a 65 per cent success rate.

> FOR ME, **PERSONIFYING AND DEMONIZING MY ADDICTIVE VOICE ALLOWED ME TO DISENTANGLE MYSELF FROM IT.** TO STAY ON THE RIGHT PATH, DESPITE THE MONSTER TRYING TO COAX ME OFF IT.

Once I realized that the voice inside my head that wanted me to drink was not my core self, and actually had the opposite of my best interests at heart, I could start to remove its power. Once I understood that it was trying to design my downfall, I started to rally against it.

People who use this technique often give their addictive voice a name. Trixie is a common one. I started off calling mine Gollum. Repulsive, underhand, obsessed with the ring (the drink) and willing to stoop to any means to hang on to it. Then I toyed with the idea of making my voice a troll, because its rat-a-tat-tatting reminded me of those cowardly, nasty trolls who hide behind keyboards and hurl insults at people.

But neither personification adequately captured the fearful sway my addictive voice held over my head. It was only once I called my voice Voldemort, the villain of *Harry Potter* fame, that I thought, 'Yup. That's it.' Nefarious, yet capable of being charming. Silken, but pure evil.

I know that I sound bonkers. I'm well aware that imagining Voldemort running around inside in my head, being all evil and shit, makes me sound like I'm not the brightest crayon in the box. But it *worked*.

So, what I'm going to say right now will truly complete the 'a few cards short of a full deck' picture. I started arguing with Voldemort. Telling him to jog on. I shut his sinister, abusive or fake-friendly whisperings down with logic. And he would slither away. His ghoulish face would fade into the blackness.

Sometimes I would laugh at Voldemort (as with the 'toothache' argument), sometimes I would calmly deconstruct his case for drinking with a plethora of evidence as to why not-drinking was undoubtedly a better strategy. But most of the time, in the first few months, getting fired up was the most effective strategy. I started to get angry with the voice; with my addiction.

How dare it attempt to savage my self-esteem, plunder my money, rampage through my relationships and crush my career. I became determined not to let my addictive voice get away with it any more. A burst of anger helps us gather together the gumption to unknot ourselves from a destructive relationship with a partner. Addiction turned out to be no different.

I finally got to a headspace whereby I realized that I deserved not to drink. I deserved *not* to have a life of 3am nausea and unreliability and zero money and bloodshot eyes. I deserved better.

Shutting Voldemort down quickly is what Belle meant by dehydrating, or starving the wolf. The more air-time I gave him, the stronger he got. The more I let him chat at me, the louder he got. Silencing him – zip it! – swiftly was crucial.

When I squash Voldemort and tell him NO, I make a firm decision not to drink, rather than letting the debate of 'should I drink?' ring around my head. When we make a clear-cut decision, rather than engage in the debate, our brains quieten down, says neuroscientist Alex Korb.

'Making decisions includes creating intentions and setting goals – all three are part of the same neural circuitry and engage the pre-frontal cortex in a positive way, reducing worry and anxiety.'

'Our brain likes definite decisions,' Korb continues. 'When we're torn between two possibilities, such as "do I drink tonight or not?", the limbic system is amped up. The uncertainty of indecisiveness means our limbic system has to sort through all the different possibilities of this dilemma. Once you make a clear-cut decision, you eliminate the uncertainty, and the multiple outcomes, meaning the limbic system calms down. The act of making a decision feels scary, since you may fail, but once you make a decision and set a definitive goal, the brain likes it more.'

It's why Holly from *Hip Sobriety*'s recovery motto is 'Never question the decision.' It's why she has a neat little 'nqtd' tattoo. Questioning the 'I don't drink, ever' decision restarts the debate in our heads, and hands our addictive voice a megaphone. It lets the wolf trick us off the right path. It invites Trixie in, allowing her to sit down and get her feet under the table. It gives Voldemort the floor, to present his best persuasive case.

Entertaining the debate takes my brain off the 'I don't drink' path and leads it down the 'should I drink?' neural pathway, which inevitably tends to meander to a HELL YES. The secret, for me, is to leave it well alone. To allow it to fade more and more.

Voldemort shape-shifts all the damn time. He tries out new ways to get me to drink. One of his favourite things to whisper lately is that I'm a 'loser' because I'm not married or mortgaged aged 37. Never mind the fact that I haven't yet met the man I want to marry, nor do I have any desire to be burdened by a mortgage yet. He's a tiny misogynist, who probably writes vitriol about 'washed-up spinsters' in online comments sections, whenever he's not yelling at me.

Whenever Voldemort lists all the things that are 'wrong' with me and why I 'may as well just drink' I fight back now. I list the things that are right about me. I was afraid to silence the 'here's all the things you're doing wrong, here's all the ways you are broken' voice for a long time. I thought that's what kept me motivated, humble and on the right path. Not so. It kept me down and wanting to drink.

Whenever I started becoming my own cheerleader and refusing to go down the 'you're shit, you are' neural pathway, I became more motivated, happier and kinder to others. And most of all, I stopped wanting to drink. I needed to raise my self-esteem to rise above the desire to drink.

Nowadays, Voldemort is Sylvanian-Family-sized. His mighty boom is now a squeak. And whenever he pops up in my head and jumps up and down, trying to get my attention by cheeping, 'That pink wine looks divin...' I can easily whack-a-mole splat him. 'Everyone else at this party is drinki...'. Nope. Shut your face, Voldy.

Each time I knock Voldemort down, the Lilliputian villain finds it harder to get back up, to be heard, to assemble a new argument that I haven't already rejected dozens, even hundreds of times. It's satisfying to watch him shrink.

But, there's a difference: I don't feel any fury towards him now. If anything, I think he's a sad little creature. Who no longer holds any sway over my decisions. Who no longer has the power to start a 'should I drink?' debate in my head. Because I now know that the answer is always – HELL NO.

'Now I know my beast and I know how to manage it. It's like living with a 400-pound orangutan that wants to kill me. It's much more powerful than me, doesn't speak the same language and it runs around the darkness of my soul.'

– ACTOR TOM HARDY, WHO GOT SOBER BACK IN 2003

SURPRISING SOBER BONUSES

1. I SMELL NICE
I am always surprised when people now tell me I smell lovely; literally nobody said that when I was drinking. Probably because I smelled like a barmaid's apron.

2. I GET LETTERS OFFERING ME CREDIT CARDS
Or telling me my bank account has been automatically upgraded to the fancy-pants one. I used to get letters threatening me with court over late payments.

3. I CHECK OUT OF HOTELS EARLY. EARLY!
In sobriety I have never been ousted from a hotel room an hour past the check-out time, by an angry cleaner/hotel manager.

4. NO MORE 'CAN WE CHAT' PARANOIA
'I have a bone to pick with you' was like an icy dagger being plunged into my heart. Jumpy 'beer fear' has been replaced by a luxuriously clean conscience.

5. I LOOK IN FRIDGES NOW AND SEE FOOD
Rather than automatically clocking and cataloguing the booze in there. Fridges were just enormous drinks cooler boxes.

6. MY BIRTHDAY CARDS ARE NO LONGER ALL ALCOHOL-RELATED.
I no longer open them and have to fake-laugh, when actually I want to cry. 'Is that all people see when they look at me?'

7. THE REVELATION OF 'SPARE' CHANGE
I used to spend every last £1 rattling around in there on wine. 'Spare' money was a foreign concept.

8. RAIN DOESN'T MAKE ME MURDEROUS
Shakes fist at sky I straightened my hair this morning, GODDAMMIT. Wind was a personal affront. Scorching sun was merely a global plot to melt my make-up. Now, I know that I cannot change the weather. I pull up my hood and feel happy that the flowers are getting a drink.

9. NO MORE REPLACING COATS/BAGS/CARDS/PHONES
I no longer 'lose' my belongings to the underbelly of Soho (read: chuck them on the floor). No more palaver having to replace said items, or cancel my cards or whatever. No more returning to the scene of

my boozehounding with my tail between my legs, to ask if it'd been handed in. That was fun. Not.

10. I DON'T HAVE TO WATCH TV TWICE
I spent so many hours squinting at the TV in an in-the-bag blackout. Watching telly with one eye shut so that the people stopped doubling and blurring. Rewinding a scene several times because English had started sounding like Egyptian. I watched the last two seasons of *Breaking Bad* while drinking. I couldn't tell you what happened. I have no idea how it ended. *No idea.* Was it a good ending?

11. MY HANDWRITING IS LEGIBLE
My handwriting started to look drunk. I remember ripping up a birthday card once, because my spidery scrawl was ungiveably messy.

12. I ORDER MILKSHAKES IN BOUTIQUE CINEMAS
The point of going to a swanky vintage cinema now is to sink into the velvet seats, eat artisan food and enjoy the film; rather than mainline wine.

13. GOODBYE RANCID FAKE-TANNED SHEETS
I no longer plaster fake tan over my puffy face, red eyes and toxin-ravaged skin. I was like a zombie trying to blend into the human crowd. I no longer want to get into bed greasy and smelling nasty. I have put my own comfort above what people think of my Irish skin. That seems unrelated to sobriety; but it's totally related.

14. BEGONE UNEXPLAINED BRUISES
I was constantly finding mysterious ink-blotches on my thighs or, even more creepy; fingertip-shaped stains. I used to tell myself that I 'bruised like a peach.' Nope. I don't. I can't remember the last time I had a bruise.

15. I GET REFUNDS ON UNWANTED ITEMS
By the end of my working day, I was either on the starters-block to get to the pub, or too hungover to face it. And the 28-days-return window would snap shut.

16. I DON'T HAVE TO RUN TO THE TRAIN STATION IN HEELS
Getting out of bed every morning used to be such agony that I always had to half-walk-half-jog to catch the train.

17. NO SWEAT
Unless I'm playing tennis or something, when you're supposed to sweat.

18. I DON'T KNOCK OVER PINTS OF WATER IN THE NIGHT
In fact, I don't need any water beside the bed. Because I'm actually hydrated, rather than waking up at 4am with a raging-inferno thirst.

19. I DON'T HAVE TO COVER UP 'ALCOHOLIC FLUSH'
I would look in the mirror and squeak with horror. Not only did I have shaking hands; my fire-engine-red cheeks were sounding the alarm too.

20. I TAKE MY MAKE-UP OFF EVERY SINGLE NIGHT
No smoky eyeshadow on my new seersucker sheets, or skin clogged with foundation. I even floss (sometimes).

21. I HAVE A FIVE-STAR UBER RATING
I am really, really nice to the drivers. I would have been kicked off Uber (and Airbnb for that matter) by now, if I was still drinking.

22. MY CLASSPASS ATTENDANCE IS 100 PER CENT
I have never been fined for non-attendance. I always use my five classes per month. *Flicks imaginary dust off shoulder*

23. I NEVER, EVER WEE IN ALLEYWAYS AT 2AM.
(You know you've done it too.)

24. FOOD TASTES BETTER
I always thought that wine enhanced food. Turns out booze numbs your taste buds. It makes the food *less* tasty. Huh.

25. PARANOIA WILL DESTROY YA
I can now see people without the soul-eating paranoia of what I did or said to them last time I saw them.

26. I READ ABOUT TEN TIMES MORE BOOKS
I can even remember the plot. Sometimes. Kinda.

27. THE LEVEL OF MY FRIEND'S GLASS IS NOT A FIXATION
Funny thing: I never ever feel like ripping my friend's head off when she pours herself a centimetre more elderflower cordial than me.

III: NATURE, RATHER THAN NIGHTCLUBS

DEATH OF PARTY GIRL

Open scene: Saturday, a house party, Camden. I'm five months sober and this is my first sober party. I am there with my boyfriend-of-the-time and have enlisted the help of a wingwoman, Susan.

The party gets off to an awkward start, with me having to turn champagne down and ask for cola instead, in front of a kitchenful of people all clutching champagne. Aargh.

When Susan shows up, I'm delighted, but she's on the verge of tears over a boyfriend debacle. She drinks one, two, three, six vodka and tonics. She becomes Party Girl.

We are in the living room. Susan has hijacked the music and put some obscure German happy house on. She's dancing around in the middle of the room, despite the fact nobody else is dancing. Everyone is looking at her with shiny-eyed admiration, or at least, that's what I interpret it as. She is so cool, so free, so unshackled.

Meanwhile, I have had three colas and am superglued to my seat in the midst of a sugar-fuelled social panic.

Susan, arms in the air: 'Cath, this is a TUNE. DANCE!'

Me, grinning manically to disguise the fact I'm crying inside. 'Oh, no, I'm OK, honestly.'

Susan tries to pull me off my chair. I grip it desperately. The makeshift dancefloor may as well be shark-infested waters.

My boyfriend: 'C'mon Cath, DANCE.'

Me: 'Noooooo! Leave me alone!'

They exchange a look. Or, I imagine they do. A 'she's-lame' look.

Five minutes later we have the exact same conversation again.

I feel intensely uncomfortable, like I have 'buzzkill' in lights above my head.

I'm not used to being the boring one. If I was drinking, I would be up there with Susan, and everyone would be regarding me with shiny-eyed admiration too. I have long been the dancefloor-starter. But dancing sober feels impossible. I feel supercharged with 'flight' adrenaline. Simultaneously frozen and electrified with anxiety.

I go and hide in the toilets for 15 minutes and pray they will have stopped dancing, and stopped trying to make me dance, by the time I emerge. I peep around the door frame. They're still dancing. Motherfuck. I duck through a bedroom and head out into the garden to take big gulps of air and talk to some people who won't try to make me dance.

They eventually stop dancing. I am thrilled.

I'm ready to leave the party at midnight, since that's what happens when you don't have booze coursing through your veins, but I succumb to their 'don't leave! It's early!' pressure pleas and stay until 2am. I am exhausted and feel like a total loser. I eye up the open window next to me. We're on the first floor, but I swear, if there was a skip to break my fall, I would cannonball out of that window.

On the night bus home, amid drunk people scarfing junk food and shouting at each other, I pretend to nap and secretly have a silent cry, my face turned to the window so my boyfriend can't see. I am no longer the Party Girl, and I'm now mourning her death.

THE NEXT DAY
I wake up feeling happy again. Last night was rough, but I did it, and I feel a swell of satisfaction. I go on a bike ride, see a wildlife photography exhibition, make a big Sunday roast and write. I reach out to some sober friends and tell them about my crushing disappointment in myself.

They remind me that I haven't been to a party sober for oh, about 20 years, and I need to give myself a break. That the challenge shouldn't be underestimated. That we are relearning how to navigate the world without Party-Girl-transforming tonic. Which is hard. We feel the way we feel. If we don't feel like dancing, there is nothing we can throw down our throats to make that change.

I tell them that I felt like everyone was staring at me, like I was the epicentre of anti-fun. They remind me that I'm only the centre of my own night; not everyone else's. That it's likely that no one else even noticed my acute discomfort in the face of the 'DANCE' badgering. Huh.

Susan emails me later in the week, saying she couldn't remember the end of the party and that she didn't recover until Tuesday. So. Swings, roundabouts. I realize that ruining two full days for the sake of an hour or so of Party Girl 'wooo' is not worth it.

I was always the last girl to leave any party, if I ever managed to leave. Most of the time, I wound up unconscious on a sofa somewhere, waking up the next day to a strange house and an awkward social predicament. I thought I was a night owl, whose natural habitat was the booming-bass world of bars and clubs. What I didn't know was that I have never been a fan of parties or nightclubs. The bait that was reeling me out of the house was the shiny lure of the bottle, not the feather boa of a nightclub. That was why I went *out*-out four times a week. The drinking. Not the club scene.

While drinking, Day Fun was anathema to me. Birds sounded like banshees. Kids laughing sounded like the stabbing violins from *Psycho*'s shower scene. Fire-sky sunsets left me cold, shrugging, uninspired. Long walks were just joyless impediments to my drinking. Road trips were white-knuckled snorefests until I could get close to booze again. Sitting in a pretty cafe having an ice-cream sundae just seemed so pointless. I could spend this money on wine! Where's the wine?

My weekends were just: drink, sleep, hangover, drink, sleep, hangover, repeat. Days were all about endurance, not enjoyment. Whenever I could, I would sleep until 1, 2, 3pm on weekends, to make the days as short as possible, as well as recovering from the night before. Daytime: meh. They were black-and-white, compared to the acid-bright, bombastic colour of nighttime.

We're programmed by society to look up to the Party Girls of this world. It's a key scene in any coming-of-age movie (*She's All That, Clueless, Dirty Dancing, Save the Last Dance*) whereby the gawky, mousey girl manages to peel herself off the sidelines after a shot or two, and join the party. Yeah! Watch her go! She's finally cool! These messages burrow deep into our brains.

And the way I tried to get there, to that arms-in-the-air dancey place, was by drinking. Now that I don't drink, I rarely get there, unless it's a magical trifecta of the right music, the right friends, the right vibe.

And that's OK. Because it's real, when I do get there, rather than a chemically induced sham. I'm now completely chilled about being the girl who's in her PJs by midnight, rather than a hot mess on the dancefloor. The price tag of being the Party Girl was – and is – too expensive. I was never really her anyhow.

> **SO, IN SOBRIETY, DAY FUN GIRL WAS BORN.** INSTEAD OF LIVING FOR THE RELIEF OF NIGHT FALLING AND THE CLUB BASS THRUMMING INTO LIFE, I STARTED LIVING IN THE DAYS.

Going for cream teas in posh stately homes; doing a mad obstacle-course race where I had to crawl through tunnels around Battersea Power Station; blustery walks alongside stormy seas; deep-diving into Aladdin's Cave vintage shops for bargains. All while my former underworld buddies slept their Saturdays and Sundays away.

Now I can enjoy daytimes without the drag of the 'when can I drink'? undercurrent. And when evening falls, I no longer have to go out, in order to legitimately drink my face off. I've done enough going out to last me a lifetime.

RIP Party Girl. I no longer miss her. In fact, I do pirouettes on her grave.

THE TRAPDOOR TECHNIQUE

When I told my sober tribe about my crying-on-the-bus departure, they said I stayed at the party way too long. That I should have left when I wanted to leave. That the most triggery thing a newly sober person can do, is to stay at a party too long and feel like a Debbie Downer. That's when we're most likely to reach for a drink.

Alcohol ups our social stamina. Without it, parties are louder, brighter, more tiring. We fade more quickly. And we get tired at the normal time. Like, midnight. Why wouldn't we? We're not jacked up on anything, other than tonic, elderflower or a diet cola. A canapé doesn't give you the ability to party until 3am.

Given their advice, I start using the 'trapdoor technique', an Irish term that means vamoosing out of the party without saying goodbye to anyone. Because if you do say goodbye, you're going to get 'stay!' pressurized into not leaving. But isn't that terribly rude, leaving without saying cheerio to everyone you know? Um, no. It's much more rude to get wasted and cry and knock breakables over and shout at people who try to take your cider off you (actual story of mine). D'you know how many times people have noticed that I trapdoored on their party? Zero. Zilch. And believe me, nothing great happens in a bar past midnight. I did my research. On about 50,000 different occasions.

Obviously, your mates or the hosts need a heads-up that you may well vanish. This is an actual message I sent at six months sober, before heading to a party:

Yeah, that's cool, will be fun, but as long as I have your permission to trapdoor when I need to. There's something about being sober, when you need to leave a party, you need to leave right then. Otherwise you can be liable to drink. You can suddenly get tired and ratty and everyone around you is on a different level because they're boozing. You obviously stay for as long as you like! I'll get a cab back on my own.

I start being financially, logistically and mentally prepared to leave a party alone, if needs be. My escape route is planned out before I even arrive.

The trapdoor technique saved my skin in early sobriety more times than I can count.

KNOCKED-NAKED MARGARITAS

AUGUST 2015: ON A ROAD TRIP IN AMERICA'S DEEP SOUTH WITH A FRIEND WHO DRINKS

I had a wobble today. I have watched Lucy drink hard for three nights. Without apparent consequence.

We've been in New Orleans feeding our dollars into Zoltar (of Big fame) fortune-predicting machines, marvelling at the delicately wrought French balconies of Bourbon Street, listening to honky-tonk at The Spotted Cat and sitting at a revolving bar made from a vintage carousel. New Orleans is one of my favourite places on the planet. But the drink flows fast.

We're now in Natchez. My thinking has been wonky all day. I've been feeling drab.

And then, earlier, we looked around this resplendent Plantation house. The guide was a charming local Natchez lady called Gay. She told us, 'While you're in town, y'all have to go to Fat Momma's for a knocked-naked margarita! Y'all can't leave town without one!'

My addictive voice found a megaphone. Normally, at this stage in sobriety, I can dismiss the 'you can't leave Natchez without a knocked-naked margarita' voice. I can spank it and send it on its way. But I half-listened. And Lucy (as I would have done when I was drinking) went on and on about going to Fat Momma's, trying the margarita and getting the 'I was knocked naked at Fat Momma's' t-shirt.

I started feeling panicky, angry and deprived.

I wanted to pretend I was OK. To stop 'being silly' and to go on down to Fat Momma's. I couldn't inconvenience my friend out of her t-shirt. She has to fill her boots with knocked-naked margaritas! Gay said so! My brain was shouting at me to stop being such a baby, and get my arse to the margarita bar.

What I actually needed to do this evening was this: have some time alone, meditate, find my sweet, serene spot once more, think hard on all the reasons I am grateful to be sober, think hard on how horror-show scary drinking got for me and not go to Fat Momma's.

At nearly two years sober, I can now genuinely have fun in bars. I can be around drinking and not crave it. I can be friends with people who drink regularly. I love these people dearly; they are far beyond the drinking buddies I no longer see.

But I also need rest days, otherwise I am fatigued. And when I'm fatigued, I'm vulnerable. Like a deer who has fallen short from the herd and can be picked off by a wily wolf. And after three nights of hanging in drinking establishments, I needed a rest day.

I dropped the 'I'm OK!' pretence and told my friend how I was feeling. I told her I needed to be alone for a while, eat a faceful of food and not go to a bar tonight. She looked after me, she didn't drink and we ended up watching a life-changing Mississippi sunset. We got heckled by the politest carload of teenage boys ever, who rolled down the window and hollered 'y'all look nice today'. Lucy later wondered why she would ever want a slightly rapey sounding 'I was knocked naked at Fat Momma's' t-shirt.

The lesson of today: pretending to be 'swell!' when you're feeling triggered is just bad, bad news. And going to a margarita bar when you're half-listening to the 'maybe just one margarita' voice is a horrible idea.

THE NEXT MORNING
I down some coffee and go for a run at sunrise, watching a steamship chug happily beneath a steel bridge so monstrously huge, it makes the ship look like a toy boat.

Ahhhhh. The thundercloud in my head has passed. Mental blue-sky once more. Tonight I might be game for going to a bar. I might not. I will see how I feel.

Party Girl would have earned that 'knocked naked' t-shirt by living up to its promise, no doubt. She probably would have picked up some sleazy guy in the bar last night. She would have gone back to his house, to feed her skeletal self-esteem the only way she knows how. And she would now be unconscious in a stranger's bed, missing this ethereal sunrise.

I much prefer Sober Girl, who runs at sunrise. Who feels like her heart might burst from the beauty of the neon-streaked sky. And who is never knocked naked by margaritas.

HELLO, SOCIALLY AWKWARD TEEN

Imagine a Russian doll. Those wooden dolls-within-dolls. When I was drinking, all I knew was my outer doll. The drunk, shouty, glitter-eyeshadowed party girl, who'd been belligerent at parties since 1993. Who threw birthday parties of 20-plus people and peacocked around them in a too-tight dress. That was me. Or, so I thought.

When I sobered up, I got a shock. My painted outer shell fell away, cracking wide open, and inside her was a surprise doll. A socially awkward, bookish, introverted doll. The likes of which I hadn't seen since I was 12. I eyed this hidden doll with bewilderment. I didn't recognize her. I thought she'd buggered off 16 years ago and here she was, back in my life. She was a lot nicer than my party-girl doll, who could be a bit of a wanker, but she was also startlingly different.

Instead of beelining to the nearest party and strutting around, my new self wanted to write, curl up with a dog, hang out one-on-one with people in parks or read a book and go to bed at 10pm. Big, loud groups of new people? A nightclub? Forgetaboutit.

My friends found it difficult to reconcile the shift in me. 'You've been up since 7am? You don't want to go to the party? You want to go to a museum? Who are you?!' I remember earnestly telling one friend that I'd discovered I was in fact an introvert, and she snorted so hard with laughter that she choked on her tea.

So, I was an introvert now. Huh. I started researching it. Turns out it's all about blood flow in our brains. Extrovert brain blood flow is directed to the regions of the brain concerned with interpreting sensory data – making sense of the outside world. Whereas introvert brain blood flow is more pronounced to the frontal lobe, which deals with the internal processes of decision-making, memory, solving problems – our inner landscape.

Introverts often appear to be daydreaming, but that's because their internal landscape is a buzzy metropolis, which takes up a lot of their energy. They're not zoned out, they're just attending to their inner landscape. Introverts turn inwards, while extroverts point outwards.

Another study found that extroverts' brains get a buzz from human faces, whereas in comparison, introverts' brains are indifferent to them. Introverts like looking at flowers as much as faces. Basically, introverts can pretty much live without people. They're happy to sit in a field with some daisies. They've already got a hive of activity in their head to attend to. Which is why masses of external stimuli, say a packed train station, can give an introvert 'Overwhelm'.

When I was drinking, I remember saying to people, 'I can't spend more than a couple of nights alone.' It wasn't unusual for me to attend three or four parties or nightclubs a week. The reality was, I couldn't spend more than a couple of nights without drinking. I didn't have FOMO, like I thought. I had FOMOOW. Fear of Missing Out On Wine.

When I was drinking being alone meant the self-loathing set in. I had wanted the distraction of other people, because I didn't like myself. Sober, I started to *love* being alone.

CONFIDENCE CHEAT CODE

Here's what I realized. It was a sun-breaks-through-the-clouds realization for me. As a teenager, I was painfully shy. So guess what I did? I drank to manufacture fake confidence.

I used alcohol as if it was a computer game cheat code. I didn't need to learn how to motor through levels three to seven. All I had to do to take me from level two (terrified) to level eight (bouncing around a dancefloor to Blur) was to *drink*. So I did. With gusto. Until I was utterly reliant on it for any sort of socializing.

When I sobered up, I found that I had to relearn how to relax at parties, how to carry small talk with strangers and how to venture onto a dancefloor (more on that later on page 152).

How? Simply with patience, time and some grit. Just as you would crack a computer game. It's trial and error. Eventually, with sustained stabs at it, you learn to navigate Tiki the kiwi through the mazes of *New Zealand Story*, or to give Yoshi wings in *Super Mario World* or to steer the stunt tubes in *Grand Theft Auto*.

You'll learn how to party sober, just as you learned how to crush a job interview, or to give a presentation, even though you were a nervous wreck the first time around.

I wish I could offer you a shortcut, but there isn't one. That's the thing. We were looking for a shortcut in alcohol, but we got lost by taking it.

Be gentle with yourself. Carry a soft drink at all times, to avoid the 'drink?' conversation if you wish. It's completely normal to be nervous before meeting a bunch of new people.

But when it does click, when you can enjoy parties sober, when you can leap around a dancefloor without sambuca in your system, you'll feel the most unbelievable buzz. Because it's genuine confidence, a genuine desire to dance, a genuine belly laugh at a joke, and a genuinely good time. Without the nightmarish hangover afterwards.

INTROVERT TIME OUT

If you're an introvert too, as 50 per cent of people are, you'll find you need to be judicious with your energy. You'll soon learn that parties are indeed fun sober, but they are also draining. You'll learn not to say yes to every party. To save your socializing credits for those who you really want to spend them on. Parties are expensive.

Think of the metaphor of a plug in a socket. Extroverts are the plugs; they get energy from social interaction. They feel electrified by it. Whereas introverts are the sockets; they lose energy while socializing. They may well love it, but it costs them dearly and they need time to recharge afterwards.

It's my responsibility to guard my energy and use it wisely. So, I never schedule in more than four social things in one week. Otherwise, I'm frazzled. If I go on holiday with a friend for a week, I carve out some time to myself. No matter how much I love that person – and I definitely do if I'm on holiday with them – I will not be able to do seven uninterrupted days with them.

I try to get my own room on holiday, always. At the very least, my own bed. I go out for runs when I'm staying with family. After the run I lie in a field and look at trees for a half hour. I take lengthy baths. I don't tend to go and stay in anyone's house for longer than a couple of nights. In the mornings, I get a coffee and go back to bed for an hour to read the *Guardian*, the *Pool* and the *Huffington Post*. I need to not talk to people for chunks of the day. That's just how I am. What about you?

With these tweaks, I stay topped up. I've learned to protect my energy fiercely and unapologetically, because when my reserves dwindle, I grow ratty, snappy and depressed. So, I'm doing everyone a favour, in the grand scheme. Also, when my red lights are flashing and I'm socialized out, I'm more likely to think about drinking.

'Almost everything will work again if you unplug it for a few minutes, including you.'
— ANNE LAMOTT

SIGNS YOU'RE A SECRET INTROVERT

- After an intense group holiday, you'd happily go to a cabin atop a glacier for three days of completely alone time.

- An impromptu house guest rocking up at the door? Just no.

- Charades is your idea of hell-in-a-party-game. Karaoke freaks you out.

- When people sing 'Happy Birthday' to you, you're secretly gritting your teeth and waiting for it to stop, because you don't like being the centre of attention.

- You fling your phone across the room in fright when someone dares to spontaneously Facetime you.

WATERFALLS AND TREES BECKON

My best friend called me the other day and asked, 'Are you staring at trees again, Cath?' Yes. Yes, I was.

My happy place used to be dark nightclubs. It was very easy to drink my fill in nightclubs, and they stayed open really late, and everyone else was generally hammered too. I loved them.

Under the misnomer of wanting to 'dance', I would badger whatever friend/s I was out with to stay out with me and go clubbing. I didn't want to dance; I know that now. I wanted to drink.

Now that I'm sober, I look into the nightclub world with horror. People stumbling around, crazy prices, dirty toilets, disgruntled queues, sticky floors, migraine-making decibels.

Now, my happy place is running through a sylvan glade. Gawping down into a valley from atop a mountain, watching as the fog lifts and the trees are etch-a-sketched in. Strolling along a beach at sunrise, watching the pinks and oranges bloom through the sky like watercolours. Doing yoga on a deck beside a sinuous, silvery river lined by embroidered flowers.

Spending time outside in nature has proved to be a huge part of my recovery. I can finally see all the beauty on the planet; beauty that I was blind to before.

I was completely stuck inside my narcissistic hangover and didn't see outside myself. I was barrelling to the pub and failing to notice Hyde Park gleaming at me, or lying in bed with alcohol poisoning as a beautiful summers' day passed me by.

My urge to be outside and surrounded by green pastorals, vast landscapes or the swoosh of water, is no mistake. My body has been telling me to do it. I've felt that unmistakable pull since very early on in sobriety.

And this could be why. A study took two lots of people and showed them traumatic scenes of people getting hurt in the workplace. Directly after the painful video, they showed Group A a nature film of babbling brooks and sunrises and suchlike. They showed Group B a film reel of urban scenes, city tower blocks, traffic, that sort of thing. Group A recovered much quicker from the traumatic scenes than Group B. Ergo, people heal faster from trauma (and active addiction is trauma, make no mistake) in the countryside than in the city. It's as if my body *knew* that, on some cellular level.

It's even been shown that hospital patients recover more quickly from surgery if they have a window view of a tree, rather than of a brick wall. Mind-blowing stuff. And recovering from addiction is not dissimilar to healing from an operation; it's a physical and mental ordeal.

Then there's a review of several studies, which shows that exercising outdoors improves people's mood and self-esteem after just five minutes. Yep, that quickly. Environments with a watery element (a river, the sea, whatever) were shown to be especially engaging and mood-lifting. If you can't get outside, even looking at pictures of green space will make a difference.

I clearly remember the first time I really *saw* nature again, in early sobriety. I was around three months sober, and back in my family's home village of Cushendall, in Northern Ireland. They filmed a lot of *Game of Thrones* around there, because it's full-on majestic, with soaring cliffs and curvy glens. There's a waterfall park there called Glenariff.

I have been many, many times, but this time I really saw it. Without the jonesing to get to the pub at the foot of the waterfall and throw back some wine. Because I wasn't impatient to get back inside and back to the booze, I could really wander for hours and soak up all of the magnificence. The goodness of its thundery waterfalls. Ancient trees that look like a giant's hand has burst out of the ground and tried to grab the sky.

I totally relate to what Eminem has to say about nature. 'I speak to Elton [John]. He's like my sponsor....He was saying things to me like, "You're going to see nature that you never noticed before." Shit you'd normally think was corny but that you haven't seen in so long that you just go, "Wow! Look at that fucking rainbow!" Or even little things – trees, the colour of leaves. I fucking love leaves now, man. I feel like I've been neglecting leaves for a long time.'

No more neglecting leaves.

ANIMALS AND KIDS KNOW

I strongly believe that animals and children have a sixth sense that picks up on addiction. Once children grow into adults, that sixth sense seems to dull.

When I was angry-drinking, I can think of so many examples of cats skittering off scared, or dogs that never growled, growling at me.

When I was angry-drinking, children eyed me warily. 'You smell funny,' my then four-year-old nephew once said, when I was reading him his bedtime story. He knew.

Animals know. Children know.

When my angry-drinking wilted to despair-drinking, and when my swagger stumbled into a stagger, the animals and children changed towards me. It was as if they could feel my deep reservoirs of sadness and self-loathing, and they wanted to help me out.

I vividly remember spending one day on a wild bit of heathland in Surrey, around six months before I found sobriety. I had spent the day drinking white wine out of a water bottle, crying, having arguments with people in my head and lying down on a quiet bit of the heath, telling myself that I was getting some 'fresh air'. I was drinking on a heath, wearing expensive designer wellies, and had keys to a rented flat in my bag; but that was the only distinction between me and a homeless person on a street corner.

I love horses, and there were three grown horses and a yearling in the field on the heath. I didn't have any food, and yet they all came to me. And stayed with me. Bowed and let me hold their beautiful strong heads. Breathed me in with twitching noses and licked my open hand. The mother even let me stroke her yearling; a huge, rare compliment. I spent an hour in that field, with those horses. It was like a love-huddle. They pulled me out of the mire of my own mind, and into that field with them, into the present moment, when I needed it most. On that day, I had been feeling especially suicidal.

During the same dark period, there was a notable change in my ex's dog Bruno. Bruno was not a clingy, cuddly dog, in the least. He was a bouncy, fighty, impish terrier through and through; much happier wriggling out of your grasp and bowling out to the garden to chase rabbits. Or playing tug-of-war with his brother.

But, when I was beset by suicidal thoughts, Bruno could tell. He would abandon digging up flowers in the garden, or crunching determinedly on his bone, and sit with me, all day long. He became a lapdog. Even when I went to the toilet, he would try to jump on my lap. He would stare at me, pouring the wine, with his tail flat and his ears down and his face mournful, pleading with me not to do it.

> HE WAS LIKE MY SAD, SOULFUL LITTLE SHADOW IN THOSE SUICIDAL DAYS. **IT WAS AS IF HE WAS GUARDING ME FROM MYSELF.**

And when I had a good run of sober days, or when I was still drinking but having a good day without dark thoughts, my shadow was gone. On those days, Bruno was always out in the garden, barking joyously at squirrels, or running around the house happily peeing on things he shouldn't pee on. He could feel it. He knew I was OK, and that he needn't look after me.

It's proven that dogs are as smart as two-year-old children, but I would wager that they're even smarter than that emotionally. They intuit how people feel, and want to comfort the sad.

When I quit booze, the animals and kids that once left six feet of distance from my angry-drinking, started getting all up in my grill. They could feel that my energy had changed, from toxic to calm.

HOLIDAYS

AUGUST 2010: A TYPICAL DRINKING HOLIDAY
I am sitting on a plane back from Barbados, after ten days in my cousin's gorgeous luxury villa.

'Are you…OK?' The guy next to me asks. My heart sinks. Shoot. He has noticed that I am shaking too much to eat the tiny meal with the tiny cutlery. The only thing I can manage is to stuff the bread roll into my starving mouth. I want to eat the whole meal, I need to eat it, after ten nights straight of heavy drinking. I can't eat it.

'I'm fine,' I reply, defensive. 'I've just been overdoing the partying.' He looks more concerned than I think he should be. I fail to mention that my friends left four days ago, I wanted to stay on longer to 'relax' alone. I thought I was going to hit the gym, get early nights and read. That didn't happen. I've spent the last three nights 'partying' by myself. I'm still devastated over the split with Seb.

I think back over the holiday.

I remember sharing far too much information when smashed. I remember being told off for being arrogant when wasted. I remember searching people's faces to see if they were annoyed with me. I remember going to a ridiculously lavish restaurant, The Cliff, for cocktails, and not enjoying it at all, despite the fake smile painted on my face. I couldn't wait until we got back to the villa where the wine was on tap, rather than agonizingly dispensed by the glass.

I remember lying in bed and thinking, 'How am I going to get through today?' even though I was in paradise. I remember sleeping in until at least midday every day because my aching body needed it, having been up drinking until 3am/4am/5am. I remember trying to exercise my hangovers away, but the exercise had stopped working.

I remember merely gritting my teeth through the stunning day we had out on a yacht, during which we swam with turtles in the duck-egg turquoise sea. They nibbled at our toes, thinking we were food. The others squealed with delight, but I freaked out and had to get out of the water. I was scared I would vomit into the snorkel. All I could think about was the vodka below deck, and why wasn't anyone else tempted, and whether I could have some without attracting judgmental comments.

I look around the plane and see people who are glowing, relaxed, with sleepy half-smiles. I am grey and broken, with bloodshot eyes. My tight white dress, make-up and gold sandals do nothing to detract from the rot of a ten-night-strong hangover.

What is wrong with me? Why can't I get a plane home from a holiday looking and feeling like those people? I turn my head so that the guy next to me can't see the silent tears rolling down my cheeks.

He might ask if I'm OK again. And I really can't have that.

MAY 2014: A TYPICAL SOBER HOLIDAY

I'm on the train back from Wales and feeling hot-damn fine. I am glowing, relaxed and have a sleepy half-smile on my face. I don't have doom rolling around inside my brain, sky-high anxiety or a bruised body. I feel amazing. I think back to the people on the plane back from Barbados, who looked all blissed out. Now I know how those people did it. They don't drink themselves sick during their holidays.

I think back over my first sober mini-break in a quaint Welsh fishing village, Solva. On the first day, I woke up at 5.30am because I was so excited. Feeling box-fresh despite only having had five hours' sleep. I went for a walk along the beach to watch the sun rise, and took pictures of a sweet fishing boat named the Curious Cat. I can't get over the fact that the wretched, infected feeling inside is no longer there; it's been replaced by a serene, still pool.

When we went out for dinner, I actually tasted and enjoyed the food on my plate, rather than fixating on the level of my wine glass and how to get more (always more).

We hiked 26km one day along a dramatic coastal path, which I never would have been able to do when drinking. I felt electrified by it, rather than seeing the hike as a boring chore before I could finally attend the main event – the pub.

I didn't spend an astronomical amount of money on cocktails or taxis. I didn't wake up in any strange beds. In fact, I did nothing to warrant disgrace, whatsoever. I told no lies. I remember everything.

Sitting on the train home, I realize I don't feel like I need another week's holiday, to get over the holiday. I feel refreshed and ready to go back to work.

I choose sober holidays.

I choose sober.

IV: BEING NICER

A GRATITUDE ADJUSTMENT

'People generally see what they look for, and hear what they listen for.'

— HARPER LEE, TO KILL A MOCKINGBIRD

In order for you to understand how much nicer I am now, you need to understand what I was like when I was drinking.

One of the biggest epiphanies I've ever had, was hearing the Anne Lamott quote: 'Expectations are resentments under construction.' And boy, did I have expectations. I treated people badly, but expected them to treat me like an empress. When others disappointed me, you better believe I kept that slight. I stored it away carefully and revisited it regularly.

Y'know how people build memory palaces, in order to remember stuff? They'll place capital cities in the courtyard, tuck mathematical equations into cradles in the nursery and neatly slot the elements of the periodic table into herbal cubby holes in the pantry. Well, I built a memory palace too, except it was made out of resentment. The foundations consisted of the tall poles and wide rafters of my unfulfilled expectations.

I placed painful memories from my teens into glass cabinets and returned to look at them as if they were ornaments, while swigging cider. I put my romantic rejections into chests in the attic and mainlined wine while rummaging through them. I would wander the labyrinthine rooms of my vast memory palace of resentments, barefoot in a torn cocktail dress, muttering expletives like a Tasmanian Devil, slugging from the bottle swinging from my arm. Drinking at the people I blamed for the contents of each room.

It was not fun for me to get lost in this derelict palace; but it did provide a great excuse for me to drink. I had to get the heck out of that melodramatic, cobwebbed relic in order to stay sober.

I didn't know how to leave the palace, though. Until I saw a post in a sober group I'm a member of, about how resentments keep us stuck in the same-old drinking patterns, but 'a grateful heart never drinks'. It was a shout-out for members to join a 'gratitude group'. At a newborn and discombobulated two months sober, I leapt at the chance. That group was to become one of my most treasured recovery tools.

The ten of us tentatively, and then fiercely, bonded, through emails, phone calls, gratitude lists and video messages. Although the rest of the group are based in the States, I've managed to meet up with most of them; we've had mini-breaks in Bruges, Carmel on the Big Sur, San Francisco and London. We've sniffed each other's tonic water at big parties to make sure the bartender didn't mishear and slip gin into it. We've floated together in sulphur-rich water under the stars at 2am at a hippy 'clothing optional' bathing retreat. We've supped tea together after biking the Golden Gate Bridge. We've shared more with each other than we tell some of our closest friends. The group is now four years old and I don't believe it's a coincidence that many of us got sober in the very month of the group's formation.

Some days are pregnant with things to be grateful for. Heaving with them. They're easy days. On others, you have to grope around to find the slivers of beauty in an otherwise shitty day. Those are the tougher days, and arguably the more important ones. Hunting gratitudes alters the way you see the world; when you seek the good, rather than point out the bad, everything looks rosier.

Here are some examples of gratitudes I have posted in the past. It wouldn't have even occurred to me to be thankful for these everyday things before I joined the gratitude group. For real.

- I'm grateful for dishwashers! They're awesome. And for washing machines. Dirty clothes in, meadow fresh clothes out. Goshdarnit, those little cavepeople would have been delighted with a dishwasher. A washing machine would have made their primordial minds burst with joy.

- Today I saw some fox cubs rough 'n' tumbling in a field like toddlers in a jungle gym.

- I'm happy that I have hot showers and a bed. Some people wash in a bucket and sleep on the floor. They really do. I have to remember that.

- I'm grateful for dogs. Sometimes when I'm sad, a little dog comes up to me and I think, 'How can I ever be sad, in a world that has dogs.'

- Grateful for my Granda's witticisms. 'I sleep a lot, but y'know, I'm 89, so that explains it.' And his political observations. On Nigel Farage: 'I don't like his face.' On Putin: 'That there fella's a wee *bastard*.' On Obama: 'I *like* him.'

- I'm grateful for frost. I'm up on the Scottish border and the ice is making the lacy flowers sharp. It's making the trees look like they've been dusted with sugar by a giant sky chef.

- Today I saw some gorgeous Indian women wearing a rainbow selection of silk saris, heading to a wedding. They reminded me of those flags you see atop Mount Everest.

- Grateful for the Lego present my three-year-old niece gave me earlier. It was red, white and blue. 'Here you go, I made you a Tesco.'

- Grateful that even though I feel poor, I'm still in the top one per cent. I *always* have a roof over my head and enough money to buy food. My friend Holly reminded me of that today. 'You're not poor. Don't say that.' She's right.

THE SCIENCE PART

Firstly, it's important to point out that our negatively biased brains are just doing their jobs by finding everything that's *wrong* with the world. It's well documented that our brains are programmed to scan the horizon for threats. In the olden days, this saved us from being eaten. Now, this brain reflex just stops us from being happy. As Albert Einstein said, 'The most important decision we make is whether we believe we live in a friendly or hostile universe.'

There's a staggering wealth of research and experts that confirm gratitude is life-changing. Here I present the mere tip of the iceberg.

A 2008 study analyzing the relationship between gratitude and sleep, found that 'Gratitude predicted greater subjective sleep quality and sleep duration, and less sleep latency and daytime dysfunction.' In laymen's terms, gratitude-ing made their sleep a helluva lot better.

In eight totally separate studies, gratitude was shown to lessen feelings of depression.

In one study, just writing down three good things about the day, led to 92 per cent of participants feeling happier.

While a 2013 study which taught a bunch of elderly people positive psychology methods, including gratitude, found that the subjects 'showed a significant decrease in state anxiety and depression as well as an increase in specific memories, life satisfaction and subjective happiness.' I mean, blimey. It actually increased the power of their memory.

And it's not just mental. The wins are physical too. Researchers have found that a positive outlook can strengthen your cardiac health. They compared the immune systems of healthy, first-year-law students and found that, by midterm, the students who displayed 'optimism' had higher levels of the blood cells that defend the immune system, in contrast with their more cynical peers. Moreover, the University of Miami carried out a study whereby they had some participants write about what they were grateful for. Compared to control groups, the grateful group experienced more contentment, exercised more and had fewer doctor visits.

'The benefits of gratitude start with the dopamine system, because feeling grateful activates the brain stem region that produces dopamine. Additionally, gratitude toward others increases activity in social dopamine circuits, which makes social interactions more enjoyable,' says neuroscientist Dr Alex Korb, author of *The Upward Spiral: Using Neuroscience to Reverse the Course of Depression*.

'One powerful effect of gratitude is that it can boost serotonin,' he continues. 'Trying to think of things you are grateful for forces you to focus on the positive aspects of your life. This simple act increases serotonin production.' And what does serotonin do? It makes you feel glorious, that's what.

He says it's all about the bounty-hunting, rather than the actual finding. 'It's not finding gratitude that matters most; it's remembering to look in the first place. Remembering to be grateful is a form of emotional intelligence.' As the brain gets used to seeking out the positives, it becomes more efficient at finding them, he explains.

'Then, it simply takes less effort to be grateful. Everything is interconnected. Gratitude improves sleep. Sleep reduces pain. Reduced pain improves your mood. Improved mood reduces anxiety.' It's a daisy-chain of benefits.

ENTER POLLYANNA

Some of my friends were startled by my new rainbow-bright, Pollyanna attitude. 'Aren't you taking this grateful thing a bit *far* Cath?' is a direct quote. I guess people had grown accustomed to moany, downtrodden me. Drinking Me eye-rolled gratitude, but her snarkiness was just a smokescreen for deep sadness. And some people see positivity as deeply uncool. Shrug it off. They can jog on. The keepers in your life will love your new, shiny, happy attitude.*

One important thing I have learned is not to leave my gratitude locked in my computer. I realized around three months in that I was writing long, generous odes to people in my life, but not actually telling them what I'd said. So now, whenever I mention anyone in a gratitude, say my aunt for having a bunch of tasty non-boozy drink options in, I've made a pact to send it on to them. I want them to feel my gratitude: they can't read my mind.

So. I've left the memory palace of resentments. I've put down the bottle, taken off that derelict cocktail dress, left the grim grandiosity behind and ventured out into the forest instead, to plant seeds of gratitude. It feels colossally good to be out here, with the sun on my face, yoga shorts on and an overpriced smoothie in my paw. Watching tentative saplings of gratitude grow into mighty oaks.

Don't get me wrong. I'm not immune to being pissed off. I still head back into the resentment palace sometimes, with a shiny slight in my hand that I want to place on a mantelpiece, as if it's a trophy of victimhood. 'I can't believe he said XYZ to me!' It's tempting. But those are the times when I'm most in danger of drinking, because there are half-drunk wine-mines all over the palace.

When I'm spending time in the palace, I have to remember 'oh yeah, this is bad' and bolt back out into the sunshine. To plant some more seeds.

*As long as you don't start grabbing people's arms and earnestly telling them 'Today is a gift. That's why it's called the present.' Too far.

I GIVE UP MY
FAVOURITE BLOODSPORT

'A person who has good thoughts cannot ever be ugly. You can have a wonky nose and a crooked mouth and a double chin and stick-out teeth, but if you have good thoughts they will shine out of your face like sunbeams and you will always look lovely.'
– ROALD DAHL

Let's time-travel back to 2008.

I'm working at Glamour *magazine. I am out for drinks with a workmate for the first time. Our mojitos arrive. I take a long draught. Cocktails are too small. Too much ice. This one has nearly gone already. Anyway, back to my friend. I can't wait to find out who she hates! We can unite in our shared hatred! Bitch to bond. 'So what do you really think of so-and-so? And what about whatshisname? Can you believe what thingymajig said the other day?!' I grill her.*

Eventually, with a weary expression, she puts a hand up and says, 'Cath, I really didn't come here to talk about people from the office.'

I'm stumped. What the frick will we talk about then? Ugh. I struggle to think of topics of conversation. I feel cheated.

It was the last time we went for a drink. She never took me up on the offer again. Which was a pity, since I was always looking for workmates to drag to the pub once the clock had ticked 5.30pm.

When I was drinking, I was the mistress of Schadenfreude. 'Did you see what she was wearing today, she does not have the figure to pull that off.' The girl in the spiky heels with the spiky comments, designed to generate a cheap laugh.

I would pick over people's misfortune like a vulture. I hunted out prey. Her fiancé cheated on her, you say? Ooh, juicy. He got sacked? Mmmm. I could always be relied upon to spread the gossip. Positioning myself on a pedestal above the people who'd done things wrong. Never mind that I was doing things wrong myself, constantly, and often the very same things I was criticizing in others. 'Look at them. What they did.' *Points*

I would remonstrate over the friend who had started dating my ex without checking I was cool with it, all the while conveniently forgetting the fact I had done the exact same thing, because, well, that was 'different'. When a friend came to me with a problem, I would stoke up the drama like I was poking a hornet's nest. 'He did what?!' They invariably left my company spoiling for a fight with their boyfriend/ boss/whoever.

Of course, it was all peacocking. Flashy feathers and prancing around and showing off. To distract from the fact that beneath my smartass comments and punchy putdowns, I was hiding an ever-growing cache of self-loathing. Savaging other people allowed me to escape from it, get a hit of smugness, a gleeful buzz.

Ironically, even though I thought people were seeing me as oh-so-moral while I dissected other's misdeeds ('She didn't!'), I was actually making them more inclined to think poorly of me.

Richard Wiseman, a psychologist and author of *59 Seconds: Think a Little, Change a Lot*, says, 'When you gossip about another person, listeners unconsciously associate you with the characteristics you are describing, ultimately leading to those characteristics being transferred: to you. So, say positive and pleasant things about friends and colleagues, and you are seen as a nice person. In contrast, constantly complain about their failings, and people will unconsciously apply the negative traits and incompetence to you.'

Don't get me wrong. I wasn't round-the-clock mean. I could also be ever-so-sweet and thoughtful towards my friends. I had a lot of friends during this bitch-on-heels time. I wasn't 24/7 obstreperous. But whenever I patiently counselled them through a break-up, or bought them a really lovely present, or did them a favour, it was in a tit-for-tat manner. I expected the same in return. I was furious when I didn't get it. Because, obviously, I was such a good friend to them. That's not friendship; that's a business transaction.

When good things happened to people, say a colleague got engaged, or got a big promotion, I felt cheated. Why not me, why haven't I got that? Where's my engagement ring and my fat pay rise. I thought there was some big treasure chest of 'good things' being dispensed out to people. And that when lovely things happened to others, there was less for me. Outrage! Hey, treasure-chest-keeper, where's mine? *Holds out hand* Elizabeth Gilbert calls this not-enough grabbiness a 'wretched allegiance to the notion of scarcity' in her marvellous book, *Big Magic: Creative Living Beyond Fear*.

> SOBRIETY HAS CHANGED ME, LITTLE BY LITTLE, DAY BY DAY. I AM NOW GENUINELY HAPPY FOR OTHER PEOPLE WHEN GOOD STUFF HAPPENS TO THEM.

It doesn't mean there's less to go around. As I've worked on my own self-esteem, I've felt less need to seize upon other people's defects. As I am kinder to myself, I have grown kinder to others. It's an inside-out sort of a process.

I bare my vulnerabilities now, from telling people I don't drink 'because, y'know, raging alcoholism', to admitting that I constantly feel I'm never doing enough, to confessing all about how my ex used to call me 'Frodo' because I have little hairs on my toes.

Turns out people really like vulnerable people. Hobbit-toed people. In fact, a study found that people found a person who knocks over a coffee 'more likeable' than one who doesn't. Mistakes are endearing. Flaws are cute.

Every now and then I find myself excoriating somebody's character. Or thinking something catty about someone I meet. The difference now is, afterwards I feel dirty, like I need to scrub myself clean. To make up for it, I write a list of nice things about them so that I can flip my focus to their positives, or I give them a compliment. The nice nixes the nasty.

Most of all, I actively avoid those who love to bitch. I recently was witness to a conversation between two perfectly nice acquaintances. 'Oh, she can't write for shit. And she's just...weird. And her clothes... OMG.' I could see what they were doing. It was a bitch-bond. And I couldn't have been less interested in pitching in on the trash-talk. I sat on the sidelines, silent.

I've given up my bloodsport of choice: bitching.

MY 'BE NICER' MISSION WORKS

Don't just take it from me. It's easy for me to say I'm different, but what do other people think? I asked two of my closest friends to write about how Drinking Me compares to Sober Me.

(I highly recommend this as a sober-refuelling strategy. My sober fuel was sitting at 85 per cent before reading these letters. It then soared to 97 per cent.)

FROM KATE:

You are so much nicer now you're sober. Before, you would have laughed and said 'nice is overrated'. But now I know the real you, the girl underneath the cider-spiked fighting talk, I can confirm being nice wins.

When we met 15 years ago, we bonded over our writing ambitions and workplace woes. And of course we bonded over cheap white wine, because that's what twentysomethings do in their first proper jobs. You were funny and smart and always up for a good time. Until that inevitable point of the evening when you picked a fight over nothing.

Often it was money-related, because you never seemed to have any. But that didn't stop you drinking. Your signature move was ordering a round, then calling on me when your card was declined, begging me not to embarrass you. Or flagging down a cab and only ever realizing you didn't have any cash when it was time to pay, leaving me to cover it. You always promised to pay me back, but rarely volunteered the money; I grew tired of awkwardly reminding you.

You had an insatiable appetite for drama, picking arguments with everyone: colleagues, our boss, your flatmates, friends and boyfriends. You saw it as confronting the truth, but often truth had little to do with it.

You were my only female friend who I never bothered to see safely home at the end of the night, because it meant keeping up with your drinking for hours beyond my physical capabilities. But I always worried about you when you were smashed and alone, because you were forever getting into scrapes. Scrapes which got darker.

Even on a press trip to Edinburgh when I thought we were back at our hotel and therefore safe, I was woken at 3am by a call from the PR organizing our trip. His tone was urgent: you'd gone back to your room with three men after the bar closed, could I do anything to help him open the door so we could check you were OK? You did open the door for me; but told me to go back to bed. The three men were behind you, deep in unnerving lad banter about who could undo your dress first.* At breakfast the next morning you crept in late and would not look at me.

Though you've always been a talented writer, you were held back by constant flakiness. I covered for you when you were late, when you turned up with another bizarre story for our boss explaining why sliding into the office at 11am was absolutely, definitely not your fault. What bothered me was that you lied to me about why you were late. Even the time after you crashed at my flat and we stayed up drinking until we heard the birds singing. In the morning you refused to get out of bed because you had the flu. A flu that only a sausage roll and a can of cola could cure.

Over the years I became wary of you, knowing that one of our nights out would lead to an almighty hangover for me, and probably a showdown at the end of the night when I wanted to go home. I joked about avoiding you – 'I can't risk getting Cathed' – and put it down to an old office friendship moving on.

I'm pleased to say our friendship has moved on. Now you are sober, you are the friend I turn to for insight and reason, and we have fun talking about our writing, walking in the park and playing with my daughters. We chat about relationships, travel and yoga. We are grateful for each other's friendship. You have relaxed into yourself and encouraged me to do the same. I have learned so much from your sobriety because you are truly honest about everything you've been through.

Sobriety has made you a better person all day long. Not only do you actually get out of bed for weekend coffee dates, but you turn up with endless patience for playing with my daughters, making birdhouses and reading stories. It's never an all-about-me rant of someone who did you wrong last night. When we go out for dinner, you actually eat

*I don't remember this. At all. As far as I'm aware, nothing bad happened. But I do recall being so hungover that I was scared I would vomit on the hotel breakfast table. Which would explain my downcast vibe.

dinner and are totally relaxed about whether I want a wine or not. You listen generously, make me laugh, give me a clearer perspective and know exactly the right moment to call it a night. We never argue any more, unless it's to insist that we want to buy the other a coffee. Afterwards, I always text to plan our next meet-up, instead of waking up thinking 'never again'.

You are still smart and funny, but also kind, thoughtful and very, very nice.

Love, Kate.

FROM ALICE:

I was introduced to Cath when we were in the first year of university, 17 years ago. She had long, curly, red hair that reached down to her bottom like a medieval princess, a pretty smile and a confident, long-legged walk. She was the coolest person I had ever laid eyes on. And I could hardly believe she wanted to be my friend!

Those days were some of the best, most carefree and exciting of my life. Some would call it wild. Which is why what unfolded was so hard to navigate. We bonded in ways that can't be undone, sharing our darkest secrets and brightest dreams.

After we left university, Cath continued to excel at life. She just had this attitude that life was an adventure and nothing was going to stand in her way! She was one of the first of any of us to move to London's Hoxton, living in a grimy neighbourhood which she'd somehow re-spun in her mind as quirky. She had the coolest job as a writer at *Cosmopolitan* and was kind enough to share some of the perks with her closest friends.

As we got older, and everyone finally got their lives together with long-standing relationships, new homes, promotions and more, it became obvious that Cath's was somehow falling apart. For a time, it simply looked like we'd all caught up and perhaps even overtaken her early successes. Then increasingly, it became clear that her life was spiralling downwards like a corkscrew.

All this happened around the time we lived together again in London. I was grieving from the death of my boyfriend when we decided she would move into my flat. She'd often been selfish but I noticed it much more now. The first anniversary of his death was a tough day for me, but Cath decided to invite her boyfriend over to stay that night anyway. It's the most hurt I've ever felt by someone I loved. Then again, everyone had warned me that moving in with Cath was a terrible idea.

In terms of our friendship, we'd have fights, sure! Something which is completely normal of best friends. But I'd begun to notice that nothing was ever Cath's fault. In fact, it was always my fault. And yet, when I discussed these minor incidents with other friends, they were regularly surprised that I didn't defend myself more. I hated confrontation. It was easier to let her win.

There was the time that Cath passed out on our sofa after a party and I let some friends take her bedroom. Naturally, it was my job to protect her living quarters and not her own, despite her being incapable of looking after herself once again. That one resulted in her not speaking to me for a week. The time she passed out and left the door wide open to our flat all night long in central London was definitely not cool.

Eventually, the years of awkward conversations and difficult make-up texts turned into long and frequently vicious emails. I never knew when our generally bright and easy friendship was going to turn dark and angry again. I was tired of being hurt, and it was clear that our friendship had become unhealthy. About ten years after we first met, when she quit her job and moved out, I secretly decided to take a break. It broke my heart since I've always tried to be a loyal and loving friend. I busied myself with other relationships and told myself that 'what's meant to be will be!'

Fortunately for me, Cath has come back into my life and I couldn't wish for a better best friend. At first when we reconciled, she'd go out of her way to make big statements and declarations of love as if to make up for her past mistakes. She told me it was important to her to apologize and build bridges with the people she loves. For me, those gestures were completely unnecessary. You see, I'd always loved her but I just didn't know how to be friends with her sometimes. Like when a family member loves you, but doesn't always like you.

The best part was when her old personality started to shine through again. Her sweet, caring and sometimes motherly nature. Her abundant love for animals and trees! I loved the debates we'd have about important topics in the world. I'd completely forgotten how brilliantly smart and knowledgeable she is! It was like watching a rebirth and I was glued to the screen.

Then there were the smaller things, how thoughtful she became. Making presents which she'd hand-crafted and laboured over for hours. And when she came to stay, I was surprised by how considerate she was around the house; tidying up before I came home or making a delicious dinner.

These days I find it hard to tell how much of it's her DNA; that she naturally enjoys caring for others. Or how much is driven by her feeling she has to repent. But I guess like anything, if you do things often enough they become a habit.

Without hesitation, I would go through the whole incredible and painful journey again to have her as my best friend in all the world. Because I firmly believe that what doesn't break you simply makes you stronger.

Alice

MY RESPONSE:

These accounts were hard, important and incredibly touching to read.

It's chilling how little of this I actually remember. I don't recall having my boyfriend over on the anniversary of Alice's boyfriend's death. I must have erased my own bad behaviour from my memory. Denial is powerful.

Alice hit on an important point. While I had an illustrious launch in my early 20s, towards the end of them, I started to feel left behind. Like my life was frozen in amber, in suspended animation, while everyone else was evolving around me.

I am so infinitely grateful that Kate and Alice are still in my life. I don't deserve them to be, but somehow they are, and I'll never, ever treat them with such clumsy thoughtlessness, cruelty or disregard again.

V: SOCIALIZING SOBER

BEING AROUND BOOZE

'Start by doing what's necessary; then do what's possible; and suddenly you are doing the impossible.'
– ST FRANCIS OF ASSISI

Building up your long-term tolerance to boozy situations is like building up a muscle. You need to go s-l-o-w-l-y at first. Gently, to avoid hurting yourself. It's all about taking it one crunch, one curl, one rep, one party at a time. And ducking out from under the bench press altogether if you feel your muscles buckling. But with time, you'll be able to go to almighty booze-ups and barely feel a twinge.

I never avoided bars or parties. I continued to go to gigs, and birthday drinks things, and whatever, even in the first few months. If my friends were having their birthday in a bar, I was going to go.

But I did bail early, when I felt my muscles growing weary. It was my responsibility to listen to myself and get the hell out of Dodge.

Thrusting yourself into drinking situations is not what builds this muscle up. I'm not suggesting you constantly hang out in bars. It's all about paying attention to your cravings, triggers and romanticizing.

Having misty-eyed visions of enjoying a gin and tonic in a beer garden as spring begins to chirp and bloom? You're going to need to dismantle that fantasy before you sit in a beer garden. Fantasies of being able to moderate? Get down and give me 20 examples of when you tried moderation and utterly, irrevocably failed. It's a mental muscle which is steeled by fighting fantasies with reality.

SEVEN MONTHS SOBER

I've booked the hotel in Mexico for Sam's wedding. I've emailed the hotel to say that it's really important that they remove the in-room optics with bottles of liquor. I do not need a miniature bar in my room, complete with 160 units of hard alcohol.

A friend, Dan, asked me why I'm not comfortable with the in-room liquor, given I 'seem so solid' in my sobriety. I thought about it for a while. And then explained that it's like having a big fat spider in a cage in your bedroom. You know rationally that you're not going to open the cage. You know the cage is secure and the only way the spider can get out is if you open the cage. But who wants a big, fat spider eyeballing you? While you sleep? Not me.

EIGHT MONTHS SOBER

I've realized that I've stopped clocking who around me in the restaurant is drinking and who isn't. I was like a drinking detective for first six months, I could have recited who had what drink and how many, at any given party. (Professor Plum, in the study with a martini).

When I was watching Sherlock, I would notice when the camera panned back and showed a wine glass fuller than it was a second before. When they moved the vintage cognac bottle, I was like 'aha!' They should have given me a job spotting alcohol-continuity errors.

One of my dear recovery friends advised me in early sobriety to see boozy parties as an anthropological observation. With me as David Attenborough, observing drinkers in their natural habitat. That helped me. As did the ever-so-slightly sadistic tactic of fast-forwarding to how all of these people will feel in the morning, like an imagined Party versus Hangover split screen. That makes me realize, 'Boy, I'm glad that's not me.'

A brilliant book has also helped me soothe my pre-party anxiety. The Chimp Paradox by Professor Steve Peters. In a nutshell, he presents a mind model whereby our panicky, irrational, paranoid limbic brain is 'our chimp', whereas our logical, rational, fact-driven frontal brain is 'the human'. 'Our chimp' is fastest to react and loves to catastrophize.

I've started personifying my limbic system as a flappy, frantic bird trapped within my chest. I've learned to soothe it, talk quietly to it, stroke it and tell it everything will be OK, just as I would with a pet. It's my animalistic daemon, Philip Pullman style, not an internal enemy.

TEN MONTHS SOBER

OK, so, I need to be better about setting boundaries re: getting other people drinks, and I'm glad I recognized that. On Friday we went to see my cousin Jake (who I was reading Roald Dahl books to yesterday, it feels like) and his band, White Room, support Paul Weller at a huge concert.

Then my stepdad asked me to go get him a beer, which was a fair request, given he has an artificial leg (motorbike accident) and the bar was a ten-minute walk. I went, and as I was approaching, my panic was rising. It was like he'd just asked me to go catch him a piranha with my bare hands. I felt like I would not be safe carrying a beer for ten minutes. It would be oh-so-easy to lift it to my lips.

Anyway, there was a humungous queue, of about 100 people, so I felt justified in coming back and telling him that. I think I'll need to explain to people in the future that I can't fix them drinks, or go to the bar for them. It's just not worth it. Surely they'll understand? I hope so? But in general, risking them being a little narked versus relapsing? No contest.

ONE YEAR SOBER

At one year sober, I still treat alcohol like an unexploded bomb. I don't touch it. I don't go near it. I don't even look directly at it. It's lurking, but I don't want to even give it a chance to obliterate me. Alcohol cannot hurt me if I don't pick it up. Simple.

My 'unexploded bomb' approach to booze seems to be helping. There is a box of Bulmers out in the garage that belongs to my mum. I used to love Bulmers, it was my second tipple of choice. I haven't even looked at how many there are, or touched it, or read what flavour it is. I know that if I look at it, it can worm its way into my head.

On the flipside, I'm going to a big, boozy party this weekend and I'm not remotely nervous about it. No future-tripping at all. I know it will be fun. I'm not catastrophizing. I'm beginning to understand that when I tell myself something is going to be really hard, it turns out to be really hard. Whereas, if I just shelve it and think 'I will worry about that when I get there' I never worry about it, because I get there and everything is fine.

CHRISTMAS

I am so out of sorts today. I'm up at my aunt's house on the Scottish border for Christmas. I wondered why, and then a few hours ago my aunt said to my mum 'try this wine, it's gorgeous' and I flinched.

Then I realized. Normally I am only around drinking about twice a week, but it's been in my face ('try this coffee liqueur everyone…oh') for the past five nights, constantly from 4pm, and I am knackered.

Normally, if there's wine in my vicinity it's tucked away and unopened. Now it's open, in the fridge or on the kitchen counter, within easy swigging reach. And that is harder. Deep respect to those of you who deal with this all the time in sobriety.

A WEEK LATER
Hard times in sobriety seem like a wall. But they're just a cardboard wall. That you have to punch your way through to get to the magical stuff in the next room. I'm really learning that if you just sit with the discomfort and trust it will pass, it always, always does. And then really great times roll in. It's as if the universe rewards you.

EIGHTEEN MONTHS SOBER
Guess what I did today! Ran past an off-licence I used to buy wine from. And it didn't even occur to me until five minutes later. At six months sober, this exact scenario was like running past an abusive ex in the street.

NINETEEN MONTHS SOBER
Sobriety is just feeling, as my lovely friend Jen would say, like the new normal. I am doing things now that would have flipped me into panic attacks, or totally foxed me before. I really do feel generally solid being in bars with my friends. I enjoy it, even. A discarded half-full drink in the toilets does not call my name. I get downright bored if I don't have something to do in said bars (food to eat, darts to play, pool to shoot) but they are no longer the minefields they once were.

My local Bruges barmen know that I don't drink. They make jokes like 'Another soda water. Haven't you had enough?!' or 'Do you want me to find some cookies to go with your kids' drink?' I am enjoying being back on the nightlife scene, even if I do turn into a tired pumpkin around 1am and need to roll myself home.

TWO-AND-A-HALF YEARS SOBER
I am now half-living with a very tall (6'5') Belgian man who I call my Big Friendly Giant (GVR in Flemish). He's lovely. He also has about ten bottles of wine, 75 bottles of beer and 15 bottles of spirits in his house.

He had the spirits on display, as most people do, as if they were pretty ornaments. I explained to him that that was like having boxes of cigarettes stacked on the dresser, for an ex-smoker. He put them in the cupboard immediately. I don't want them in my eye line.

Two and a half years ago, I never would have believed it was possible for me to be in such close proximity to said amount of booze, without fixating, salivating, plotting, romancing, obsessing. I would have thought about these bottles literally hundreds of times a day. But it seems: the obsession has gone, people. I know now that my thoughts don't have to lead to an action. I'm feeling more and more safe. I'm not afraid of myself any more. Now I am really beginning to trust myself again; and have faith that my actions mirror my intentions.

DECEMBER 2014: I GO TO MY FIRST SOBER CHRISTMAS PARTY

I'm feeling comfortable in my sobriety these days. I'm excited. Not nervous. I know I won't drink.

The company throwing the shindig are minted. We are greeted by a band dressed as drumming toy soldiers. I'm delighted when my friend tells me the theme is 'Toytown'. There are Willy Wonka-esque displays of ginormous neon meringues, presented for the Augustus Gloop-style grabbing. A person-sized Operation game. A gigantic Scalextric. A karaoke stage made up to resemble a Fisher Price 'my first cassette player'. Twenty-foot-high dancing robots on podiums beside the stage. A nice man in a striped outfit dispensing candy floss. Fairground horses, which we play with for a long time. It is the best party I've ever been to.

We bound around, whooping when we discover what's around the next corner. I clock that the bars are all five-people deep, and hear that it's a 45-minute wait. I see the sheer need in the eyes of the people in the queue. Maaann, I would not have enjoyed this magical party had I been drinking. As it is, I'm free from all of that 'where's the next drink coming from?' stress. At one point I mislay my water. So what? If that had been wine, I would have been crushed, and annoyed for the next hour. I probably would have regaled my friend with how miffed I was, for an hour too.

I allow my friends to coax me onto the dancefloor. They are playing my favourite; '80s cheese. I look around. Nobody's staring at me. They're too busy having fun. So, I do the same. I don't die.

Afterwards, my mate tells me I remind her of someone out of The Fresh Prince of Bel-Air *when I dance. I think she means Carlton, rather than Will. I grin. I don't care. 'Is that a paid actor?' I say, pointing at a Buzz Lightyear on a podium, busting out some extravagant moves. 'No, that's just a dickhead from the office,' she replies.*

I'm in bed by 2am with a peppermint tea and a book. I've had the best time. I can't sleep from the adrenaline. I think back to Christmas parties of years gone by.

Beforehand, I always felt a curious mixture of anticipation ('endless free drink!') and fear ('what will I DO tonight. Must not get drunk. Must. Not. Get. Drunk.' I always got drunk.

Arguably the most stupid thing I have ever done at a Christmas party, and there were many, was getting into a hot tub topless with a bunch of co-workers, both male and female, when I was working at Glamour magazine. The rest of them were in their underwear. I wasn't wearing a bra with my backless dress. I stood by for five minutes gripped by FOMO, and then I just whipped my dress off and got in anyway, unsuccessfully trying to cover my boobs. My appalled boss heard all about it the next day.

There was also the time I fell asleep at the Christmas party while talking to my boss. Which was great for my career, as you can imagine.

It's such a thrill now to head out into the night and know that I'm in safe hands. My own. To be able to trust myself, and know that I won't do anything crazy, or job-threatening, or offensive.

TELLING PEOPLE

I vividly recall my addiction counsellor saying to me, when I was around two months sober, that I seemed 'very concerned as to how other people would react to my non-drinking'. And I was. I was fixated, in fact. What would People think? People! *What about The People?!*

Their opinion was gigantically important to me. I orbited their opinions slavishly, because I had no self-esteem-centre of my own. I was Planet Earth to their Sun, constantly looking to them to shine on me. Their opinions had the power to light me up, or plunge me into darkness.

I would say that the fear of What People Will Think keeps millions of us drinking. Whenever you don't smoke, drink tea or eat Doritos, nobody gives a damn. Nobody asks you 'why not?!' huffily, as if they have a right to know.

> BUT, WHENEVER YOU DON'T DRINK, PEOPLE SEEM TO FEEL THEY DESERVE AN EXPLANATION. **AS IF YOUR STORY IS PUBLIC PROPERTY.** IT'S WEIRD AND AT TIMES, VERY ANNOYING.

Saying 'no thanks' to drinking often invites questions. Lots of them. Particularly in booze-obsessed Britain. You often need to justify your decision not to imbibe. A dear friend of mine is eight months pregnant, and she's finding that she's having to defend her decision to drink zero. She went to a party laden with prosecco and ended up holding a glass of prosecco and secretly ditching it, since her prosecco-less presence was making people jittery. Despite the NHS now saying you really shouldn't drink at all during pregnancy, nope, not a drop (I'm paraphrasing, but that's the gist) my pregnant friend says that people seem to be affronted by her decision not to drink.

However, things have improved somewhat. My mum told me that when she was pregnant with me in 1979, she drank throughout. When she asked her Irish doctor if it was OK to drink, he said 'Oh, jeepers creepers, absolutely! People only say that you shouldn't drink in case you fall over!'

THE SOFT-DRINK REQUEST

Everybody in recovery will remember, with pin-perfect clarity, the first time they had to ask for a soft drink in front of a crowd/table/kitchenful at a party. It's heart-stopping. For me, it was at a gig, at two weeks sober:

David half-shouts across our dozen-strong group: 'What are you drinking Catherine?'

Me: 'I'll have an OJ please.'

David: 'A what? An OJ?'

Me, turning scarlet: 'Yes please.'

In my head, this is what happened. Several people swivelled to stare at me. They could barely contain their gasps. Like that moment when an out-of-towner swings open the door of the Western saloon. The piano plinks to a stop, poker play ceases, as everyone about-turns in hostility.

What actually happened? David didn't hear me properly. Nobody cared much. Sometimes we do conjure the sober social awkwardness out of our own heads; other times it's very real.

'WHY DON'T YOU DRINK?'

The almost-inevitable 'why?' Answering that question is probably the scariest thing about sober socializing. Saying 'no thanks' to a drink and being confronted with a 'why?' in response, is like having to turn yourself inside out, and let the crowd have a look at your soft secrets.

It's so much easier to say 'yes'. Saying 'no' is crazy hard, socially. Because of the questions. Which is why droves of trying-to-be-sober people wind up making up excuses about taking antibiotics, being on fitness or diet missions, driving and so on. I totally understand why they do it. I did it too.

It's thick with irony, our self-consciousness around not drinking. I was more than happy to get so lashed that I was unable to stand, unable to get food successfully into my mouth, unable to say intelligible words, unable to remember my address, unable to undress myself for bed.

But when we're drunk, we're socially anaesthetized. We don't feel the social disgrace of these things. However, when we're sober, we feel every awkward silence acutely. And that takes a lot of getting used to.

WHAT I SAID TO PEOPLE

I went through several stages. The first was the 'I'm training for a triathlon!' stage. This was, indeed, true. I did a triathlon. (I came 144th out of 160 competitors, yeeha!)

I kept that excuse up after the triathlon was over too. The problem with my triathlon excuse was that it was all too easy to lob out of the window. People tried to persuade me to drink. And I let them. Repeatedly. 'Because, triathlon' thrust me into a sucky spiral whereby I kept bouncing off the wagon and clambering back on a few days later, tattered, battered and bruised.

It didn't work. For me, I had to be way more honest than that, and stop cowering behind 'health' reasons. (*Just me*. Others are different. In fact, please read everything in this book with a 'just me' disclaimer.)

I also went through a stage of pretending I was drinking, when I wasn't. Asking for an elderflower pressé to be put into a wine glass with ice, so it would resemble a white wine spritzer. Or saying, 'Oh, there's vodka in it!' if I was challenged by somebody for drinking cola. I remember going to one party in the very early days, where I was *the only person* who knew I wasn't drinking.

I soon realized, after a very real white wine spritzer was plonked in front of me by somebody buying a round, that it would be a very short segue from pretend-drinking to real-drinking. I 'misplaced' that drink, but what would I do with the next one? I had to look the fear of the questions dead in the eye, if I wanted to stay sober. I had to tell the truth. I had to shuffle off the shame. I wasn't drinking.

THE FULL TRUTH STAGE

Here's the thing I discovered. When I started stepping out from behind the 'triathlon!' toot-a-toot bravado, and showing chinks in my 'health reasons!' armour, the People started reacting a lot better.

Instead of dismissing me as a 'health bore' they started softening up. 'My body is a temple' virtuousness turns most people off. They try to topple your smugness, they try to push drinks on you, they don't relate. 'I was a nightmare and now I'm trying not to be' is a much more likeable package. Vulnerability is attractive. It really is. And you'll find people show you their soft spots, in response. In a non doctors-and-nurses way.

THE SWOOSH-SEND METHOD

So, I decided I was going to be vulnerable, tell people the truth, and tell *everyone*. Leaving no pockets of people to drink with. This was the blanket 'tell-all' stage.

After a few teeth-grittingly bad conversations where I dropped the sobershell in person, I decided that the best way to do it was by text or email *before* I saw said people. For some reason, the swoosh that tells you a text message has gone, or hitting the 'send' button on an email, was much easier all round. Done. No undoing it. No chickening out.

My go-to message became something along the lines of, 'Looking forward to seeing your face. Heads-up: I don't drink any more, because I realized I'd grown hopelessly addicted. I'm very happy being sober, so now there's more for you, woo, let's have fun tomorrow.'

It worked like a charm, meaning that the recipient of the sobershell had time to absorb the information, collect their thoughts, and arrange their face into something less panicked-or-pained. It meant we could both avoid a bum-clenchingly bad conversation whereby they scrabbled around for what to say. They didn't feel judged or preached at, and I'd made it clear that they could of course continue to drink. If they wanted to talk about it in person, I always did, but some people avoided the subject entirely.

It also meant that I didn't show up and find a glass of wine already awaiting me. Or that I wouldn't fold like a house of cards whenever they chirruped, 'drink?'

I was always super nervous the first time I saw that person as Sober Cath. Just as your first sober gig/party/wedding is a major milestone, so is your first time seeing significant friends and family. They don't know what to expect, and nor do you, because you've always been half-in-the-bag when you saw them before. They're worried you'll glower at their Sauvignon Blanc or start hissing and throwing holy water at them while they do shots. But, once you're over the first meeting, the second time is a gajillion times easier.

Around a year in, I hit the 'super-honest' stage. I started just taking the armour entirely off, rather than just showing a few chinks in it. When people asked me why I had quit, I would matter-of-factly tell them I got seriously depressed and felt suicidal. Did they know the contemplation of suicide is 120 times more common in alcoholics?

Crikey. All true. But, turns out that's a bit of a...buzzkill. Yeah, people didn't gravitate towards me at parties. Hmmm. That chat is probably more suited to therapy sessions or sincere one-to-ones with loved ones on a misty evening walk, than birthday dinners, fireworks night or small talk with Emma-who-you've-met-twice. So, yeah, I rethought that one.

RANDOM ACQUAINTANCES

What about when waiters at weddings, acquaintances at parties or supermarket liqueur-pushers try to give you a glass, assuming you must of course be a drinker? My golden rule here is: as few words as possible. *You don't need to explain.*

In early recovery, I felt self-conscious ordering a tonic water in a bar. But I finally reached the 'and what' unapologetic stage. The first time I smoothly said, 'Oh, no thanks, I don't drink' without feeling a hint of embarrassment or half-whispering, was on a plane when an air stewardess offered me red or white. A year into sobriety. For the first time, it felt like no biggie. It just rolled off my tongue. Lots of people heard me say it. I didn't care. I wasn't hangdog about it. Why would I be? I'd turned a corner.

Now, I'll deliver the 'I don't drink' line with a half-smile, without offering an explanation. I'm proud. Not scared of their opinion of what I choose to put in my body. Technically, it's no different to being vegetarian, or gluten intolerant, or not drinking fruit juice. That wouldn't upset other people, so why should people be upset by my not drinking?

THE 'WOKE UP IN MEXICO' MODEL

I wanted to shoot for honest and vulnerable, yet light-hearted, with potential new friends. A couple of years into sobriety, my best friend inspired me by telling me about a non-drinking guy she'd met who said, 'Well, I went bar-hopping in Edinburgh on a Friday night and woke up in Mexico on Monday.' 'You want a disarming story like that,' she said. 'Everyone fell about laughing, and that was the end of it. Nobody challenged him on it.'

So, now I say things like, 'Y'know Lindsay Lohan. Yeah, so I was basically the British version.' Or, 'Well there was that time I woke up in a jail cell in Brixton. On a work day.' Or, 'Why don't I drink? I once got into a hot tub topless at my work Christmas party.' Or, 'Once I slept on the toilet floor of my office in Soho because it was 6am and there was no point in going home.' Or, 'I have snogged a band member of Goldie Lookin' Chain.'

People love these lines, these tales of ignominy. They're like, 'Woah, hells bells, haha, no wine for you then.' They rarely dig for more dirt; I've gifted them with the dirt jackpot already, ker-ching, so I'm not stuck in a big explanation conversation, and we move on with our night.

SOBRIETY IS A REALLY HANDY DICKHEAD DETECTOR

If only. Yeah. Well. Some people won't let it go. Imagine I have just handed you a magic wand, a nifty little gadget, that will go 'nerrrrrrrr' every time you talk to a dickhead. Just as a metal detector goes 'nerrrrrrrr' every time it comes across a (bad) penny. Sobriety is that. Sobriety is a dickhead detector.

I used to be that dickhead. I remember when I worked on *Cosmopolitan*, my mates and I invited a lovely, funny freelancer to the pub. Once there, I found out that she was in the midst of doing six months off alcohol. I was appalled. Offended! I mean-girled her. 'What's the point of you being here if you're not going to drink?' I pushed, I prodded and I sneered, until she finally left. (Sorry Anna.)

Why? Her non-drinking made my drinking feel threatened. I felt judged. I felt intensely uncomfortable mainlining wine while she supped a fizzy water. After she bailed, I said something along the lines of 'I don't trust people who don't drink.' And got a laugh. I mean, what? That's an idiotic thing to say, and yet it's a frequently wheeled-out line. I even saw it on a fridge magnet once.

So, it's somewhat karmic that I have encountered my fair share of 'nerrrrrrrr' dickheads along my path. They're Sober Shamers. They try to make you feel small about your sobriety. People have said, 'So you quit because you couldn't handle it?' with a sly smile. As if you've bailed in the middle of battle, or run from the field during a big game, and left the collective in the lurch, like a traitor or an AWOL deserter.

I've even had 'I know someone else who doesn't drink, and they're strange too.' Nice. But, this says way more about them, than it does me. They're just backed into a corner and feeling like they have to fisticuff, just like I used to. They feel vulnerable, attacked by my sobriety.

Sobriety is also a Drinker Deflector. I remember going to a house party once and finding that two of the people who used to seek me out as a partner-in-crime, were now completely avoiding me. It was like they couldn't stand to be within ten feet of me. Every time I walked into a room, they left it, as if I carried a forcefield around me that they couldn't enter.

It's *their problem*. Not mine, or yours. When somebody is that irked by your not drinking, they definitely have a twisted relationship with drinking themselves. Shrug and leave them to it. They'll figure it out, eventually.

WHAT PEOPLE SAY
THEY SAY: 'YOU'RE NOT THAT BAD'
This was what many of my friends said, when I told them I was an alcoholic and had quit drinking. One even called me a 'fake-a-holic' for a while, despite him having had to physically carry me home, deal with my hissy fits, and answer my 'what happened?' blacked-out queries. Who knows why they say this. Maybe they're trying to reassure, or maybe I don't fit into their cardboard cut-out vision of what an alcoholic looks like. I latched onto the 'you're not that bad' comments and allowed them to drive a couple of my relapses.

Eventually, I started responding to the 'you're not that bad's by telling them things they didn't know. Like, how I'd started getting to the pub early to get a shaky drink down myself before they arrived. (Which shocked them in and of itself, because I am not known for my early timekeeping.) That once we'd said goodbye at 11pm on a school night, I would often have often gotten another mini-wine on the way home, having still not drunk my fill.

That started to erase the 'you're not that bad's. My friend Kate said to me, 'You were my big-night-out friend. I guess I just didn't realize that you were everyone's big-night-out friend. That you were having a big night every time you went out.' An ex-boss from *Cosmopolitan* said to me. 'Oh my, I had no idea. But now you've told me that, that actually makes a lot of sense.'

THEY SAY: 'WHAT HAPPENED?'

Most people expect a moment where thunder and lightning illuminate the sky, and 'fuck, I need to quit drinking' is there written in the stars. Most people expect a big story. Where you wake up in a shopping trolley outside a supermarket wearing a flower-pot as a hat and clutching a can of super-strength lager. They ask you, wide-eyed, *what happened*? You have to tell them that nothing actually happened. Well, thousands of things happened, and they filled up a bucket of despair drop by water-torture drop. Until finally the bucket just capsized.

THEY SAY: 'I'VE KNOWN FOR AGES'

A couple of my closest family said this to me. It was absolutely their right to, given they'd been worrying about me and watching me for years. But, I felt very small and very stupid when they said it. Which was probably my bruised ego, but there you have it. Maybe you relate.

THEY SAY: 'CAN'T YOU JUST HAVE ONE?'

Oh, man, I never thought of that! You're a genius! Just one, you say? Rather than five or six? Thanks, Captain Obvious.

Heavy sarcasm aside. Asking an addicted drinker to just have one? Imagine a starving medieval peasant stumbles across a king's banquet, unattended. That's like asking him to just pluck the apple from the pig's mouth. Im-fricking-possible.

When people ask questions about addicted drinking, I often use food as a parallel. So, I say: 'I can put a packet of crisps in a cupboard and forget about them. I often throw out stale cake. I sometimes eat Easter eggs in August. I love food, but I really do not obsess over it. I stop eating when I'm full. I have a little of whatever I fancy, and that's it. I'm very lucky in that I have never seen food as a psychological solution, or over-used it for comfort.'

I ask them if there's anything they find they can't get enough of, whether it's chocolate, online gambling, clothes shopping, whatever. Then I say that the wine in the fridge for me is like the chocolate in the cupboard, or the clothes in the shop, or online poker to them. It won't shut up. It's all 'come play with me' whispering, until I give in. They usually get that parallel. (Of course, this changes over time. I now cohabit with my housemates' booze and don't hear the whispers.)

THEY SAY: 'I DID BANUARY/STOPTOBER/HAVE BEEN PREGNANT, SO I KNOW EXACTLY HOW YOU FEEL.'

I love these people for trying to relate to me. But it's not the same. At all. When this comes up, I try to remember that they're just trying to find common ground between us, rather than belittle the Titanic struggle of getting sober.

THEY SAY: 'YOU'VE JUST BEEN HAVING A ROUGH TIME OF IT'

Well, yeah, I'd royally screwed up my life in the last few years of my drinking. But that was not the reason I drank. It was *because* of my drinking. It was the cause, not the effect. Even when things were peachy in my world, I drank too much.

THEY SAY: 'I DON'T HAVE A DRINKING PROBLEM, AND HERE'S WHY...'

Some people will respond to your 'I don't drink' as if you just flashed a badge and announced 'I am the drinking police! I suspect you are addicted to alcohol!' They will tell you in great detail about how they are definitely 'innocent!' of alcoholism, as if you're about to bundle them into a van and take them to a recovery meeting. How they can easily have one or two, how they only drink for the taste, how they only drink three nights a week. Just nod and smile. It's about them, not you. They're not lording their 'moderate' drinking over you; the likelihood is they're worried about their drinking too. And presenting you with their 'alibi' is their way of keeping themselves cozily deep in denial.

THEY SAY: 'CAN YOU STILL GO TO BARS?'

Because socializing in Britain tends to revolve around pubs, bars and restaurants, some will be flummoxed as to how you spend time with people now that you don't drink. I've also been asked 'Can you still go to parties?' It just demonstrates how drinking is so deeply stitched into our socializing culture. It also shows that people think that sober folks must be living in a state of constant craving. As if they think you'll rugby-tackle the waiter with the wine, should you go to a restaurant. Or sit in a corner rocking, should you be made to go to a bar.

THEY SAY: 'NOW YOU'RE HAPPY, SURELY YOU CAN DRINK AGAIN?'

This is similar to the 'rough time' reasoning. I simply say that the entire reason I am happy is because I quit drinking. Remember the upside-down triangle? That.

THEY SAY: 'HOW BAD DID IT GET? WERE YOU DRINKING IN THE MORNING?'

How I respond entirely depends upon the person who asks me this. If I get a gossip-gathering, gawkery vibe from them, I snap shut like a protective clam. But if I get a genuine, gentle enquiry, or an 'I'm worried about my drinking too' person, I tell them that yes, I did drink in the morning on several occasions to stop the shakes, but that was only towards the very end of my drinking.

Why the latter disclaimer? Many people who ask this question want to know how bad it got, so that they can say, 'Oh, so I'm OK because I don't drink in the morning'. They want to use you as an 'abnormal drinking' benchmark, so that they can position themselves as 'phew, normal'. So I'm always careful to establish that I didn't drink in the morning for many, many years...until I did. I didn't drink straight spirits other than shots bought for me in bars...until I did. I didn't get the shakes...until I did.

I'm careful to tell them that I didn't drink every night either, even during the final descent, so that they know that an addicted drinker isn't necessarily always the 'drinks every night and drinks in the morning' archetype.

In general, when people dig for dirt, I would say this: your decision to not drink isn't something you have to explain in depth to others. They're on a 'need to know' basis, not a 'right to know'. I'm pretty much a wide-open book (certainly now, hello world!), but you don't have to be.

THEY SAY: 'DO YOU WANT ME TO PUT THIS IN A WINE GLASS?'

Again, consider this with a big 'just me' disclaimer above it, but I really have no desire to pretend that I'm drinking. Some of my really sweet friends give me soft drinks in wine glasses. They think I don't want to feel left out. But drinking out of wine glasses actually freaks me the feck out. It reminds me of a really traumatic time.

When I accidentally bite into cakes with liqueur in them, I spit them out. Whenever I catch a whiff of wine, I grimace, rather than lifting my nose greedily towards it. To me, faux-drinking would be like a car-crash survivor wanting to hop into a car-crash simulator.

Some sober people do like alcohol-free beer or whatever, and that's fine, and that works for them. I don't. Whatever works.

THEY SAY: 'OH, YOU POOR THING'

Usually accompanied by a cocked head. Aargh. This does my head in. I recently said to a 'poor you' lady who I'd just met, 'It's really not a sad thing, so don't feel bad for me. I'm a million times happier, I'm healthier, I have way more money, my relationships are much better. It's actually a joyful thing, that I don't drink any more.' She looked distressed, said, 'Oh do stop it' and swivelled her wine glass away from me like she was protecting a newborn baby. Again, her response was about her. Not me.

THEY SAY: *TUMBLEWEED AND CRICKETS* NOTHING

Some friends and family never bring it up at all. Even when I mention it or joke about it, they shrink away from the subject. That's up to them. I leave them to it. It clearly makes them uncomfortable, or they think it will make me uncomfortable, asking.

Hey guys, if you're reading this, I really am more than happy to talk about it. It's actually my biggest accomplishment to date, so I *want* to talk about it.

THEY SAY: 'GOOD FOR YOU. I'M PROUD OF YOU. DO YOU WANT A SPARKLING WATER?'

These people are golden. And rare. Tell them how much you appreciate their unquestioning support. Many of my friends and family reacted this way, which makes me a very lucky duck indeed.

'WHY ARE YOU NOT DRINKING?' ONE-LINERS

Being badgered? These lines are neat ways to stop people's shot-shoving.

1. See that girl over there? The one spilling her drink and talking too loudly? That was me when I was drinking. I prefer to be *this* girl.

2. I didn't have a drinking problem as such. I was great at drinking! It was the stopping. I had a stopping problem.

3. Drinking seriously impairs my decision-making abilities. Once I decided it was a good idea to [insert crazy decision].

4. If I drink one, I want five. So now, I just don't have any. *Cheery shrug*

5. Y'know how kryptonite weakens Superman? Wine is my kryptonite.

6. I found that alcohol makes me pull people I don't fancy.

7. I searched everywhere *gestures to entire body* and couldn't find my Off Switch.

8. After my 100th visit to Chicken Cottage at 1am, I decided it was time for a change.

HD SOCIALIZING

Sober time with friends is so much more…real. And that scared me, at the start. Do you remember when HDTV was introduced, and the picture was *too* clear, too real, too unfiltered? 'I don't like it,' said viewers, across the globe.

That's what it feels like, when you first socialize sober. You no longer have a veil. You can't plug those little infinitesimal cracks with the social Polyfilla of booze, which used to fill in the tense silences, or smooth overlapping sentences, or obscure jokes that fall flat. It's so real, so clear and so pin-sharp.

But the only reason alcohol is a social Polyfilla, is because it dulls your brain. While also dulling your wit and vibrancy and compassion and intelligence. It takes a while to acclimatize to socializing in HD, but once you do, you wouldn't go back to the old blurry picture. You start to forget that the new picture is HD at all.

RESULT: MORE GENUINE FRIENDSHIPS

When I was nearing rock bottom, my best friend, Alice, came to the pretty riverside Surrey village where I lived, for a day out. I had a drink before she arrived, naturally, but that half-a-glass of wine at the bottom of the bottle was not enough to hide the torment. We walked my boyfriend's dogs, went for lunch and then finally, in the late afternoon, had some wine. The entire time, I couldn't look her in the eye for a full heartbeat.

She knew me so well that I felt naked, under threat, and exposed. Like I had a red, flashing sign saying 'I AM NOT OK' above my head. It was imperative that I maintain the appearance of being OK, because if I didn't, she might ask why I wasn't. Which would threaten the very thing I thought was holding me together – the drinking.

Now, I can look my friends in the eye without flinching. I have nothing to hide. I am OK. I really am. I can also actually hear what they say, and be interested, rather than their voice being drowned out by the internal chatter of 'Oh, they've taken some more wine, that means there's not enough wine, I'm going to need to go get some wine, oh I'm drinking my wine much faster than them, slow down on the wine, when will we go get more wine, they poured themselves more wine than me, need more wine, WINE, WINE, WINE.' Now I can hear my friends.

Socializing is also a lot more efficient. Eight-hour drinking binges from 5pm to 1am become three-hour lunches in sobriety. And you do, oh, about ten times more bonding in that time, because it's authentic, rather than chemically altered.

Drunk bonding is like a glue stick. It's cheap and it sticks quickly. But it's also easily torn asunder. Whereas sober bonding is more like cement. It takes a heckofalot longer to set. More effort. But once it's there, it's solid as a rock. Ain't no shifting that bad boy.

WHAT IF THEY THINK I'M BORING?

There's nothing more frustrating to a former hellraiser than to be pigeon-holed as a pious bore. I can't possibly top Sacha Z Scoblic's writing on this topic in *Unwasted: My Lush Sobriety*, so I'll hand over to her:

'What I was really thinking was: Don't even for a minute think I'm vanilla because the truth is I am so hardcore I had to quit. I drank so much it was a matter of life and death. I'm like a rock star compared with you… you should look at me with a touch of fear and awe because I am such a badass you would quiver just to think about the amount of rot gut I've ingested over the years. So step off with your preconceived notions, okay?'

As for the fear that people were going to like me less without alcohol, that it was making me funnier, sexier and more charming. That seems laughable now. Alcohol doesn't make people funnier, it only makes them louder. Alcohol doesn't make people sexier, it only makes them *feel* like they're sexier. Alcohol doesn't make people more charming, it makes them less charming once they cross the three-drink mark. Which I always, always did.

WHY I TELL EVERYONE

Some people don't feel comfortable with people in their lives knowing why they don't drink. That's up to them, and there is *no right way* to do this. For me, however, I feel ill-at-ease when people don't know.

'Don't burn bridges' is a popular phrase. However, sod that. Some bridges should absolutely be burned. They should be torched until all that remains of them is charred embers whirling around on the wind. Personally, I had to douse the 'return to drinking' drawbridge in petrol, throw a match on it and watch it explode. When the 'return to drinking' bridge remains intact, I think your non-drinking mission becomes infinitely harder. Why make life harder for yourself?

Everyone in my life knows that I don't drink, and they also know why. That makes me feel safe, secure, anchored. Like an epileptic carrying a diazepam pen just in case they have a seizure, or somebody who wears an 'allergic to penicillin' necklace, or a tattoo that denotes type 1 diabetes, it's crucial to me that people *know*. It makes me feel less imperilled. It means they can help me stay sober. It means that they pour me elderflower tonic at a dinner party, without me having to issue excuses about driving, or antibiotics, or whathaveyou. And some of the golden ones even remember my soberversary and send me congratulations every year. Keeping your reasons for sobriety on lockdown may well mean you don't need to get vulnerable, disrobe or risk judgment, but it also means you can't share your successes as well.

SOBRIETY INSPIRES RESPECT

Once your dickhead detector (nerrrrr) has cleared all of them out of your life, you'll find that your sobriety will inspire respect, more than anything else. Side note: once you stop being ashamed of it yourself. People pick up on the shame, and mirror that, but if you start feeling quietly chuffed, even proud that you don't booze any more, you'll find that you'll get a lot more 'well dones'.

The only people who think recovery should come with a side order of shameface tend to be the same people who think immigrants should all go back to their own countries, or think women who don't want kids are 'unnatural', or that a dress size says something about a person's worth. They are gobshites. So why would we care what they think?

Now, when I tell someone I'm in recovery and they mysteriously vanish from my life, I think, 'Good riddance, pal'. (This very rarely happens. The few friends who I thought had disappeared have always come back.)

SOBRIETY IS A SUPERPOWER

A few years after my sober-shaming of the non-drinking colleague in the pub, when I was about 27, I'd started to become scared of my drinking. I'd started to lie awake fretting about it. I turned up to a birthday party one evening feeling rancid from the night before, but as usual, wearing a slip of a dress to detract from my pained expression. Look at my boobs, people! Not my face!

At the party, I met a man who'd been sober for two years. I remember my brain being utterly unable to grasp the idea of somebody not drinking for two years. I was finding it tricky to string two days together.

Rather than acting like a fuckwit as per, and pressuring him into drinking, I was wonderstruck by him. It was as if I'd met a real-life wizard, a wizard that I lionized. I regarded him with awe and admiration, as if he was some sort of social superhero. He was able to be warm, funny, laid-back and engaging, without drinking. I mean, what?!

I asked him loads of questions about not drinking. He told me some brilliant stories about waking up in odd places and ultimately deciding his life was better without drinking. He struck the funny-vulnerable mix perfectly. I didn't feel he was judging my drinking; I felt like he was an ally. I then watched him from afar the entire night. I noted that he left at midnight happy and sober, while I was reaching the staggering-around stage. In-ter-esting. I thought about him for a long time after that night. Years, in fact.

Once you learn to socialize sober, you will inspire that same wonder in those that you meet. Being able to socialize without drinking is like a superpower that you should be proud of. We're not afflicted, we're liberated. Let's remove our imaginary cones of shame. Right now.

'When you no longer need approval from others like the air you breathe, the possibilities in life are endless. What an interesting little prison we build from the invisible bricks of other people's opinions.'
– JACOB NORDBY

DRY DANCING CHEAT SHEET

When I first found myself staring reluctantly down the barrel of sobriety, I thought I would never dance in public again. I put it on the 'things that will now be impossible' list. Oh well. No more dancing for me.

Before I'd had a few drinks, I was like an inert hand puppet. I could have no more sprung onto a dancefloor sober, than a glove puppet could magically jump up and start to bust out some moves. Alcohol animated me. It enchanted me into movement. It was the hand up my... um, I'm beginning to regret this metaphor.

I decided that the solution to my 'learn how to dance sober' mission was to learn how to dance *properly*. I'd long ago decided that I was a bad dancer, so maybe if I had some moves, I would feel more comfortable striding onto a dancefloor.

I bought two DVDs: a Tracy Anderson dance routine and a *Dirty Dancing* one. I tried to follow them. I was rubbish. I discovered that I can't street dance like Madonna, or do the steps of the merengue, à la Jennifer Grey. Epic fail.

Then, I finally realized the truth. The reason people dance is because they like the music and *it's fun*. Once I stopped caring about what other people thought of my dancing, I was able to leap around on dancefloors with wild abandon. Here are my sober dancing shortcuts.

1. THE STICK FIGURE MODEL

When I was in my first few months of sobriety, one of my dear sober friends Brigette said something that really stuck in my head. It helped me tremendously. She said that in our own heads, we're giant stick figures, while everyone else is a little stick figure.

But, here's the thing. In other people's heads, they're the giant stick figures, and we are miniscule, amid a sea of other stick figures. People are so wrapped up in themselves, that you are pretty insignificant.

There's a beauty to be had in this tininess. On the *Buddhify* app, there's a guided meditation called 'Universe'. In it, you imagine flying above your room, above your house, above your city, to see how small you are in the big picture. You then zoom out into the stars, outside the

Milky Way. It's a gorgeous mental journey, because it helps you see how minute we actually are. For me, that's a comfort.

When I feel self-conscious now on a dancefloor, I think hard on how much I've noticed the girl-in-the-green-dress and her dancing style. Barely, generally. She looks like she's having a good time and I like her dress, that's about all I've noticed. Yet, in her head, she's the big stick figure.

Look around, when you're dancing. Is anyone laughing at you? Does anyone even care? Nope.

2. START WITH YOUR FAMILY AND FRIENDS

When I was about a fortnight sober, I went for a long run. I was feeling the need to dance. So I jumped around a deserted field, watched by some confused cows, to 'Blister in the Sun' by the Violent Femmes. It felt incredible. I then started showing my parents my terrible dance to Will Smith's 'Miami' in the family kitchen, which features a lot of hula hands and *Pulp Fiction* style V-eyes (I believe those are the technical terms). I started twirling around the living room with my niece.

My 90-year-old Granda once said to me, with his trademark twinkle, 'If I could still use my legs, I'd get up and show you how to dance properly.' Yeah, I can't dance. #sorrynotsorry.

I went on holiday to do a scuba-diving course in the Philippines with my best-friend-from-school Sam. We had a dreamy little log hut on stilts overlooking a peacock-hued lagoon, with our own section of private beach. On lazy days after diving, we would take turns to perform mock-serious dances for each other, starting from the floor and opening up like a flower, like a *Fame* dance student. One day, we saw the bushes shaking. The hotel staff were watching us, and laughing so much the leaves vibrated. We waved at each other, we all cracked up and they ran away.

3. ACKNOWLEDGE THAT YOU CAN'T CHANGE YOUR MOOD

When you're in the mood to dance, you're in the mood. When you're not, don't force it. 'No thanks' is a complete sentence. Sometimes it's hard to explain to people who are a few drinks in, but you don't really have to explain. 'Knock yourselves out, I'm fine here' works.

Also, it's really, really difficult to dance to music you don't like when you're alcohol-free. When I was a year-and-a-bit sober, Alice and I were in a candlelit basement bar in Bruges. We started chatting to a couple of (cute, but totally age-inappropriate) twentysomethings. We played darts with them. They invited us to a nightclub. We went. It was full of people even younger than them. They led us straight onto the dancefloor and started to dance to the techno music. I hate techno. I stood there, frozen. Alice was dancing, too. I tugged her sleeve and said, 'I need to leave.' We made our excuses and did one. Lesson? I can't dance when I hate the music.

Another time I've said, 'Hell no'. When I was two and a half years sober, I went to a wedding. There was a game on the day, whereby each table had to perform a song. Most tables did a sing-song, with half of the table standing up (extroverts) and the rest sitting and looking mildly traumatized as they mouthed along (introverts). I was sitting on the fun-times people table. My table decided that we were all going to stand in the middle of the room and do the Macarena, in front of about 90 people, to the Spice Girls' 'Wannabe'. I was horrified.

I can't do the Macarena. I don't know it. I'm mal-coordinated at best. Awful at following scripted dance moves. And the idea of standing up in front of all of those people? Just – no. I tried to wriggle out of it, but they were having none of it. I felt more triggered to drink than I had done in oh, about a year and a half. As irony would have it, at that exact moment, a glass of wine was placed in front of me by a waiter. I asked him to take it away, finished my food and went to my room for a nap while they were performing the Macarena. 'It was so fun,' they told me afterwards. 'You would have been fine.'

It's like Stephen Covey, the author of *The 7 Habits of Highly Effective People* says, 'You have to decide what your highest priorities are and have the courage – pleasantly, smilingly, nonapologetically, to say "no" to other things. And the way you do that is by having a bigger "yes" burning inside.' My bigger yes (which was much, much bigger than wanting to do the Macarena and not be seen as a wet blanket) was to stay sober.

Later that night, I danced for about four hours. On my own terms, without a seated audience. Don't be afraid to say no. (Or to hide in your room.)

4. TRY THE FIRST DANCE IN PRIVATE
Another thing that works for me, is buggering off once the dancing starts, and kicking off my dancing in private. At another wedding, I went into the roomy bathroom cubicle, put my headphones in,

played a song-I-can't-not-dance-to ('People Everyday' by Arrested Development, or 'Last night a DJ saved my life' by Indeep) and danced. Then I went outside and continued. I've also done this in hotel rooms. It works, for some reason.

Another thing that works, is something my ex Tom suggested to me, 'Just think of it as exercise'. Rather than some sort of crowd-impressing performance, akin to a bird-of-paradise display.

He hit upon something. I feel zero self-consciousness in a trampolining exercise class, or sweating through a savage HIIT session that features burpees and star jumps. I started thinking of dancing as exercise. As a result, my dancing now involves rather a lot of jumping. Like a kid hopped up on too many sweets. I'm desperately uncool, and frankly, I don't give a damn.

'If you think it's uncool to be dancing foolish, forget it! I'll be dancing like an uncle at a wedding'
– RIZZLE KICKS, 'COOLER THAN THIS'

31 DECEMBER 2016: DANCING ON NEW YEAR'S EVE

Drinking Me LOVED New Year's Eve. It was the one night of the year, when I felt like the gloves were off, the limits became unlimited and everyone got absolutely blitzed, not just me.

It's like Sacha Z Scoblic writes in Unwasted: My Lush Sobriety. *'It was a night that made my desires normal, that evened the scale between my behaviour and the world's. Like how freaks and malcontents can blend in on Halloween. New Year's Eve brought the world to my doorstep. Welcome my pretties. Now we can fetishise alcohol together.'*

Sober, I was confused. Nervous. How would this look? Ringing in the new year without a champagne glass.

I ended up cancelling my first sober NYE party. I'd agreed to go to a big house party in Brighton, where there would be dozens of people who didn't know I'd quit drinking, and to whom I would probably have to explain my newfound sobriety. As the party rolled towards me, I grew more and more clenched. I didn't want to pack, I didn't want to book a train, I didn't want to go, if I was honest. I wasn't sure I wouldn't drink. So, I didn't go. I stayed in and ate roast chicken instead.

The following year I did go, taking with me an ally in the shape of my best mate. Everyone knew by then that I no longer drank. Alice and I bailed at 1am. The next morning, I awoke at sunrise and went for a walk along Brighton beach, slipping and sliding into the pebbles, as I watched the golden sun-crown rise behind the spiky, haunting silhouette of the West Pier. I nodded to dog-walkers and smiled at early-day runners. Felt madly proud of myself, for having done the entirety of 2014 completely sober. Marvelled at how many other people were also up and enjoying this gorgeous morning. Who knew?

Then I passed a nightclub that was still open at 6am, vibrating with bass. Swarms of shouting people sat on the beach outside, still drinking, or passed out. The Morning People gave them a wide, wary berth.

I walked past a still figure lying on the beach. He stirred and shouted, 'Alright darling'. I walked on. I heard something behind me. I turned and saw him running at me, full pelt, blood streaming out of his nose. Like something from The Walking Dead. I ran as fast as I could, to get away from him, and back towards the wholesome Morning People. He tripped, fell and lay on the floor, groaning. I watched him from afar to check he was OK, and then walked on. Phew.

Anyway, back to this NYE. I'm in Edinburgh with other-best-mate, Sam, and her family. We're having a splendid time. I love the high-trash versus high-class clash of Edinburgh. The way that the neon spinning chair-ride twirls impudently in front of the sombre 20-storey Gothic monument; like a mischievous child twirling in a party dress in front of a stern Queen's Guard.

We go for quesadillas and drink virgin mojitos. There's a street party; The Charlatans are playing. Sam is six months pregnant. At one point she sits down on the pavement for a rest, among the throng. 'Dance for me,' she says to me. I do. I'm ridiculous. I don't care.

Later, we all bounce around to the music. Nobody is looking at me; nobody gives a flying fig what I'm doing. I'm in bed by 1am, happy AF. And up again the next morning for a run down to the seafront of Leith, to watch circles of squawking seagulls fighting over last night's chips.

ATTENDING WEDDINGS

AUGUST 2011: A TYPICAL DRINKING WEDDING

I wake up in the wrong place, again. I am meant to be at my best friend's house. Instead, I am in a man's bed. Mercifully, a man I know well, a good guy, who lives in the same town as my best friend, Alice. It is 11am. We are meant to be leaving for the wedding right now! Fuck, fuck, fuck. I chuck clothes on that reek of stale beer, appraise my puffy, red face in the mirror with disgust, and jog-walk to her house. How could I let this happen? Snatches of memory come back to me.

Alice leaving the bar at 11ish. Asking me to leave with her. Me refusing, insisting that the night was yet young, and that I wanted to go clubbing. Stumbling around a dancefloor to Bon Jovi. I remember little else.

I arrive at Alice's. She is kind but stern. 'Just get into the shower. We're leaving in twenty.' I arrive at the wedding half-ready, shaky, bloodshot-eyed, stubbly-legged and desperate for a drink.

During the speeches, my drinking is referenced. It goes along the lines of, 'The bar is well-stocked, so it shouldn't run out, unless Uncle X or Catherine get to it! The crowd roars with laughter. 'Stand up Uncle X and Catherine!' Uncle X stands up and takes a dramatic bow. I stay glued to my seat in horror, trying to laugh along. I just want to cry.

By 9pm, I am in blackout again.

THE NEXT MORNING

I wake up in the wrong place, yet again. I am meant to be in a hotel room with Alice. Instead, I am in a man's bed. Mercifully, a man I know well, the groom's brother. Doubly mercifully, I am clothed. I try to recall the wedding and the reception.

Disembodied moments – an offended man, Alice forcing me to eat to try to sober me up, sweaty dancing. I take inventory of my possessions – phone, check, purse, check. It's rare that I wake up with both. But with a stab of sorrow, I realize I have lost a treasured seashell bracelet that Alice gave me for my 30th. Noooo. I smack myself repeatedly on the forehead.

But I can't let the humiliation fold over me. I simply need to firefight. The most immediate fire: getting the hell home. Where am I exactly, and how do I get home?

APRIL 2014: FIRST SOBER WEDDING

I have been nervous about this day for, oh, a fortnight. I am going to a wedding alone, sober, where I barely know anyone, save the bride and a few of her buddies whom I've gotten banjaxed with a few times.

My mind has been in overdrive, imagining disaster predicaments (and then someone will ask me why I don't drink in front of the entire table!) and idealized movie-reel moments (maybe I will own the dancefloor! Lead a conga!). The train slows to my destination and I realize I'm holding my breath; I take deep gulps of air to try to find c-a-l-m.

I'm in the church, trapped deep in the pews, and the heavy doors are shut. This is when my panic attacks are most likely to strike: social or work situations where I feel pinned in place and unable to leave. Meetings, elevators and train journeys have all become adversaries. The panic starts rising in my throat and I stuff it down. I feel like I'm about to throw up.

My heart starts ba-bumb-ba-bumbing so hard that I think it's going to punch through my chest like a sci-fi alien. A white roar reverberates around my head like a mighty ocean, which is threatening to suck me into its depths. I feel the urgent need to leave. I want to race for the doors and run forever. But, I can't leave.

I sit with my eyes closed and try to regroup. I remember what my addiction counsellor said about bringing myself back to the present. I alight on something I can see (blue flowers), something I can hear (birds tweeting) and something I can smell (liberally applied aftershave, with a hint of last night's wine, from the man sitting next to me). I fix my attention on these small details. Panic locks me within myself. Often, the key to unlocking myself from the panic prison is swivelling my gaze back to the outside world.

Another tool my counsellor gave me is box breathing. When I panic, I am almost always holding my breath, which makes my body freak out even more. I breathe in for a count of seven, hold it in for seven, breathe out for seven and hold the exhale for seven. It forces my breathing from shallow and fast, to deep and slow. This tells my survival-oriented limbic system that it's safe to move out of 'flight' mode, apparently.

My friend. I manage to focus on my friend, the bride. The service is so touching that I end up with soft tears. In the past, the church was always something to grit my teeth through, a boring ball-ache, before finally arriving at the champagne-sigh. Today, it's my favourite part.

I realize that I felt that way about everything that wasn't drinking. It was just a prologue. I sat through The Lion King, twitchy, until the interval drinks. I walked around the Tate Modern feeling empty, until I could fill myself up with wine. There was always a lack, a restlessness, a feeling that my hand was way too empty.

Cocktail hour: holy cow. I forgot about cocktail hours. I can't see anyone I know. Oh, there's someone, but they're in a group, and they're all holding champagne. I don't have a soft drink, and I'm too nervous to go to the bar. The only thing twirling around on trays is champagne. I flinch every time the tray comes near me and move away from it. I hide in the toilets for half an hour.

I am starving, and I know that's a trigger for me. I need to eat. I squirrel myself away in a corner where no one can see me and beg the bar staff to make me an emergency sandwich. 'We're not serving food darl,' the manager says. 'The wedding breakfast is soon.' He sees the plea in my eyes and relents. I sit and eat. I feel immediately better. I call a sober confidante. She reminds me why I don't drink, ever. I feel fortified after our chat, like I have an invisible shield around me now. I can do this!

Dinner, finally. I am sitting next to a lovely lady. The waitress's eyebrows shoot up when I say no to the wine. 'Would you like red instead, that's just coming...' I ask her to take away the glasses instead. I feel like I have a neon sign over my head saying 'Failed Drinker'.

My neighbour and I settle into easy conversation. I relax. None of my worst-case-scenario imaginings are coming true; they never do. An hour later, which is just the right time, she asks me why I have refused the wine. I feel mellow about telling her the truth.

She is intrigued, non-judgmental and sensitive, so we end up having a great conversation about when regular drinking segues into addiction. 'I would have been the girl who was a bottle of wine in already, by now.

I'd be cracking catty jokes. Flirting with the groomsmen. Later, I'd have been the girl who was first on the dancefloor.' She says she wishes I had filmed it, so that she could see it for herself, since she can't imagine me as that person. That? Is an enormous compliment.

A champagne flute is placed in front of me for the toasts before I can deflect it. I subtly move it into the centre of the table and feel instantly better. The dancing starts. I would rather walk across a canyon on a tightrope, than walk onto that dancefloor. It is the scariest place in the world, right now. I feel as if I'm a different species from the people around me, whose inhibitions have been blurred by the booze. Can I leave? Is it rude to leave? I want to leave.

I leave. I call a taxi. They are going to be half an hour. I stand outside on the country road and feel myself decompress, slowly. I watch sheep grazing a field, underneath heavy thunderclouds. I did it. I feel utterly relieved and thoroughly wrung out.

> I ALSO NOTICE SOMETHING I HAVEN'T FELT SINCE I WAS MAYBE 18: **THE MEREST SUGGESTION OF SELF-RESPECT.**

THE NEXT MORNING
I wake up in the right place. I wake up where I'm meant to be. I always wake up here, now that I don't drink. I wake up safe, happy and with a full memory of what I've done, where I've been and who I've seen. It never, ever gets old. I burrow deep into the duvet and smile.

JULY 2015: SECOND SOBER WEDDING
I know by now that the first sober anything (date, concert, party, birthday, holiday) is by far the hardest. And that the second is way easier. And that they get incrementally easier, from thereon in. In the past 15 months, I have worked at wrangling my future-tripping. It's now under control. So, I have tried my damnedest not to imagine this event in advance, either to catastrophize or romanticize. It helps.

Just before arriving, I have a few minutes of rising panic, but I use my clever friend Anna's alphabet tool (A for Albania, B for Belgium, C for Cambodia. You choose a topic: countries, clothes shops, anything). It calms me and takes my mind off the hamster wheel.

Best of all, I have enlisted a precious, hilarious buddy as my plus one, and we spend half an hour doing a 'let's pretend we're in Haim' band-style photo shoot around the gorgeous Jane-Austen-esque venue and manicured gardens, laughing so hard we double over.

I do go to the toilets to escape some socially awkward moments; but I don't hide in them. I know now that I am bad at small talk with strangers, so I let my friend take the lead. I reach for elderflower cordial instead of champagne and feel zero awkwardness about it.

The question, 'So, how come you're not drinking?' is asked, by an ex-colleague who is used to me drinking the world. I'm honest with her. I trust her, she's nice. I have stopped being ashamed of being sober. I actually feel proud. She tells me she admires my decision and thinks she should probably quit herself. We talk about my/her social anxiety and bond over it, big time.

When the dancing starts, I don't freak out. Nobody is looking at me; I know that now. They're much more concerned with themselves. I dance with a boy. Aged two. I eat and eat and eat delicious food. I genuinely do not hanker after the wine on the table; not once. We leave three hours after the first dance.

On the way home, my friend and I stop in the New Forest to talk to the ponies. Turns out the New Forest ponies are more psychopathic than sweet. They surround and besiege the car, shoving their gnashing faces into the car windows as we try to wind them up, squealing. It's more The Shining, *than* My Little Pony.

We speed away beneath a rhubarb-pink sunset.

JULY 2016: THIRD SOBER WEDDING, NEARLY THREE YEARS SOBER

There's only one thing you need to know about this wedding. I was flinging myself around the dancefloor so energetically to 'Teenage Dirtbag' and 'Semi-Charmed Life' that two people asked to sniff (and even taste) my tonic water.

They didn't believe I could be having that much fun sober.

WHERE TO PARTY SOBER

As we know from page 71, it's advisable to swerve free-flowing booze-fests in the first month or so. Here are some bars and parties that are totally alcohol-free.

MORNING GLORYVILLE: an incredible sober morning rave featuring sets from the likes of Fatboy Slim and Basement Jaxx. Expect hugs from the 'wake-up angels', free massages and yoga, an 'eco-glitter station', superfood and smoothies, plus of course, a 'banging dancefloor'. It's a total riot and everyone is totally stone-cold…nope, *sunshine-warm* sober. www.morninggloryville.com

OFF THE ROCKS: Mocktails, mingling, guided meditations and intention-setting. Run by a sober lady called Ruby Warrington, who like me, wants to show people that being sober rocks. These events are already a success in NYC and now they've come to the UK. www.joinclubsoda.co.uk

SHAKE AWAKE: Feelgood alcohol-free morning rave in Scotland, that replaces dark, sticky dancefloors with yoga, massages, light installations and dancing or zumba lessons. www.shakeawake.org

REDEMPTION: A bohemian alcohol-free bar and restaurant in West London (and another venue in Shoreditch) that is a hotchpotch of upcycled vintage furniture, neon signs, bare brick walls, a 'nearly vegan' menu and zero alcohol. www.redemptionbar.co.uk

FITZPATRICK'S 1890 TEMPERANCE BAR: A teetotal establishment in Lancashire which was founded during the temperance movement of the 19th century, and feels like a step back in time.

SOBAR: Nottingham's food and drink establishment that comes 'without pressure or hangovers' in a sleek setting with vibrant pops of colour. www.doubleimpact.org.uk/cafe-sobar

THE BRINK: A casual, friendly bar/cafe in Liverpool that has 'taken alcohol out of the mix' and hosts local musicians, poets and performers. www.thebrinkliverpool.com

VI: THE BOOZE-FREE BODY AND BRAIN

THE BRAIN BOUNCES BACK

'Addiction is a neural reality, not a mental illusion'
– ANNIE GRACE, THIS NAKED MIND: CONTROL ALCOHOL

When I was first trying to be sober, my brain felt like a foe. I didn't want to drink, and yet my brain was suggesting I drink. Over and over and over. It was utterly confounding. I didn't understand why my intentions and brain were at odds. Why they were locked in a maddening debate.

But, like so many aspects of sobriety, once you whip back the curtain and see the wizard, you'll be like, 'Huh, not so scary after all'. What was once mythical, all-powerful and intimidating, shrinks to become a little old man in a bad waistcoat. Understanding the machinations of the addicted brain was, for me, a total revelation.

THE EXPERTS
Obviously, I am not a doctor, a neuroscientist or an addiction expert of any kind. So I called on the help of the following.

- Dr Alex Korb, a neuroscientist who has studied the brain for 15 years. Author of *The Upward Spiral: Using Neuroscience to Reverse the Course of Depression, One Small Change at a Time.*

- Dr Julia Lewis, a psychiatrist who has worked in the addiction field for 12 years and acts as a consultant for Alcohol Concern.

- Dr Marc Lewis, a neuroscientist and retired professor of developmental psychology. Author of *Memoirs of an Addicted Brain* and *The Biology of Desire: Why Addiction is Not a Disease.*

WAS MY BRAIN BROKEN?
My brain felt like it was bust, like it was malfunctioning, when it was repeatedly barking 'DRINK' at me like *Father Ted*'s Father Jack. But it wasn't. My brain had just learned that alcohol was the solution. All the time. Always the solution.

'Something I wish more people would realize, is that addiction is not the brain being irrational,' says Korb. 'It's the brain doing its job. When you have anxiety, your brain says "alcohol is the solution to that", because it has worked in the past. With many years of repetition, that sticks, so that the brain then automatically suggests it. Your brain is merely trying to solve your problem.'

Marc Lewis is in agreement. He says that addiction is less of a brain disorder, and more of a 'cognitive adaptation'. But that doesn't make it any less of a neural reality. Oh no. It feels extremely *real*. Because it is.

'Alcohol is extremely addictive primarily because of the way it affects the brain,' adds Dr Julia Lewis. 'Alcohol re-sets the brain, hijacking its basic circuitry, so that it becomes alcohol's biggest fan.'

A HABITUAL NEURAL PATHWAY FORMS

'The more you drink to soothe social anxiety, the more that "drinking is the solution" gets encoded into the habit centre of the brain,' explains Korb. 'And the more appealing it becomes in future. Eventually becoming something that is no longer pleasurable, and is just a compulsion. It becomes a coping habit written into the brain. The brain then gets stressed when you don't choose the drinking coping habit. So when you don't drink, you feel stressed about the not-drinking. It's a catch 22.'

Then, the lying, the calling in sick, the infidelities (all crazily common side effects of addiction) create yet more stress to drink on. 'The social habits that accompany addiction, like lying to yourself and others, mesh so very easily with the self-soothing (or self-feeding) habits that make up the addiction itself,' says Marc Lewis. So around and around we go; where we'll stop, nobody knows.

THE WANTING INTENSIFIES

Dopamine is often misrepresented. This neurotransmitter has long been depicted as the pleasure vehicle. The fun wagon. And while it is indeed the driver of addiction, it's actually more aptly described as the brain process that creates the 'wanting'.

Marc Lewis says that 'dopamine is the fuel of desire, not fun' and that 'wanting something is not the same as liking something'. This is why it's such a misconception that addicts are merely tireless pleasure-hunters. They want the booze; even when they no longer like it. *Addicts are not having fun anymore.* The fun broke long ago.

'Over time, only the user's substance of choice is capable of triggering major dopamine release (or reception) in the brain regions responsible for motivation and meaning,' says Marc Lewis. 'Other goals such as work, self-care and healthy relationships generally fade into insignificance. Particularly if they interfere with the addictive goal.'

The booze becomes centre stage in your mind. Your 'I want' drive to succeed at work, to shower, to work out, to make your partner happy, dims. 'Dopamine decreased in relation to other formerly pleasurable activities like sex, food, and watching your kids grow up,' he says.

THE BRIDGE VS THE ADDICTIVE ENGINE

Imagine your brain as a ship. Marc Lewis calls the pre-frontal cortex (PFC) 'the bridge of the ship'. It's crucial for self-awareness, insight, judgment, logic, building new perspectives and adjusting previous decisions. The Bridge is ideally steering your life.

In alcohol dependence, the PFC loses its control. Some sources say that the PFC shrinks in addicted drinking, but Marc Lewis says 'it's more accurate to say there is a loss of synapses in certain areas'.

Meanwhile, deep down in the hub of the ship is the striatum. This is where addiction is generated. 'It's the area responsible for pursuing rewards,' explains Marc Lewis. 'The hub of impulse, desire, craving and automatic responses. It's fuelled by dopamine.'

In our ship analogy, let's make this the Addictive Engine. The fuel chugging around it is dopamine. The heart of it is the *nucleus accumbens* (the NA). 'Certain activities (e.g. eating, having sex) light up that area and are perceived as being "pleasurable",' says Julia Lewis. 'The NA then connects to the movement control areas of the brain and the activity starts to become habitual. With time, not only the activity itself, but the anticipation of the activity (such as through memory, visual or other reminders of the activity) will also light up the reward centre and this leads to a "drive" to complete the activity.'

However, the Bridge is still in control. 'The PFC monitors everything else that is going on, combines feedback from the environment with knowledge and memories, and then decides whether to act on the drive being created by the NA,' she continues.

Where there's a fully functioning Bridge in the picture, the Addictive Engine gets overruled. 'So, you go to the pub with your friends and they buy that pitcher of mojito (which reminds you of that nice holiday in Rhodes) but you order a cola for yourself because your PFC reminds you that you are the designated driver,' says Julia Lewis. Sorry, Addictive Engine. No can do. No mojitos for us.

With regular drinkers though, the Bridge stops being able to override the Addictive Engine. 'The pathways between the NA and the movement control areas in the brain become stronger with regular drinking,' says Julia Lewis. 'The response to triggers, such as sight, smell, memories, and emotions, become virtually habitual. The pathways from the PFC to the NA become weaker. This means that the poor old PFC struggles to moderate these responses.' In other words, the Bridge has stopped steering the ship.

THE 'DRINKING IS THE SOLUTION' PATHWAY

Way back in my first month sober, I read an academic paper called 'Addiction changes the brain's communication pathways'. It changed everything for me. I finally understood what the devil was afoot in my brain.

The paper says that neural pathways in the brain, including addictive pathways, are formed in a similar way to hiking trails. The more a hiking route is used, the smoother, wider and clearer it becomes. It becomes the default, easiest route. Should you need to forge a brand new path through the forest (or form a newborn sober neural pathway), the paper points out that it will be arduous initially. 'At first, this new path will be narrow, difficult, and slow…Over time, it will become a well-worn, comfortable path. It will be just as easy as the original path.'

> THIS MAKES ABSOLUTE SENSE TO ME. IT'S WHY THE LONGER YOU ARE SOBER, THE EASIER IT IS TO BE SOBER. **IT'S WHY THE FIRST MONTH IS THE HARDEST.** YOU'RE FORGING A NEW PATHWAY THROUGH A TANGLED FOREST. TRAMPING DOWN A NEW NEURAL ROUTE.

Marc Lewis describes addictive pathways as such. '[Synaptic patterns] show up as networks – villages or towns connected by dozens of little roads. But the networks become more robust and more efficient with repetition, and the learning gets deeper. Think of the dozens of little roads being replaced by several main roads and maybe eventually a freeway.' Imagine a motorway coursing through the mind. That's what is carved into the brain of a dependent drinker.

THE SOBER BRAIN

When people put together building blocks of abstinence, 'their neuroplasticity returns,' says Marc Lewis. 'Their brains start changing again – perhaps radically.' Your brain literally restructures. But this takes time. 'Which is why it's very rare for people to get sobriety on the first try.'

Another way to think about it is thus. Drinking has become our socializing mother tongue. Learning how to socialize without drinking, is like learning a whole new language, say Spanish. And having to resist using our mother tongue. 'It's a brilliant analogy that has struck more than once,' says Marc Lewis. 'I've used this analogy.'

'The language analogy is a great one,' adds Korb. 'The brain wants to respond with the easiest, reflexive route. If your first language is English, your instant knee-jerk will be to respond in English when someone asks you a question. Responding in Spanish instead takes more effort and requires the PFC to intervene. If you're trying to learn Spanish (to be sober), it makes sense to hang out in Spanish-speaking (sober) circles. If you just hang out with English-speaking friends (drinking buddies), then it's so easy to slip back into habitually speaking English (drinking). This is why it's a good idea to stick to alcohol-free environments in early days.'

Marc Lewis agrees that it's a good idea to give bars and nightclubs the swerve for a while, while your brain is restructuring. 'Sensory cues such as the smell and sight of alcohol, as well as sounds you associate with it, can trigger a flow of dopamine,' he explains. And remember, dopamine is the 'wanting' neurotransmitter. See booze, hear booze, smell booze; want booze. Out of sight, out of mind is absolutely true.

BRIDGE 2.0

In *The Biology of Desire*, Marc Lewis cites one study that suggests that the brain bounces back quickly. 'A study published in *PLOS ONE*, the journal of the Public Library of Science, in 2013 showed that the reduction of grey matter volume in specific regions of the pre-frontal cortex…reversed over several months of abstinence.' This particular study showed that grey matter volume returned to a normal baseline level within six months to a year of abstinence. Encouraging stuff.

But then, they discovered something surprising. 'Grey matter volume (synaptic density) in these regions (or closely related regions) continued to increase, beyond the normal baseline level, the level recorded for people who've never been addicted.'

So basically, the Bridge may experience an upgrade, thanks to the effort the sober mission requires. As Marc Lewis, puts it, 'the bridge of the ship may become more elaborate, or sophisticated, or flexible, or resilient.' He attributes this to the 'sustained and seasoned cognitive effort' that being sober takes.

WHY MODERATION WON'T WORK FOR ME

Here's my theory behind why moderation isn't an option for me. We know that the brain remembers addiction. So, if I was a whizz on the violin when I was a child, I could go 20 years without playing, but when I picked a violin up again, it would eventually all come flooding back to me. Those dusty neural pathways would re-illuminate. They'd start to blaze and ping once more.

My 'drinking is the solution' motorway is now disused, deserted, its grass banks choked with weeds. But it's still *there*, even though it's not being used. I just choose not to drive down it. Ever again.

I much prefer the new sober road through my mind. It's still not as wide and entrenched as the massive motorway, but it's a stunning coastal road nonetheless. A road that was established back in 2013.

- To read the full version of 'Addiction changes the brain's communication pathways' see www.mentalhelp.net

- This chapter is merely a simplified depiction of what happens in the addicted brain. The best thing I've ever read on the neuroscience of addiction is *The Biology of Desire: Why Addiction is Not a Disease* by Marc Lewis. Check it out if you want a fantastically detailed description.

PHYSICAL WINS OF QUITTING

Turns out that my body *hated* me drinking. Hated it, with a passion. As a result, I hadn't felt physically 'normal' in years. Even when I wasn't hungover from the night before, I was still struggling from the night-before-last. I didn't know this. But I always felt middling-to-terrible. And no wonder. I was abusing my body like a rock star trashes a drum set.

We're not meant to put alcohol into our bodies. It's like putting diesel into a petrol engine. And our poor bodies have to work crazy hard to cleanse the neurotoxin out. Traditional thinking says that a hangover lasts one day, but after a big session, it actually lasts for three days. 'If you have a binge, you are essentially creating a mini period of dependence, so you have a mini withdrawal after it. So, yes, 72 hours is the likely period of withdrawal,' says addiction psychiatrist Dr Julia Lewis.

I found this out because when I quit, I felt spec-flipping-tacular. I went through a phase of springing out of bed at 6am (I am now happy to announce that I am out of that smug phase). My unexpected joy in being sober felt like a stroke of serendipity, a beautiful accident and a mysterious transformation. But really, it's just science. When you stop putting a neurotoxin into your brain and body, it makes sense that you feel a heckofalot better.

I also started to look different. Better. I remember going to a party when I was about six months sober. I ran into three people who hadn't seen me for a year, who were like, 'WOW, you look great, Cath. You look so well!' They weren't just complimentary; they were gobsmacked, astonished-complimentary. I must have looked really…unwell, before.

I started to regain some pride in my appearance, in sobriety. Not in a prancing, show pony, 'look at ME' kind of way. But more in the way that I would take some time doing my hair, wear a nice dress I'd actually ironed and feel semi-attractive. I could walk down the street without longing for an invisibility cloak.

In the last year of my drinking I hid. I had this deer stalker hat. I wore it all of the time, even on hot days, because it covered most of my face and hair. I would pair it with a voluminous parka, to cover as much of my body as possible. I took great pleasure in chucking away that hat, when I turned a year sober.

Here's a rundown of just some of the physical changes my body underwent.

1. MY EYES

For years, every morning before I dragged myself to work, I would lie back with a bag of frozen peas on my eyes for five minutes, to try to turn them from bloodshot and burning, to sparkly. It didn't work.

I recall looking in the mirror and no longer seeing myself in my eyes. It was as if my soul had been vacuumed out of me, and I was looking at a sinister stranger.

My eyes were one of the first things to come back. They literally got bigger. I guess sleep deprivation, smoke and crying made them small. Then they got smiley again. And the whites became white once more.

2. MY CHEEKS

In the last year of my drinking, I started noticing with alarm that my cheeks and chest had started to turn scarlet and blotchy. Even just two drinks in. Apparently it's because alcohol causes the blood vessels to swell, increasing blood flow.

I found out that this is nicknamed 'alcoholic flush' in medical circles. I would look in the mirror and squeak with horror, caking powder on my cheeks to disguise the telltale stain. Basically, heavy drinking inflames the tiny blood vessels in the cheeks. On my cheeks, their starburst pattern looked like fireworks. While I still have traces of these, they've faded, just as fireworks do.

3. ACNE

I was never blighted with teenage acne. People regularly complimented me on my porcelain, near-perfect skin. Heavy drinking changed that. In my mid-20s, I started getting terrible, self-esteem-crucifying acne. Of the cystic variety. Arguably the worst type. We're talking marble-sized lumps deep within my face.

Apparently, the liver is the most important organ when it comes to clear skin. 'Alcohol is actually one of the worst, most aggressive compounds to destroy your skin,' New York nutritionist Jairo Rodriguez told *Vogue* magazine. 'I always joke with my patients, "If you want to get older, go ahead and drink!"'

When the liver can't handle all the toxins overloading it, it often pushes them out through the skin. Hence, heavy drinking shows on your skin. Also, beer and cocktails are loaded with candida; a fungus that leads to outbreaks. Booze shrinks the pores, making them more prone to blockages. Finally, a weakened immune system means that bacteria runs riot on your skin. The body is too busy fighting bigger foes, to get around to the lesser task of giving you pretty skin.

While my skin is not perfect now, and probably never will be, it is dramatically better than it was when I was boozing. I haven't had a cyst since 2013. Happenstance? I think not. When I asked my dermatologist whether my drinking caused my cystic acne, he raised his eyebrows and said 'most probably'.

4. HAIR

Did you know that drinking can provoke hair loss? It depletes the body of two important minerals that are important for healthy hair: zinc and iron. Also, dehydration promotes dry, brittle hair. My hair is definitely thicker and stronger now.

5. TANNING

This sounds bizarre, but now that I'm sober I can tan. Seriously. I remember I once got a tan when I was 15, when I went abroad for the first time, to Greece. From the ages of 16 to 33, I never tanned again. Even when I was away for two whole weeks. I tried valiantly; I lay beside the pool for six hours a day and all that ever happened was that I eventually got burned, turned pink and then turned white again. My legs have always been a determined Irish milk-bottle hue that verges on blue.

Now, mysterious tanning power is mine. Even my *legs* go brown now. On my very first sober holiday, to Wales, I got a cracking tan. And that's…Wales. A destination not exactly renowned for giving people tans.

I was curious, so I researched it. Turns out that Vitamin B is a key agent to tanning. Pill tanning accelerators are loaded with vitamin B. I can only assume that because my body was so leeched of this vitamin, I couldn't produce a tan.

6. FACE

My face is different. I've always had a round face, but dogged drinking turned it bloated and puffy. A friend once told me when she was drunk that I looked like a hamster. 'But a really cute hamster,' she added, when she saw my stricken reaction.

These days it's less doughy. My jaw has become more defined. My cheekbones have re-emerged.

7. STOMACH

My skinny teen body acquired a spare tyre in my mid-20s. Like a life-ring around my middle, that turned more cellulite-like as the years rolled on. I would look at girls around the pool and wonder why their stomachs creased with flat lines, and mine didn't, no matter how many sit-ups I did. I stopped showing my stomach in crop tops.

The muffin-top just naturally disappeared when I quit drinking. Which isn't really surprising when you consider that a pint of cider is the same amount of calories as a doughnut. On nights out, I was effectively putting away five sugar-dusted doughnuts and then topping it all off by falling on fried chicken on the way home with the table manners of a coyote.

> GIVEN A BOTTLE OF WINE IS THE CALORIFIC EQUIVALENT OF TWO CHOCOLATE BARS, **I WAS EFFECTIVELY PUTTING AWAY 14–16 BARS A WEEK.**

The average wine drinker puts on half a stone a year due to the excess calories. I can now wear flirty dresses with cut-away panels, or crop tops with floaty skirts in the summer. It's nice.

8. ENERGY

I'm naturally a pretty lazy bear. I love lying in bed with a book. I don't love cleaning. Pre-dawn is a time I only see when I am catching a flight to someplace thrilling.

But, the difference between my energy levels drinking versus sober is like night and day. I remember hungover days when the act of making my bed seemed on a par with scaling K2. Now, these chores are just automatic; I don't have to scrape together the wherewithal to do them.

9. NAILS

I used to bite my nails and savage the skin surrounding them until I had to hide them under plasters, or beneath big, ugly fake nails.

They were an outward sign of my wounded state of mind. I didn't know it at the time, but it was a very small form of self-harm. Now, my nails are decent. Clean, a respectable length, taken care of. I don't need to hide them any more. My outsides are beginning to match my insides.

10. SLEEP

Ahhhh bliss, I'm so grateful for sober sleep. I remember it being a total revelation in early recovery. After around two weeks of insomnia, I started falling into luxurious deep slumber, the likes of which I had not experienced for years. And waking up refreshed and clear-headed for the first time in over a decade.

Why? Alcohol prevents us from getting enough REM sleep, the sleep stage in which our brain learns, makes and retains memories. As well as disposing of unnecessary ones. The brain makes important neural connections during this time. Rats deprived of REM had a shortened life cycle, dying in five weeks rather than two–three years.

It was a phenomenal change: putting my head on the pillow and waking up eight hours later. Rather than constantly stirring, needing to drink water. Dehydration can actually trigger anxiety, it turns out, which would explain why I would always lie awake with a piston-pounding heart at 4am on a Monday morning after a large weekend.

Going to sleep is now a pleasure, rather than something I stall. I know I will wake up feeling infinitely better, rather than infinitely worse.

VII: DATING AND SEX

I GIVE AWAY MY DRINKING CLOTHES

There has been a subtle, but powerful, shift in the way I dress now I don't drink. Unconsciously, I have begun to practise self-care on a sartorial level.

When I was drinking, my clothes were chosen purely to attract men. Getting dressed was *all* about gaining male approval. I'm not even sure if I was fully aware of this at the time. I would wrinkle my nose at tops that covered my 'wares' up too much, and would instead reach for low-cut boob-framers. My main concern when choosing a shoe was not 'are these comfortable?' It was 'are these hot?' Sequined bum-grazing dresses, shiny tops slashed to the midriff, strappy stripper heels, second-skin pencil skirts with tantalizing zips in the back. My skirts were short or too-tight. My shoes savaged and shredded my feet, leaving them bleeding and cold.

Everything was clingy, sparkly and attention-seeking. I dressed for the murky scene of bars and nightclubs that formed the nexus of my existence, even during the day. I didn't have to day-to-night transition; I was always ready for the night. I fed off male appreciation. If they liked me, maybe I wasn't so bad after all? I secretly hated myself, and clung to any compliment like it was a life raft.

Now I'm sober, tottering around with my cleavage/legs out, freezing my tits/bum off, has become a bizarre concept. Why would I do that? As my self-respect has plumped up, my hunger for approval has faded. I now get dressed in clothes and shoes that I like. Comfy, warm clothes and shoes that don't have me wincing at every step by midday.

I wear low-heeled boots lined with sheepskin that feel like foot-clouds. I pair floaty summer dresses with trainers or pretty ballet pumps. Sky-high wedges have been replaced by flip-flops on hot days. Dresses that exposed more than they covered have been edged out by demure, lacy dresses. The cramped skirts that I had to take itty-bitty steps in have vanished, in favour of those with a nice twirl to them. Shiny hot pants for tail-feather shaking, have given way to roomy tailored shorts with boyish pockets. Looking sexy has become totally irrelevant. What I like, and how I feel, now come first.

I used to wear thongs. Ouch. Now I don't care about VPL. I wear pants, world! Deal with it. I've also stopped wearing those padded bras that hoik your boobs up and turn them into domes that sit beneath your clavicle. Now, I choose soft cotton bras that don't cut into my skin and leave an angry red mark. The men of the world will now know that my breasts aren't perfectly round. Oh no! (I don't care.)

I seek the soft feel of natural fabrics rather than the grit of glittery lurex. I wear a lot of white, without the fear of staining with red wine, cigarette ash, or nasty urine-coloured cider. I no longer have to bin clothes that have become derelict through partying. My boobs remain neatly sequestered away in snuggly jumpers or high-neck Ts, rather than jiggling around in people's faces. I have stopped dressing like a sexpot, and started dressing like…myself.

> SHORTLY AFTER MY TWO-YEAR SOBERVERSARY, **I PERFORMED A MASSIVE WARDROBE PURGE OF ALL MY NIGHTCRAWLING CLOTHES AND HEELS.** I GAVE THEM ALL AWAY. I CAN'T EVEN BEGIN TO TELL YOU HOW GOOD THIS FELT. IT WAS LIKE SOME SORT OF WITCHY CLEANSING RITUAL; LIKE A BAD-BOYFRIEND BONFIRE.

As I sorted through the 'Like me, please!' remnants of my former life, I was reminded of so many dark times. Four-inch courts that I twisted my ankle in, as I tried to navigate the tube at midnight, drunk. A tiny dress that I did the walk of shame in one morning after staying out all night and sleeping with a stranger. Or a crop top which I wore to a festival, a festival where I secretly drank from the moment I woke up. The missing buttons, strange rips and alien stains all prodded painful shame-spots on my soul.

Getting rid of the reminders was so cathartic. Every single item I chucked time-travelled me back to a dark, desperate time. It's time to move forward. Without the wolf whistles, or the leers. I don't need them any more. What I think of me has become more important than what *they* think of me.

DRUNK GIRLFRIEND
VS SOBER GIRLFRIEND

MAY 2009 : I GO SEE A 'BIG HOLE IN THE GROUND'

I am fucked off. Really fucking pissed off. We only have 30 hours in Las Vegas and my boyfriend, Seb, has decided to 'surprise me' with a trip to the Grand Canyon. Ugh! I don't want to see the Grand Canyon!

When have I ever said I want to see the Grand bloody Canyon? He is so selfish. He never thinks about my needs. I sit on the coach and glare at the Hoover Dam. Hoover Whatever.

When normal people are in Vegas, they go bar-hopping and roulette-spinning and shot-slamming and nightclubbing. They don't sit on a coach for ten fricking hours to go see a hole in the ground. I make my displeasure known by stropping around like a sulky teenager.

'It's just a big hole in the ground. So what. Big hole.' Seb sighs and says it's one of the Wonders of the World. And that most people don't get to see it with their own eyes. I scowl at it. I only cheer up when we see a bar and Seb agrees to sit and watch me drink two large glasses of wine while he nurses one beer that he doesn't actually want.

We hit traffic on the way back. When we arrive at our hotel, it's gone midnight and we have to be up at 6am for our flight, so I can't go and do more drinking. I go batshit crazy at Seb and smash my hand-mirror on the floor in a fury. Seb looks scared. It's all his fault. I'm not a mercurial brat: he's a bad boyfriend who buys me unwanted gifts and buggers up my Vegas bender.

MARCH 2016: I AM APPARENTLY MELLOW AND REASONABLE

Me, writing to my sober buddies.

BAHAHAHAHAHA. Today Tom described me as a 'very calm person', 'not controlling at all' and 'very mellow and reasonable'.

When I laughed in his face, he was like 'what?!' I told him my ex-boyfriends would have said exactly the opposite. Seb used to say I needed anger-management therapy.

SOBER DATING

'When you quit drinking you stop waiting. You begin to let go of the wish, age old and profound and essentially human, that someone will swoop down and do all that hard work, growing up, for you. You start living your own life.'
– *Caroline Knapp*, Drinking: a Love Story

When I was drinking, I saw being single as a problem to be solved. A puzzle to be cracked. A malady to be cured. A plus-one sized gap to be filled, asap. I was basically sitting there, huffing, waiting for someone to save me. I used men as life rafts. When I didn't have one, I was splashing about in the water, panicking, frantically swimming around trying to find a new one.

I allowed my rampant wine habit to dictate who I chose. I'll give you a great example. In 2011 I was dating this totally lovely guy called John. John was the kind of guy who casually asked me what my favourite breakfast was, and then shopped for smoked salmon, eggs and avocado at the crack of dawn, and brought it to me in bed. Legend. John was utterly reliable, kind to a fault, clever, totally into me, crazy handsome, owned his own flat and was CEO of a company. But he barely drank. When I was suggesting a fourth drink, he wanted to go home. He raised his eyebrow at me when I started drinking cider at 3pm on a Saturday afternoon. He started trying to steer our dates towards non-drinking activities. Quelle horreur.

So I finished it, saying there was 'no chemistry'. Instead, I decided to go out with Ralph (see page 48) who was unreliable, selfish and lived with his mum (albeit also mischievous, funny and charming, because nobody is all bad). Why did I choose him over John? Because he was up for drinking and smoking fags until sunrise.

I claimed that Ralph and I had 'off-the-hook chemistry'. But the reality was, he let me drink the way I wanted to.

My addiction chose him, not me.

I remember stopping in a busy London street when I realized this, as if paralyzed by an immobilization spell. 'Oh my God.'

DRY DATING

When I quit drinking, I was terrified of dating. So terrified in fact, that after a self-enforced (and lovely) year's dating sabbatical to get my love-hooked head straight, my best friend, Alice, forced me to join Tinder. 'You need to get back out there.' She was right. I needed a push.

Firstly, how to tell them that I didn't drink? That was pretty easy. I always, always told them via text beforehand (see page 139). But wouldn't they just leg it? They didn't. I expected my sobriety to be a man-repeller. It turned out that most men saw it as a desirable selling point, rather than a faulty feature. In fact, research has shown that online dating profile pictures that show women/men boozing, are among the *least* popular among their potential suitors. They were the least liked and the least swiped-right. I was astounded when I discovered that; I always thought cocktail-chugging or beer-swilling was a desirable feature in a date. You could've knocked me down with a feather. But, there you have it. The swipes have spoken.

So, out of perhaps 50 men I chatted to online (hey, you have to swipe right on a lot of duds to get one good date), only about three ghosted me once I dropped the 'I don't drink' sobershell. Most of them were curious, but non-judgmental. A lot of them confided in me that they wanted to drink less, or quit too.

My first sober date was with a Belgian policeman who looked like a Viking. Literally. A ridiculously hot Viking. Before meeting him, I had to meditate for about an hour. I felt the panic rising, my throat constricting, my muscles clenching, and I immersed myself in my ABC game (see page 160). 'A for aardvark, B for bear, C for cheetah.' By the time he rang the doorbell to pick me up, I was stuck on Q – and pretty calm. We went for a walk around Bruges's medieval fairy-tale streets and had lunch in a cute vintage bagel shop. It was delightful.

What I've learned about sober dating, is that the anticipation is the hard bit. The couple of hours running up to it. Once I'm in the actual date, I'm fine. Great, even.

Sober dates are so much better, once you get past the initial jackhammer-heart fear. Which is easily sorted. I always, always exercise before a first date. That's my secret. It flushes the adrenaline and cortisol from my system and helps me feel chilled. I've also found that I'm much more comfortable with being outside on a 'doing' date, such as walking a dog (www.borrowmydoggy.com is brilliant), or wandering around a photography exhibition, or going for a bike ride. Sitting across from each other in a formal restaurant? Shudder. I need to move; it nixes my nerves.

> YOU MAY BE THINKING: WILL I STILL BE ABLE TO DATE DRINKERS? THAT ONE'S ENTIRELY UP TO YOU. **I DATE DRINKERS ALL THE TIME.** IN FACT, I'VE ONLY DATED TWO PEOPLE WHO DON'T DRINK, OUT OF PERHAPS 20 DATES IN THE PAST FOUR YEARS.

A lot of them ask me, 'Can I have a drink?' And I'm like, 'Of course!' Once we get to know each other better, I explain that it's preferable if, when we're together, they keep the drinking low-key. When they have more than two, we're officially on different levels. When we're apart, they can drink their socks off.

BUILDING YOUR OWN LIFE RAFT

The eternally epic Anne Lamott says, 'There is almost nothing outside of you that will help in any kind of lasting way, unless you're waiting for an organ. You can't buy, achieve or date serenity and peace of mind. This is the most horrible truth, and I so resent it. But it's an inside job.' (Watch Anne's TED talk on the 12 truths she's learned, it's glorious.)

She's right. And it's so annoying. And we've been programmed to think the opposite way, by fairy tales, romcoms, love songs, society and unrepentant love-addicted mothers (hi, Mum!). It's not our fault we think this way, that a partner is a panacea, we've been brainwashed into it. But we are responsible for our own de-programming.

Overall, I'm making progress. As my self-esteem has risen, so have my standards, while my propensity to date men who aren't good enough has fallen. I'm attracted to them, but I bail quickly now, rather than clinging to the raft with my fingernails. We accept the partners we think we deserve. I'm beginning to see that I deserve better.

Sober dating looks different to how I expected it to. Rather than my relationships getting longer, they're actually getting shorter. In the past year or so, I've finished with guys for: always trying to start arguments, not wanting to be exclusive after eight dates and being shite at staying in touch.

I'm now just like, seeyalater pal. Rather than waiting around for scraps of attention, like a dog beneath a dinner table. I've been single more in my four sober years, than I ever was in the two decades of my drinking years. My fear of being unmarried, even aged 37, has almost totally faded, like a vintage photograph. I can barely see the image of that fear now. I'd rather be single until I'm 60, than settle for second best.

I'm also beginning to learn that I should probably avoid men who frighten me, or who I feel inadequate around, rather than flying into them like a bewitched moth hurtling into a flame.

A writer called Monica Drake went viral with her quote, 'The Buddhists say if you meet somebody and your heart pounds, your hands shake, your knees go weak, that's not the one. When you meet your "soul mate" you'll feel calm. No anxiety, no agitation.' Huh. Really? My soulmate won't scare the shit out of me? Good to know, Instagram quote.

I've swivelled my focus from 'likemelikemelikeme' to 'do I like you?!' It's not about if they want to see *me* again. It's if I want to see them again. Saying no to unworthy people is the same as saying no to booze. It's a muscle. An 'I'm better than this' muscle. The more you flex it, the stronger it gets.

VANILLA SEX

'Nothing good ever happens in a blackout. I've never woken up and been like, "What is this Pilates mat doing out?"'

– AMY SCHUMER

Inhibitions. They're there for a reason. When I set about dismantling my inhibitions with alcohol, I turned from a buttoned-up, shy teenager into a sexual predator. My buttons became well and truly unbuttoned. I transformed from a wallflower into a man-climbing vine, as if in some botched botanical splicing experiment.

Once I'd removed the chains (or so I thought) of my inhibitions, I made terrible sexual decisions. Inhibitions stop you from doing things like going home with a man you've just met in a nightclub, who may or may not have a penchant for killing and taxidermy-ing the women he takes home. Inhibitions stop you from taking your clothes off when you don't even know a man's last name. Inhibitions say, 'Hey, maybe don't do that' when you are about to go house-party-hopping with two dubious men, simply because you're not done drinking. Inhibitions perk up and say, 'Ah but hang on, you don't even like him' when a man you wouldn't want to share a lift with lunges at you and tries to grab your boob. Inhibitions are like our really wholesome, at-times-annoying, smug friend who's always right, but you sometimes want to punch in the nose.

> HERE'S THE THING I'VE NOW REALIZED.
> **INHIBITIONS ARE GREAT.** THEY KILL BAD BUZZES,
> NOT GOOD BUZZES. WE SHOULD NOT WANT TO
> TURN THEM OFF. **THEY PROTECT US.**

Removing them before striding out into a night full of horny men is like disabling the automatic braking system in a car, and then driving straight into a wall. Or carefully taking off a helmet before careering downhill on a bike. Without inhibitions, we are naked and immensely vulnerable. Removing them is madness.

Circa 2007, my best friend Alice decided to intervene. Rather than saying nothing, which most people did, she stepped up and said something about my one-night-stand-prone existence.

Open scene: Alicante. I'm 27. I'm floating around the pool on an inflatable dolphin. We're discussing a very unwise sexual decision I once made.

Alice: 'When you do stuff like that, it's as if you don't respect yourself, or your body, at all.'

She's said it in a matter-of-fact, gentle way. Not a mean way. Just a 'this is what it is' way. I fall silent and slump onto the smiley dolphin. She's right. I know she's right. We're in a plush villa and I'm surrounded by friends, but I feel so very alone in that moment. I resolve to try harder, to do better, to make more grown-up decisions, to pull fewer men, to crack the three-drinks-then-home conundrum.

Then, I go into the kitchen and pour myself a sneaky afternoon sangria to try to blot it out. I don't want to feel these feelings. I'm on holiday, after all!

This conversation came back to haunt me hundreds of times in the coming years. The inflatable-dolphin-chat bobbed up in situations when I was disrespecting myself yet again. But I simply held it underwater, downed a drink with my other hand and watched with satisfaction as it drifted away. It always came back though. Damn determined dolphin. What's that saying, that nothing ever goes away until it teaches us what we need to know? Yeah. That.

I didn't like who I was, sexually. This is not to say that women who sleep around are 'bad' women, because they're most certainly not, any more than men who sleep around are. The societal double standard around slut-shaming leaves a nasty taste in my mouth.

But the confounding fact was, I didn't want to do it. Every time I woke up in a strange bed with a strange man, I lay there and felt tears sting my eyes as the slither of self-loathing set in. Not again. *I didn't want to.* So why did I keep doing it? I felt like I was being body snatched by some predatory vixen-witch, who had me swaying around dancefloors and scanning around for my next target, when all the Actual Me wanted to do was sit in a corner and chat to my friends.

To cope with my all-consuming regret, I would brag about my sexploits, turning them into funny stories. The guy who opened his wardrobe the next morning to reveal dozens of flowery shirts. The man who repeatedly said that he wanted to make babies with me, while we were doing it. The oh-so-awkward tube journey the morning after. I would paint myself as a sexual libertarian, but meanwhile, wretched 'why did I do that?' shame echoed in my head.

I pushed the shame down and told myself I was just a sexual revolutionary, who refused to be shackled by societal restraints. A man-eating rebel! Forget Che Guevara, I was Che Guyvara. Empowered, like She-Ra. Shag-Ra!

I remember when the magazine I worked on was handing out ironic awards at Christmas. When somebody else won the 'man-eater' award and I was a close second, a superior said to me 'you were robbed' with an arched eyebrow as we dried our hands in the toilets together. I thought that was a compliment. It wasn't.

The more my self-esteem and body-respect waned, the more I turned to the cause of it for comfort. Booze and men. Men and booze. Them wanting me meant I was worth something. I sought acceptance and approval in the very source of my wretchedness. Not unlike eating more cookies to feel better about eating too many cookies.

And much of the sex I was having was during blackout. Which meant I didn't remember it. At all. As the marvellous Amy Schumer writes in her book *The Girl with the Lower Back Tattoo*, 'Blacking out is NOT passing out asleep in a drunken stupor. It's quite the opposite. Your brain is sleeping like an innocent little baby, but your body is at a rave and it keeps making decisions…This is why blacking out is incredibly dangerous. You might look like a regular drunk girl, but you're actually a zombie who won't remember shit later.' She then goes on to recount her most shocking blackout moment. 'My brain was completely checked out and then all of a sudden I was back in my body…I looked southward and there was a stranger going down on me in my bed. Huh? What? Hello?!! I'll say that again. Someone I had never in my life met or seen before was tonguing my vagina like he was digging for gold. I had a boyfriend at the time and this was not him.'

HELLO SOBER SEX
Then, I stopped drinking. To my utter astonishment, and everyone else's, when I got sober I discovered that I am not an easy lay. At all. Quite the opposite, in fact. I am positively chaste. Not remotely wanton. Promiscuity – gone. I'm actually as vanilla as they come; more

of a sixth-date-after-STD-tests kinda gal. It's a revelation!

My first sober sexual experience was after ten dates, in a committed relationship, after we'd met each other's families. It was lovely. Missionary, lights-out lovely.

The blindingly obvious reason why sober sex is better is that you remember it. Otherwise, what's the point? It'd be like sleep-eating. The motions, with none of the deliciousness.

Much like inhibitions, our senses are something we don't want to disable during the sexual act. Think about it. The hair-raising sensation of somebody's hand on your inner thigh for the first time. The mmm-jolt of somebody nibbling your ear unexpectedly. The ohhhh-feeling of your bra being smoothly unclipped. You don't want to numb those moments. They're sexy as hell.

When I was drunk, I hardly noticed these tiny thrills. I barely knew my own name, let alone was capable of sexual subtlety. Numerous studies have actually shown that far from alcohol helping us 'get there' it does the exact opposite. It reduces our satisfaction, slows our sexual response and takes our orgasm further out of reach.

I felt like I was better in bed when I was drunk, but the reality is, I was all over the shop. Misjudging, clumsy, ham-fisted, out of rhythm. Like a drunk person who thinks they're killing it on a dancefloor, my perceptions of my performance were way out of whack with reality.

THE FLIPSIDE OF SOBER SEX

So, when you are acutely aware of every single square inch of your skin, and what he (or she's) doing to it, sex is infinitely better. It's obvious, non? However, the flipside is this. It takes longer, *much longer*, to get to the point where you're comfortable enough with someone to disrobe.

It was like finding yet another hidden Russian doll within myself. Beneath the old shell of the floozy doll, and inside the socially awkward doll, there she was. Another doll. A miniature vanilla one. Who I was chuffed to meet, but also had no idea what to do with. I didn't know how to play the field with this more-Skipper-than-Barbie Me. I thought Skipper had been smashed up back in my early teens. And yet here she was.

I ran away at the end of dates. 'Bye then!' When men stared at me,

I shrank away from it, rather than drank in the attention. Men edged closer to me on sofas; and I edged away. A hand would snake around my hip and I would clench. I felt clumsy in my sexuality, like it was an outfit I wasn't comfortable in yet.

I was bewildered. Who was I? I only snogged three men in my first three years of sobriety. It's no understatement to say that I probably went through spells of snogging three men a week, while drinking, particularly during the hormone-surge university years.

I just didn't really know how to do *this* sober. It was the one thing that continued to elude me.

OVER-THINKING

So, it took me a long time to settle into my sexual sober skin. And then I realized. It was an over-thinking problem, not a kissing problem. I used to tangle myself into thought knots over it. 'We didn't kiss on the first date, so we have to kiss on the second, otherwise we'll be in the friends-zone, and how will it happen, and what if I botch it, what if it's awkward, and, and, and…'

Here's what I learned. If you look at someone and you want to kiss them, just do it. I never over-think it now, or plan it, or agonize over it. If they're on a date with you, they want to kiss you. And they probably will. But I tend to be the kisser now, just because I'd rather get it over and done with, rather than live in the anticipation. As with the date itself; the fear lies in the before-bit. Once you're in it, you're on a roll.

Once we do kiss, my experience is that the rest just happens. It unfolds and uncoils and untwirls and unzips in a tumbledown way. After my second sober sexual encounter, I joked that it was like he'd hit a quick-release button and all my clothes fell off. That he'd liberated a really horny person trapped in a sober shell. Because nature does take over.

My inhibitions may be jangly and frustrating at times, keeping me away from men like a cat's bell keeps it away from canaries. I may wish that I could be more devil-may-care daring. But, I'm just not. And ultimately, it's far better to have inhibitions, than to not have them. Inhibitions are our natural intruder-alert system.

VIII: ROLLING WITH THE PUNCHES WITHOUT DRINKING

A LIFE BEYOND MY WILDEST DREAMS

DECEMBER 2015

In AA, you hear a lot about how recovery will bring you a life beyond your wildest dreams. If the sharers know there's a newcomer in the room, they will talk about this at length. Hope is a powerful aphrodisiac for recovery.

For me, this turned out to be true. I got a LBMWD and then some. The LBMWD that I imagined in my first few months of sobriety was nothing compared to what I've actually ended up with. I would comfort myself by imagining myself moving out from my mum's house into a little studio flat in London, bagging a full-time job, going to the gym, having my friends round for a BBQ in a tiny patch of garden I had planted with flowers. It seems like a humble LBMWD when I write it down; but back then, it just seemed so impossibly out of reach.

The LBMWD I now have happened so slowly. It was a result of next-right-things stacked on top of each other. Paying a bill here, doing a little work there, applying a little glue to a broken friendship.

I moved to Bruges when I was a little over a year sober, and spent most of 2015 there. Why? I spent five days there on a mini-break, to celebrate my first soberversary, and I didn't want to leave. It felt like being inside a gorgeous Gothic fairy tale. I discovered that I could get a three-storey beauty of a house with a roof terrace, for the same as a shoebox in London. I went. I wandered the serene little labyrinthine streets taking pictures, I watched the swans being fed at sunset beside the beguinage, I cycled to the Art Deco swimming pool to do laps, I hosted 25 of my friends at weekends, I ran along the cobbled canalside streets. It was bliss.

London felt like a memory map of humiliation. Everywhere I went, another bad memory slapped me in the face. The nightclub I got kicked out of, the street I did the walk of shame down once, the many many off-licences I frequented. I needed a break from London, I couldn't go back there just yet.

So, it was in Bruges that I located my LBMWD.

MY 'LIFE BEYOND MY WILDEST DREAMS' BEGINS TO BREAK

1 FEBRUARY 2016

This weekend I received some shocking, life-earthquake news. The full-time writing job that I do, which was meant to last until 2017, has suddenly been cancelled due to budget cuts from the on-high corridors of power. Yikes. Job of the past 18 months – poof, gone.

In the past, I would have drunk myself into a stupor all weekend over this. Sloshed around in self-pity, dramatically gulpy-sobbed, moaned bitterly to anyone who would listen and been so hungover during the days, that I could do nothing but wolf down a bacon sandwich and hide in bed, until sundown when I could legitimately get wasted again. That was my coping strategy.

But, I know better than that now. So, I stepped up the self-care setting to 'maximum self-soothe', cried quietly on my boyfriend's shoulder, didn't tell anyone else or dramatize it, then broke it to my need-to-know friends/family/landlady, after wrapping my head around it myself. I made a plan B, set plan B into action, lay in a lot of bubble baths, took my frustration out on a fairground game of whack-a-mole, went for long, blustery walks, ate huge plates of food and played with cute animals. Adjusted my perspective lens, by widening it to take in the dozens of other writers and editors also affected by this news, who may rely on this income even more than I do. Empathy twinges; it's not all about me. I'm lucky to have a plan B to go to, many won't.

> THE NUMBER-ONE THING I HAVE LEARNED IN THE PAST TWO AND A HALF YEARS IS THAT **EVERYTHING WILL BE OK, AS LONG AS I DO NOT DRINK.** EVEN WHEN THINGS AREN'T PEACHY, LIKE WHEN I LOST MY JOB ON FRIDAY, THEY'RE STILL OK.

Or better than OK. As long as I just don't pick up booze. It's beautifully simple, really. And I feel so fortunate that I now know that. And so grateful that I have that feeling of sober security in the pit of my stomach.

THE HEARTBREAK TUNNEL

I hate to be the one to break this to you, but sobriety isn't going to mean you're rewarded with a perfect life. People still die, men still cheat and unfair things will sideswipe you, knocking you off your feet and leaving you breathless with how bloody unfair they are.

When I was drinking, I secretly thought I deserved any bad thing that happened to me. That didn't stop me wailing and waxing lyrical about 'why, why, why?', shaking my fist at the sky. But deep down, I thought it was payback for me being an inherently 'bad' person.

When I got sober I sort of expected that I would be treated well in return. That my relationships would work out, because I was doing my very best. That people wouldn't be bitchy, or sly, or cheats, or liars, given I wasn't any more. Ahem. Yeah. Not so much. Life is vastly, immeasurably better, but it's far from perfect.

Within a couple of months of losing my job, my boyfriend of nearly a year, who I'd just half-moved in with, cheated on me.

My best friend once told me that life is like a table, and that the table's legs are finance, romance, family and health. And that the table can survive one leg being swiped away, but when two or more are kicked, it falls to the ground.

It was a rough, tough time. My table definitely fell down for a while there. But it taught me a lot. The word 'crisis' in Chinese is made up of the symbol for 'danger', but also the symbol for 'opportunity'.

When the crops you oh-so-carefully planted have been razed by a flash fire, you can either lie there and cry forever among the blackened stumps and hate everyone and give the hell up. Or, you can cry for a week (a solid week, in my case) and then start to re-plant everything again, with the unshakeable hope that this time, things will work out even better. That these plants will be even bigger and taller and stronger than the original ones.

There's poetry to be found in scorched-earth destruction. Sometimes seemingly great things have to fall apart, so that even better things can fall together.

Here are some of my posts on my recovery group from that dark time.

26 MARCH 2016
Reaching out, because I know what happens when I don't. I bottle it up, and I wind up with a bottle in my hand.

Remember the super-fine guy who I had just half-moved in with, the Belgian? We're coming up on a year and our relationship has been madly blissful. Last Thursday I left his in Belgium, to come back to Britain for a fortnight with family and friends. A friend texted me that day: 'How are things going, living with Tom?' 'Couldn't be better,' I replied. I truly thought we were at the happiness pinnacle.

So, I left on Thursday. We were in contact constantly, as per usual. On Saturday, he texted a girl he'd met in a nightclub a few weeks back (and had been flirting with via text ever since) and asked her to come round to his house. FOR SEX. While he was sober, I might add.

I know all of this because he told me. I am just so heartbroken. I thought this was The Guy. A few weeks ago, I woke up from a nap to find him gazing at me. 'I want us to get a house in Ghent and fill it with animals,' he said. 'I want the happy ever after.'

We decided to half-move in together. We decided I would split my time between Ghent and London, since I wasn't ready to live in Belgium full time. A couple of weeks in, he was going on about how much he loved coming home and having me there, going on about how much he adores me, how when I'm living there he finds he procrastinates less and is just all-round happier. I just don't get it. I cannot compute. I cannot reconcile the man I left and the man who did that on Saturday.

I am now completely torn between still wanting to be with him, and wanting to castrate him. I know I can never forgive what he's done, and yet I don't want this to be over. I'm riding a tsunami of sadness, anger, longing, loathing, bafflement and hurt.

This is the best relationship I've had to date. I gave this everything. Now, the future we'd started to dreamscape has gone. To paraphrase the writer David Mitchell, I feel like a stick of gum that has lost its flavour and been spat out. While he greedily shoves a fresh one in his mouth.

I've deleted his number, blocked him on all social media and resolved never to contact him again. Thankfully, I feel nothing but fleeting micro-urges to drink. I know now that throwing alcohol on pain is like throwing petrol on a fire. WHOOMPH. There it is. Way more pain.

1 APRIL 2016
This week has been Goddang hard.

Here's the thing I've realized. If emotional pain is a tunnel that you have to go through, then the drinking tunnel has trapdoors. In the drinking tunnel, you can check out of the tunnel for a while, sit in a hole and find oblivion. It's a bleak oblivion, but a pause in the pain all the same. But when you clamber back into the tunnel it's changed: it's even longer and more labyrinthine. You've spent all that time sitting in the hole, rather than making progress out of the tunnel. Suddenly, there are clickety clackety furry things scuttling around in the darkness. You've gone backwards.

Eventually, you use the trapdoors so often in the drinking tunnel that the pinprick of light at the end extinguishes altogether. And you have no idea if you're walking the right way or back the way you just came.

The sober tunnel is a tunnel too. But it's just a freight tunnel, rather than a horror-movie morphing tunnel. The sober tunnel is dark, it's tough, and the only way through is through. There are no trapdoors. No escape from feeling what you feel. But it's an honest-to-goodness, clean, finite tunnel. No rats. And the light is always there at the end, even if it does seem very far away at times. You know you will get to the end, if you just keep putting one foot in front of the other.

So I'm not drinking this weekend. I don't want to go to the tunnel with the trapdoors and the unseen beasts. I like this tunnel a lot better.

I went for a long, hard run today and I feel my inner warrior returning. I've deleted all of our texts, so that I can't comb over them. I am ignoring his messages. I'm facing forward, towards healing, rather than ripping out my stitches over and over.

And I'm now going to watch Begin Again *as it's my favourite empowered-women-dumping-fuckwits movie, and I love the unexpected ending, and I love Keira Knightley even though no one else seems to.*

A YEAR LATER

I don't regret trusting Tom. I don't wish I could time-travel back and check his phone, or be suspicious when he stayed out all night, or question him about the women I saw him texting, while we lay on the sofa together.

I will still approach all relationships with 100 per cent trust. That's the kind of relationship I want.

IX: UNPLUGGING FROM THE ALCOHOL MATRIX

SOCIETY IS A DRINK-PUSHER

There's a jaw-dropping scene in the film *The Matrix*, which sums up, for me, how it feels to unplug from our alcohol-centric society. It's a swooping sci-fi shot which shows an endless field of people plugged into a fake reality.

It takes around a year to unplug from the world of drinking, but once you do, that's what it feels like to look back at heavy drinkers. It's shocking, depressing and startling.

'Blimey, they've been duped. That's not real life at all.'

But, as a sober person, you're in the minority. And it's a battle to stay sober, sometimes, because as social creatures we want to run with the herd. We don't want to be *different*. We don't want to peel off from the pack. We want to be in the middle of the throng, wind streaming through our hair, surrounded by our pals, thundering down a dusty savannah, whooping.

Why is it hard to stay sober long-term? Society is a drink-pusher. Everywhere you look, there is encouragement to drink.

DODGING THE ENABLERS

You walk down the street. Signs outside pubs and cocktail bars say things like, 'I don't want to get technical, but according to chemistry, alcohol is a solution.' Or, 'if you didn't drink, how would your friends know you love them at 2am?' Another sign points inside the pub, promising 'Booze, food, fun.' It then points outside the pub, at 'Real life' with a big, sad face. Did pub signs just tell us that answers, love and fun sit at the bottom of a bottle? I think so. You'll be safe in Starbucks, surely? Nope, Starbucks have started selling wine.

We'll be safe at home, non? NON. We turn on the TV and watch Alicia Florrick in *The Good Wife* swigging gigantic goblets of red wine every dang night, and then somehow going into the courtroom every morning and killing it. In the final season she even upgrades from wine to tumblers brimming with tequila and triple sec. Her jolly drinking clearly tips over into needy drinking in the final season, as she admits, 'I was going to smash the bottle if you couldn't get it open', nodding to a corked bottle of spirits. And yet she still crushes her career. A wildly unrealistic picture of somebody who drinks eight-unit-full tumblers. The implication we're left with is that falling in love with Jason Crouse (Jeffrey Dean Morgan) curtails her thirst. JDM is smokin', it's true, but hot men can't cure alcohol dependence, even if it is only psychological.

We watch the *Scandal* cast engaged in sharper-than-a-razor repartee over dirty martinis. Does Olivia Pope ever have a hangover? Nope. Her weakness for wine is seen as attractive, humanizing, giving her tin-woman-work-machine image a heart. 'Everyone has a tell,' Quinn says to Olivia. 'Yours is wine. Red wine. Rare, complex, fantastic red wine.'

It's heavily implied in *Homeland* that Carrie Mathison successfully winds down from her stressful job and daily struggle with bipolar disorder by using: white wine. It was reported in the *New York Times* that real female CIA agents were outraged by the implication that you can drink like a fish and be a successful secret agent. 'The CIA sisterhood is fed up with the flock of fictional CIA women in movies and on TV who guzzle alcohol as they bed hop and drone drop.'

In *Gypsy*, bourbon is like the gateway to Naomi Watts's devil-may-care alter ego. She orders tequila when she wants to have a wild night of hotel sex with her husband. Her husband repeatedly refers to her as 'drunk' when she has perfect make-up, diction and hair, which is not what 'drunk' looks like. Spirits are portrayed as her rebellion passport. Booze is constantly held up as a feminist rebellion, like bra-burning.

Meanwhile, in *Fearless*, Helen McCrory plays a spitfire lawyer who slays at upholding justice, even though she up-ends tumblers of spirits into her gob every evening. She appears to have vodka for dinner.

In the male character camp, we have the tankard-swilling Tyrion Lannister of *Game of Thrones* who's always drunk but fun; Hank Moody holding it together in *Californication* despite his blatant alcoholism; and the liquor-reliant but utterly smooth and capable Don Draper from *Mad Men* ('We drink because it's what men do,' says Roger Sterling). Incidentally, back in real life land, Jon Hamm, who played Don Draper, checked himself into rehab for issues with alcohol.

Let's take a look at comedies. Hard-drinking Jules from *Cougar Town* holds a funeral for a goldfish-bowl-sized wine glass, now smashed, called Big Joe. RIP Big Joe. The cast of *How I Met your Mother* spend every evening in the Irish pub downing round after round, with zero negative fallout. The *It's Always Sunny in Philadelphia* characters are rampantly regular day-drinkers. Jess from *New Girl*, Sharon from *Catastrophe*, Valerie from *Casual*: all partial to enormous glasses of wine, but mostly whole bottles. All likeable, successful and wholly unaffected by their high intake, aside from the odd clownish hangover. I honestly can't think of one significant female TV protagonist that doesn't drink.

> AND THEREIN LIES THE PROBLEM. ALCOHOL IS RARELY SERVED WITH A SIDE OF CONSEQUENCES. THESE FAST-DRINKING, GOBLET-INHALING TV CHARACTERS **DON'T REFLECT THE REALITY OF HEAVY ALCOHOL USE.**

They never lose jobs, get dumped by partners for being drunken nightmares, have their kids taken off them or get arrested for driving over the limit.

They represent an El Dorado that the viewers go mad trying to find: consequence-free constant wine.

Let me present an alternate universe. Alicia doing lines of cocaine in the boardroom with Will to celebrate harpooning a whale of a client. Olivia romantically cradling a 'rare, complex, fantastic' crack pipe. Carrie dropping MDMA after a hard day at the terrorist-fighting coalface.

Just picture it. Imagine these shows portraying the habitual use of these drugs without career blowback, without it impacting their friendships, without it blunting their quick wit, without it affecting their glossy good looks. This would *never happen*. All other drugs come with consequences in TV land. Alcohol is the only addictive drug that is still rampantly glamorized.

It gets inside our heads. A study found that films and TV which show drinking in a positive light, make people more likely to want to drink. A no-brainer, really. The study leader asserted that between 80 and 95 per cent of films portray alcohol in a positive light.

ADVERT BREAK

Then you have adverts. The current Advertising Standards Authority (ASA) code in Britain says that alcohol adverts on TV must not imply that drinking 'is a key component of social success or acceptance or that refusal is a sign of weakness. Advertisements must not imply that the success of a social situation depends on the presence or consumption of alcohol.'

A clue to how wonky our society is lies in the line: 'refusal is a sign of weakness.' Why would refusing an addictive drug ever be portrayed as a 'sign of weakness'? 'No crack for me thanks, I'm too weak to handle it.'

Adverts must not 'imply that alcohol has therapeutic qualities' or 'portray alcohol as indispensable or taking priority in life'. The guidelines go on to say that adverts must not link alcohol with 'sexual success or seduction, or imply that alcohol can increase attractiveness'. However, it's OK to link alcohol with romance and flirtation.

Recently, Facebook (having figured out I mention alcohol often, but not the non-drinking context) kept firing a Corona advert at me. Under the banner 'This is living' the ad flipped through images of surfing, a bikini-clad woman paddle boarding in a dreamy cove, a grinning model wearing a scuba mask and gorgeous people lounging in hammocks.

Because none of the women were drinking in the shots, presumably this passes muster with the ASA, even though this advert clearly implies that 'drinking is living'. Despite it being a life-threatening choice to go paddle boarding, surfing or scuba-diving once you've had a few beers. Bizarre. Imagine an advert for cigarettes with the same images, and the same 'This is living' message. Drinking while doing watersports is not living, people.

If 'This is living', then why do 64 per cent of us want to drink less, or none at all?

NEWSFLASH: ALCOHOL IS REALLY ADDICTIVE

Society has a blind spot when it comes to the addictive nature of alcohol. A French addiction awareness campaign demonstrated this dramatically. They set up a hoax Instagram account, using an ultra-chic model under the fake name Louise Delage. In it, she's on boats, browsing for pastries or posing in a pool. She gained 60,000 followers in just two months. Nobody noticed that in every *single shot*, she has a drink in her hand/in the frame/a bottle of wine poking out of her bag. Once you see the omnipresent alcohol, it's impossible to un-see it. But their point was: people didn't see it. The campaign was ironically called 'Like my Addiction'.

Nobody is surprised when people who start off smoking socially, progress to smoking in the morning. Nobody is shocked when an occasional heroin user becomes a daily heroin user. Because we openly acknowledge that cigarettes and heroin are addictive. We know they're bad guys. Yet, talking about alcohol as a villain is socially taboo. You're seen as a wet blanket, a joy-slayer, a party pooper if you do so. It's a mass delusion of millions.

So, society pushes an addictive substance on us (sometimes literally chanting, 'drink, drink, drink!') and then, when we quit, is like: 'Woah, you became addicted?' *Backs away looking alarmed.* 'You weren't supposed to do that! You're supposed to be able to take or leave the addictive substance, not become addicted to the addictive substance! We were only joking when we endorsed drinking in the morning!' (Please note: drinking in the morning is acceptable when it's mimosas on holiday, you're getting ready for a wedding, or you're downing Bloody Marys at a fashionable brunch spot. Got that? Cool.)

When people become addicted to alcohol, it's seen as their failure. They didn't pass the 'moderate use of an addictive drug' challenge. They failed at drinking! Society expects us to regularly use an addictive drug, without becoming addicted to it. Alcohol is the only drug where, the second you stop taking it, you're seen as being too weak to handle it. It's truly bizarre.

If I quit eating cake, would people make jokes about me 'not being able to handle cake'? No. I don't think so. If I quit imbibing cheese because I wanted to commit suicide after eating cheese, would people ask, 'Can't you just have a little bit of cheese? Just one piece of cheese?' *Pleadingly offers up the cheese* HAVESOMECHEESE.

As the brilliant Sarah Hepola, author of *Blackout: Remembering the Things I Drank to Forget*, has written in *Jezebel*, 'I cannot imagine my friends—who grew up to be lawyers, and journalists, and lawyers, and lawyers—saying things like, "But what if you just did heroin on the weekends?" Or, "You really just need better product." But heroin is darkness and filthy mattresses in squalid hotel rooms, and alcohol is celebration and party streamers descending from the ceiling (or so the movies say). Heroin is estrangement, and alcohol is inclusion.'

When we give up alcohol, it's like we've chosen to leave the party. Boo hiss. Which is why non-drinking can be perceived as a mark of shame, rather than a badge of pride. Ex-smokers brag about their former pack-a-day habit and how many smoke-free years they have, whereas sober people tend to apologize for their non-drinking.

THE FACTS

A colossal 84 per cent of British men and 43 per cent of British women want to drink less. This rises to 83 per cent among women who are drinking above the weekly recommended limit of a bottle-and-a-half of wine a week. Another survey found that a quarter of female drinkers want to quit – for good.

I would actually say most women fall into the above-the-weekly-limits camp. Because, who can drink just a bottle-and-a-half a week? Show me these elusive unicorn women! I don't know any of them. All of my friends bust the limits, if not every week, then most weeks. I suspect the bottle-and-a-half-max drinkers are sylvan myths, that skitter off into the shadows when you actually try to see them.

'HMRC data shows that people are buying twice as much alcohol as they admit to drinking,' says Dr Ian Gilmore. 'If you divide the total amount of alcohol bought by the number of non-teetotallers in this country, you find that people are drinking an average of 25 units a week.' Unless those people are storing booze in secret bunkers for the zombie apocalypse, it's safe to assume that people either underestimate how much they drink, have no idea what a unit is or they are fibbing.

One in six of us is developing health problems from drinking too much. Probably because 38 per cent of regular drinkers exceed 14 units in just one drinking session (at least once a month).

> IN 2002, 200,000 BRITISH WOMEN LANDED IN HOSPITAL DUE TO BOOZING. IN 2010, THIS **MORE THAN DOUBLED**.

It's an epidemic that everyone is trying to ignore. That we continue to sleepwalk towards.

The reason society wants to brush the 'alcohol is highly addictive' fact under the rug, is because most people are addicted to it to some degree. As we've already established, addiction is not a 'normal drinkers' versus 'alcoholic' division; it's a spectrum.

Even drinkers that would be classified as 'normal' in the eyes of a doctor, would find it unimaginable and horrifying to never drink again. That, friends, is a sure sign of addiction. It may only be a thrice-a-week psychological addiction, or an 'I have to drink at parties' dependence, but it's a bet-your-bottom-dollar dependence nonetheless. If you can't live without something, it's an addiction. The inconvenient truth that we conveniently ignore is this: it's practically impossible to drink alcohol without it getting its hooks into you. Because it's addictive.

ALCOHOL IS NOT REMOTELY GOOD FOR YOU

A team of British scientists controversially announced in 2009 that alcohol is more dangerous than crack or heroin, and almost three times as deadly as cocaine or tobacco.

They scored each drug out of 100, with 100 being the most harmful. Alcohol rolled in at 72 on the harm scale, heroin was a distant second at 55, crack rolled in at 54, while crystal meth came in at 33, cocaine was scored as 27 and tobacco hit 26.

Professor David Nutt, the British government's chief drug advisor, and a key player in this report, was asked to resign the day after it was published. The British government were furious with him, for reasons that were unclear. He said, in the wake of the scandal, 'My view is that, if you want to reduce the harm to society from drugs, alcohol is the drug to target at present.' He wanted to put alcohol in the dock, above all other drugs, even face-rotting crystal meth.

Consider the above figures for a second. Let them really sink in. Cigarettes are socially abhorred. Smoking is now banned in outdoor public places. Kids are shown terrifying pictures of people with holes in their throats. Cigarettes are hidden away in unmarked cupboards in shops, rather than displayed. And yet tobacco is around a third as dangerous as alcohol, says this scale.

Loving parents give their 12-year-old kids sips of their wine, whereas they wouldn't dream of giving them a drag on a cigarette. Responsible adults smuggle teens bottles of cider at parties, whereas they would never chop up a line of cocaine for them. And yet cocaine is far less dangerous. Right now, I'm looking at a picture of a toddler on Facebook clutching a bottle of wine, which has garnered 67 likes among my friends. There is something very wrong with this picture.

A big report published in 2015 showed why the government is so keen to silence the Professor David Nutts of this world. It showed that the total costs of alcohol use in England (including the NHS, police and welfare) amount to £3.9 billion. While alcohol taxation in England rakes in £10.4 billion.

So, heavy drinkers make the country £6.5 billion, after the costs of taking them to hospital, policing them or giving them benefits. A tidy profit indeed. Now it becomes clear why the British government don't want people to stop drinking. 'Shut it, Professor Nutt.'

Then there's also the money we don't know about; money exchanged in the corridors of power. 'Let's not forget that the alcohol industry contributes major funding to the government. The harmful effects of alcohol will only ever be muted,' says addiction psychiatrist, Dr Julia Lewis.

PSEUDO RESEARCH

'But, I saw a link on Facebook the other day that said gin is good for you!', I hear you cry. What's that all about? I don't want to get all #Trump on you, but it's fake news.

'People don't get a clear and consistent message about the level of risk around drinking,' explains Dr Julia Lewis. 'That's partly because one side of the debate is able to shout louder than the other. The alcohol industry is a very powerful one with oodles and oodles of cash at its disposal.'

Its reason for being? To flog booze. 'So, what do they do if there is a new piece of research out there suggesting that your product isn't a good thing to buy? They come up with a counter argument,' says Lewis.

'There's good research and there's bad research,' she says. 'The first thing I look at in a piece of research is whether the researchers have any affiliations to organisations that might bias their interpretations of the findings. So, I would put less weight on a piece of research on 10 people, sponsored by Budweiser as opposed to a piece of research on 500 people by totally independent researchers published in the *Lancet*.'

'But the public don't know this,' she continues. 'If it's reported in the *Sun*, most people assume it's legitimate research. Every time a piece of medical research is published about the risks of alcohol, social media gets flooded with counter "research" promoted by the drinks industry.'

For instance, when the weekly UK guidelines for men were lowered to 14 units, she says 'there was a deluge of counter stories on Facebook. And when you looked at the small print, the counter stories all had links to the alcohol industry.'

But what about this gin thing? 'Consider the recent push among women to be healthy – yoga, running, Pilates, so on. Is it a coincidence that the alcohol industry has been promoting gin as a sophisticated women's drink? I think not. I see sensible friends of mine sharing this nonsense.'

'I got really angry once,' she continues. 'Not long after Alcohol Concern published a report into Alcohol Related Brain Damage, there was an article in the Wetherspoons magazine (that enlightened tome!) about how all this stuff about alcohol and the brain was a load of nonsense – written by someone with no scientific background at all! And you think "how the hell do they get away with this?"'

AN INCONVENIENT TRUTH
The press is complicit in this fact-twisting too.

In 2011, the World Health Organization announced that alcohol is the 'international number one killer', given it contributes to 60 different diseases. In 2014, the most recent figures available, there were a total of 8,697 deaths in the UK that could be laid squarely at the door of alcohol.

That's 24 people a day. Eight women and 16 men. Eight women a day, dead. 16 men a day, dead. Female deaths in this year were 'significantly higher' than two decades previous, said The Office of National Statistics.

You can guess how many papers ran with this huge story from the WHO. Not many. It got buried. Newspaper staff are notoriously hard-drinking, so they want to ignore these facts on a personal level, which then shapes the news content. And also, people don't want to read that alcohol is the 'international number one killer' while they're letting their nightly bottle of red wine breathe by the fire. They don't want to know. They'd much rather read enabling headlines, such as 'A glass of red wine is the equivalent of an hour at the gym!'

This particular obscure study got picked up and 'woooo!' exaggerated in practically every publication from here to Timbuctoo. Once you unpick the actual study however, you find that they're only talking about one teeny tiny element found in red wine. An antioxidant called resveratrol. Which you'd be infinitely better getting from blueberries, peanut butter, red grapes or dark chocolate, given how dangerous alcohol is. Saying you should drink alcohol for the resveratrol is like saying you should swim a swamp filled with alligators. Because swimming is good for you. It's like saying you should become a bullfighter because running is good for you. Never mind that you might get killed in the process. It's dangerously myopic.

The press also harps on about the polyphenols in red wine as being healthy for the heart. Polyphenols dilate the blood vessels and are therefore potentially good for blood pressure. Yet, a handful of walnuts, an apple or a cup of English breakfast tea have basically the same amount of polyphenols as a glass of red wine. Without the deathly drawbacks. So, saying you should drink red wine for the polyphenols would be like saying you should eat burgers because of the gherkins 'n' tomatoes. Nonsensical.

It's a colossal news blackout, driven by collective denial. The press don't want to report it, and the readers don't want to know. Some scientists in Toronto once documented this preference of the press to report studies that throw booze up onto a pedestal. And to bury evidence that threatens to topple it from said pedestal. 'We have counted how many studies are reported in the press, and there are many more reports on the beneficial link than on the detrimental link between alcohol and health,' says Jürgen Rehm, a senior scientist at the Center for Addictions and Mental Health in Toronto.

The press doesn't just wildly exaggerate, or even fabricate, the health benefits of alcohol. It also paints boozing as socially *essential*. A 2016 study sparked a forest fire of press. The headlines ranged from 'Couples who drink together stay together: sharing a bottle of wine can make your relationship happier' to 'Couples who get drunk together, stay together.' This headline was *everywhere*. Illustrated with pictures of Prince William and the Duchess of Cambridge clinking champagne glasses and grinning, or silhouettes of smooching couples with cocktails watching a sunset. You couldn't get greater promotion for drinking. 'Drink or you'll die alone!'

Obviously, as a sober person, I clicked on it with dread. Now that I don't get drunk, am I doomed to have unhappy relationships, what is this Godforsaken study?! But when you dig around in the study, it doesn't show that 'couples who get drunk together stay together' *at all*. I'll quote it directly: 'Concordant drinking couples reported decreased negative marital quality over time.'

Basically, if one of you is a massive imbiber, and the other a teetotaller, you're not going to get along. You're going to irritate each other. It's better that you have similar (both teetotal, or both heavy drinkers, or both moderate drinkers) drinking habits. It follows that closely 'concordant' (you're teetotal, he barely drinks) drinking habits would also lead to a more harmonious day-to-day existence. Which is just common sense.

Far from promoting a bottle of wine as relationship glue, the lead author of the study was quoted as saying that drinking is becoming an increasing problem, 'especially among baby boomers, who seem more accepting of alcohol use'. This study was misreported as 'get drunk together, stay together!' proof. It should have been reported as 'have the same/similar drinking habits, stay together!'

THE BOOZE-A-GANDA MACHINE BREAKS
Thankfully, the 'drinking is good, let's go to the pub!' press machine has been temporarily smashed to smithereens, in the UK at least. In January 2016, a report by the Chief Medical Officer said, 'There is no level of regular drinking that can be considered as completely safe.'

Also in 2016, the World Health Organization classified alcohol as a group one carcinogen, alongside tobacco and asbestos. We now know that alcohol directly causes eight different cancers. And that heavy drinking shortens our lifespan by between 10 and 12 years.

So, it causes cancer, guys! It really, really does. And no amount is healthy. Full stop. End of.

Relatively light drinkers don't get off scot-free either. Boston University stated in a report in 2012 that 'Reducing alcohol consumption is an important and underemphasised cancer prevention strategy'. They showed that just one and a half alcoholic drinks a day 'accounted for 26% to 35% of alcohol-attributable cancer deaths'. And yet, 90 per cent of drinkers think it's totally fine to consume alcohol in small amounts. You can legitimately drink one and a half glasses a day (if you choose something like one and a half shots of vodka, or one and a half low-alcohol bottled beers) and stay within the 14-units-a-week governmental limit.

Meanwhile, a study published in the *British Medical Journal*, found that even two bottles of wine a week can shrink your brain. They conducted MRI scans on 550 people over a 30-year period, and found surprising results. Only 35 per cent of teetotallers showed shrinkage in the hippocampus, a region associated with learning and memory, over the 30 years. While 65 per cent of those who drank between 14 and 21 units a week showed shrinkage. This overturns previous claims that a drink a day can help 'protect' the brain. A neuropsychiatrist, Dr Killian Welch, wrote that '[the] findings strengthen the argument that drinking habits many regard as normal have adverse consequences for health'.

If you want to reduce your risk of cancer and hang onto your brain, it's clear that the best bet is to drink no alcohol at all. Just as you avoid smoking and breathing in asbestos.

I used to brag about wanting to die young and leave a good-looking corpse. But really, bad stuff starts happening to your body at 55 rather than 65. You lose a decade of feel-good years and then die much younger, rather than lopping the feel-bad years off the end of your existence. You don't party hard and then abruptly die, with a sparkler in your hand and a grin on your face. You party hard and start dying slowly much, much earlier. Not at a party wearing a glittery hat.

Despite all of this 'alcohol is a carcinogen' proof, a poll showed that half of all British people still did not associate alcohol with cancer in 2016. Consider this. British people are five times more likely to die from an alcohol-related death than a car accident. We religiously wear seatbelts or buy cars with fancy air bags. And yet, we totally ignore the monster in the room that is five times more likely to kill us.

THE MYTH THAT SOBRIETY IS BORING

Drinking is celebrated as social glue. Being sober is denigrated as social suicide. Pop 'sober memes' into Google and you'll find 'Being sober. What boring and/or skint people do on a Saturday night.' Or 'friends don't let friends stay too sober'. These 'sober is lame' messages root into society in a tentacle-deep, insidious way.

Try this as an anthropological observation. Pretend you're a social scientist. Drive down the streets of any metropolis at 2am. If alcohol is the fun elixir we're all told it is, then it would follow that the people who have had the most to drink, should be having the most fun, right? Yet they're puking in doorways, abandoned by their friends. Or chewing through a kebab like a zombie chows down on a corpse.

Watch the girl getting into an unmarked car that she thinks is a cab. The people stumbling into the street, as drivers blare their horns. The crying girl being comforted by her friends. The people who look like they're still having fun, in this dystopian panorama, are actually the people who have had the least alcohol. What does that tell you? Alcohol is not a fun-giver. It's a fun-taker-awayer.

THE FUTURE IS LESS DRINKY

Millennials are increasingly choosing to swerve booze. Between 2005 and 2013, the proportion of teetotal Brits aged 16–24 rose by 40 per cent. That's enormous. Four in ten have said that alcohol is less important to their social life than their parents' social lives. Perhaps they have been put off drinking by watching their parents drink? Of those, 66 per cent of them classify drinking as 'not very important or not at all important' to their lives. Fewer than half of people aged 16–24 had a drink in the past week, compared with nearly two-thirds of those aged 45–64.

Overall in Britain, women are more likely than men to be teetotal (25 per cent of women, compared to 18 per cent of men). Sobriety rose from 19 per cent in 2005 to 21 per cent in 2013. London is the UK's epicentre, with one in three adults living there choosing to be alcohol-free.

DRINKING IS THE NEW SMOKING

Back in the 1950s, people were still smoking on planes, doctors were endorsing smoking in adverts, and it was normal to puff away at your office desk. In the late '80s, smoking was banned on planes worldwide and, in 2007, lighting up became forbidden in British pubs and restaurants. It seems unimaginable now, a decade later, for somebody to spark up in a restaurant. Who would do that?! When we go abroad, we're appalled to see people smoking in bars.

Social change is glacial, but steady. It could be that we're on the threshold of a similar shift: society falling out of love with alcohol. It may take decades, but there's definitely a leaning towards wholesome brunch and boutique gyms, and away from slurry pub crawls. The number of coffee shops has gone up by 12 per cent in the past decade and only three per cent of teenagers say that alcohol is an 'essential part of socializing'.

In 50 years' time, our grandchildren could be saying, 'I can't believe people used to drink for fun?! I can't believe people used to booze on planes, on trains, in offices!' *Grandchild widens eyes in disbelief and swigs their coconut water*

I saw an amazing advert the other day for alcohol-free drink, Curious Elixirs. A guy orders a soda water and the music screeches to a halt in the bar. A medieval peasant shows up ringing a bell and chanting, 'shame, shame, shame'. The barman snatches her bell and says 'not cool…there's no shame in skipping on the booze, people have tonnes of reasons not to drink.' He then introduces a bunch of people who aren't drinking. It closes with the barman saying that he's sober too, and owns a bar – 'Wrap your head around that.' The tagline for the brand is 'shaken, not slurred'.

For now, while the rest of the booze matrix slowly wakes up, the sober can take pleasure in the fact that they've fled the nightmarish reality of 2am. They can tuck away the happy knowledge that their alcohol-free choices slash their chances of cancer, and untimely death, dramatically. They can eye the Alicia Florricks on TV with scepticism; she's not real. Her consequence-free drinking is *not real*. The red wine she's cradling is actually blackcurrant juice.

And here's a mind-bender for you: Kerry Washington, who plays Olivia Pope in *Scandal* (the lover of the 'rare, complex, fantastic red wine') doesn't drink. Nope. Not at all. So, the next time you're admiring how charismatic, gorgeous and together she is, remember: that's what a teetotaller looks like.

MINDFULNESS STOPS ME FROM GOING INSANE

'I hate feelings. Why does sobriety have to come with feelings?'
- AUGUSTEN BURROUGHS

I soon discovered that one of the main reasons I drank my face off, was to shut my chattery mind the eff up. Sober, I no longer had that silencer. Once we don't have booze to turn down the volume of our minds or anaesthetize our moods, we need other methods.

Whenever I'm showering, watching TV or trying to get to sleep, I am constantly assailed by a tickertape of background noise. And it's infuriating. I find it remarkable that some people can just have a shower, without having to script hypothetical arguments with people. That some people can watch TV, without time-machining back to 'that time when' and plunging back into the sorrow all over again.

My brain insists that I firefight three potential disaster scenarios before I even have breakfast. My mind is like a really jumpy ex-spy. Think Carrie in *Homeland* off her bipolar meds. Complete with a twitchy eye and an itchy trigger-finger.

'Often, people drink to actually quiet down the pre-frontal cortex,' says neuroscientist Alex Korb. 'The limbic system is responsible for anxiety itself, but the pre-frontal cortex provides the worry scripts, formulating potential problems. When our mind races and catastrophizes, that's the pre-frontal cortex.'

And as we know from page 170, the pre-frontal cortex comes back online in sobriety. So, basically, it felt like my brain was trying to drive me insane. It was catastrophizing one minute and filmic fantasizing the next. I needed help with it. My moods were all over the shop, because they felt tethered to my thoughts. I felt like a slave to my errant brain.

THE CAVALRY DUO
I found my answers in the blissful guided meditation app *Buddhify*, and a wonderful book that my psychotherapist aunt gave me, called *Mindfulness: a practical guide to finding peace in a frantic world*, by Professor Mark Williams and Dr Danny Penman.

I read the latter with my mouth open. 'How do they know exactly how my mind feels?' (Probably because most people's minds feel that way.) 'Our moods naturally wax and wane,' Williams and Penman write. 'It's the way we're meant to be. But certain patterns of thinking can turn a short-term dip in vitality of emotional wellbeing into longer periods of anxiety, stress, unhappiness and exhaustion. A brief moment of sadness, anger or anxiety can end up tipping you into a "bad mood" that colours a whole day, or far, far longer.'

The worry scripts tip us into being unhappy, basically. Or we feel fearful, and we feel the need to assign a reason for our inexplicable mood. We then try to extricate ourselves from that snare by *thinking some more*. Big mistake.

'It's natural to try and think your way out of the problem of being unhappy,' write Penman and Williams. 'You try to establish what is making you unhappy and then find a solution. In the process, you can easily dredge up past regrets and conjure up future worries. This further lowers your mood.' And then you feel guilty for being unhappy, when you lead such a privileged life! 'You start to feel bad for failing to discover a way of cheering yourself up,' they continue.

And that's just it. When we feel sad, angry, annoyed, we add a further layer of negativity to that emotion, because we're like 'you have nothing to feel sad/angry/annoyed about!' There's a meditation called 'Rain' in the *Buddhify* app that had me sobbing the first time I heard it, because it's all about this negative emotion self-flagellation. 'I shouldn't be feeling X.' Why ever not? We're not *Ex-Machina* robots. The human experience comes with a side of emotions.

Penman and Williams taught me that it's all about learning that negative thoughts 'are like propaganda, *they are not real*. They are *not you*. You can learn to observe negative thoughts as they arise, let them stay a while and then simply watch them evaporate.' A fretful ten minutes of worrying doesn't necessarily have to colour the rest of the day blue. An encounter with a rude stranger doesn't have to disrupt my mood.

This was nothing short of a personal revelation. It meant that my mood remained largely even, rather than up-down, in-out, shake-it-all-about. I wasn't leashed and tugged by my thoughts to places I didn't want to go.

Here is my carousel of go-to techniques. Sometimes one doesn't work, and another does, so I switch them around.

1. NAMING, NOT SHAMING
The ever-so-simple act of simply naming an emotion (anger, fear, anxiety) takes the sting out of it, say numerous studies. 'Consciously recognising the emotions reduced their impact,' explains neuroscientist Dr Alex Korb. Emotional labelling is even used by FBI hostage negotiators, to calm volatile situations.

Suppressing negative emotions is futile, says a study from Stanford University, which concluded 'trying not to feel something doesn't work'. When people are asked not to think about polar bears, they think about the Arctic alpha way more than those who are allowed to think about them as much as they want.

2. THE B&B MODEL
This mindfulness technique is based upon the poem, 'The Guest House' by Rumi, which is all about welcoming in our emotions or thoughts as if they are 'visitors', even if they're unwelcome ones. Treating each guest with kindness, as a (good) B&B owner would, rather than arguing with them or trying to shove them out of the door. A frequent guest to my mental B&B is someone who I like to call Poor Little Rich Girl, who says things like, 'Why haven't they de-headed my prawns! I don't want to touch their creepy eyes!' Or, 'My lovely dress needs to be dry cleaned. Now I have to go to the dry cleaners. Poor me.' Even when she strops about, uses her tiara as a Frisbee and slams the door until the house shudders, I go about my day, just as the B&B owner would, and I don't hate on her. She's annoying and I actively disagree with some of the ludicrous things she says, but I'm polite and friendly, until she decides to leave of her own accord.

3. CHILDREN IN A CAR
One of my sober friends once said, 'Feelings are like children. You don't want them driving the car, but you shouldn't stuff them in the boot either.' Let them chit-chatter away in the back, and get on with your life. Amazing, right?

4. BIRD-WATCHING

I got this from *Buddhify*. The idea is, pretend you
In a hide, observing the birds of your own thoughts.
'Oh, there's the fear bird.' Rather than grabbing it, or fee
trying to scare it away, none of which a bird-watcher would e
you just watch it with objective curiosity. It's not a bad bird; it jus
Then, it'll fly away.

5. THE MAGIC DOORWAY EFFECT

Did you know that simply walking through a door-frame can break a
repetitive thought-loop? It literally causes a memory lapse, which is
why we leave the living room and go into the kitchen for something,
and then stand in the kitchen cluelessly scratching our heads. In a
fascinating study aptly called 'Walking through doorways causes
forgetting', professors at Notre Dame University discovered that this
worked in both virtual and real-world settings.

6. BLUE-SKY THINKING

The Buddhist nun Pema Chodron once said, 'You are the sky.
Everything else – it's just the weather.' (The me of 2013 would have
eye-rolled taking advice from a Buddhist nun.) This captures another
technique I use regularly. That malevolent moods are black clouds
in an otherwise blue sky. They don't have to gather into growling
thunderstorms. If you remember that the sky is blue behind them.

The beauty of mindfulness is that it gives you permission to feel
all the things. The dirty things, the pretty things, the ugly things.
We're allowed. We're allowed to be angry if someone cuts in front
of us in a queue, and think a little 'fuck you'. We're allowed to be
sad for no reason. It's normal to be stressed when we're on an
almighty deadline.

Trying to shove undesirable thought patterns away and be 24/7
Stepford-wife sunshiny doesn't work. It makes them bigger and
badder in our heads, ultimately. But naming, detaching and using
mindfulness-based meditation means we don't become pushed
around by our minds. We gain space within them. Mindfulness gives
us what I like to call, the 'gift of the golden pause'. In which we can
decide how to react, if at all.

ng to tell me that disaster is
ere I am. What are the facts?
check time.

eed to panic. OK, phew. Death
plant pots. I'm in Homebase; not

to feel its wonder.'

VE

're a bird-watcher.
You ID the bird.
ding it, or
er do,
is.

REAL GREETING CARDS

Isn't addicted drinking *hilarious*? These are genuine cards in a shop near you.

- Smiley woman: 'I don't see why boxed wine doesn't have a little straw stuck to the side!'

- Friendly nurse: 'This birthday, I prescribe a whole bottle of wine.'

- A 1950s mother sits over a breakfast table pouring a glass: 'That's right, darlings, Mummy needs wine.'

- A picture of five bottles of wine with the pay-off 'It's important to get your five a day.'

- 'Alcohol kills brain cells...' on the front. Inside, it reads, 'Let the massacre begin.'

- Part of me says, 'I need to stop drinking.'
  The other part says, 'Don't listen to her, she's drunk.'

- 'Drinking can cause memory loss... or even worse, memory loss.'

- Winking woman. 'If I have two drinks, I can feel it. If I have four drinks, *anyone* can feel it.'

- 'Sometimes I drink water just to surprise my liver.'

- 'Is it still alcoholism if I only drink wine rated 95 and above?'

- For the first time in a while, she was happy.
  Then she remembered she was drunk.

- Good friends offer advice. Real friends offer gin.

- 'Why the fuck would I want flowers for my birthday when I can have wine?'

- 'A wine please.'
  'Miss, this is McDonald's.'
  'OK, a McWine please.'*

- First thing on my bucket list is to fill the bucket with wine.

- Keep smiling! Wine can't be far away.

- She was astounded that the wine contained 13% alcohol. 'That means 87% of this bottle is wasted!'

- 'I never drink anything stronger than gin before breakfast.'

- I like to have a glass of wine to relax after a long glass of wine.'

- 'The doctor said I needed to start drinking more wine.
  Also, I'm calling myself 'the doctor' now.

*I'm meant to disapprove, but this one cracks me up.

X: BOOZEHOUNDS DEBUNKED

THE MYTH VS
THE REALITY OF BIG DRINKERS

The cliché of the no-hoper drinking super-strength lager on a park bench is a fallacy. Some drinkers may end up that way, but this does not capture the typical barfly at all. When I was attending AA, I noticed that recovery meetings are awash with lawyers, doctors, entrepreneurs and high-achievers. People at the top of their game.

MYTH
Heavy drinkers are on the bottom rungs of society

REALITY
They tend to be the big-earners

Re-adjust your stereotype, friends! Big drinkers tend to be the big hitters career-wise. Those who earn £40,000-plus are twice as likely to binge drink, when compared to those on lower incomes. Plus, doctors are twice as likely to be alcoholics, compared to members of the general public.

MYTH
They're not very bright

REALITY
They're clever and creative

We've already established that addiction is a brain disorder, not the sign of a small brain; intellect cannot out-think addiction.

And guess what? Studies show that people with higher IQs booze more. Meanwhile, female university graduates are twice as likely to drink to 'hazardous' levels, when compared to non-graduates (a hazardous amount is defined at 28 units or more a week; double the recommended maximum of 14 units).

Also, successful rock stars are more inclined to live fast, die young. They're almost twice as likely to die prematurely, when compared to your average person. A study of over 1,000 chart-toppers found that a quarter of them perished from alcohol- or drug-related problems. Of those who had died, the average age of death among European icons was a shockingly young 35.

MYTH
Boozehounds are weak

REALITY
Boozehounds have serious grit

I vividly remember my addiction counsellor telling me that far from heavy drinkers being 'weak', they are actually remarkably resilient characters, more akin to an athlete than a layabout.

Why? Think about it. Flip your perspective. Heavy drinking is *hard*. It takes grit to struggle through life hungover every damn day. You need to be hardcore to limp into work, after partying 'til 5am and waking up in a claw-foot tub in a five-star hotel in Soho (yep, that was me. I had to dash into Topshop the moment it opened to buy some new clothes to go to work). You need to be wilful to hang onto your energy-sapping habit. The hungover games! Quite the arena to endure.

When that athlete-esque determination, monomania and moxie are funnelled towards healthy, constructive pursuits, an amazing change happens in the ex-drinker's life. As we read about on page 170, the Bridge of the brain could even become *more* sophisticated. So, that sheer bloody-minded stubbornness has a really fantastic flipside.

MYTH
Sober people are straight-edge cowards

REALITY
Sober people are rebellious non-conformers

Some see being sober as a lily-livered move. 'They can't handle it.' Huh? It's actually more of a gangster move to choose to peel away from the pack in a world that is super drink-pushy. It's having the courage to say, 'Er, I don't want to run with you guys any more, because I think you're running in the wrong direction. Right over a cliff, in fact.'

Does anyone remember the computer game, *Lemmings*, from the 1990s? (Gah, I loved that game. Somebody buy me an Amiga so I can play it again.) Anyhow, there was always one lemming that insisted on walking away from the cliff, who refused to follow the crowd. That's the straight-edge, sober lemming. They've decided to sup tea, rather than shorten their life span by 10–12 years (see page 212). They've dared to be rare.

MYTH
Sober people judge people who still drink

REALITY
Nuh-huh. Not a chance

'Sober as a judge' is so misleading. In my experience, sober people are the *least judgmental people ever*. I don't know about those who've never drunk, but those who are ex-boozehounds? Not judgy.

There's a saying in the sober community. 'If you've shagged a zebra, I've probably shagged two.' Sums it up, neatly. Basically, please never feel like an ex-drinker is judging you for drinking. Because they've been there. And have probably done a lot worse than you are doing right now.

MYTH
Sober people feel constantly deprived

REALITY
They're relieved they no longer drink

Recently, my housemate came home from work saying that she'd had a bastard of a day, and that 'all I want to do is drink bubbles and smoke fags'. She then got a bottle of Prosecco from the fridge. As she was opening it, she looked at me and earnestly said, 'Sorry'. I said, 'Please, don't apologize!'

It was bizarre. As if she thought I was gutted I couldn't join in. I really do not feel that way, ever. I feel relieved I no longer need to do that, rather than crestfallen that I'm not popping corks any more.

As we learned on page 167, drinking creates the urge for more drinking. It sets up a drinking-craving-drinking-craving cycle. Once you stop drinking, that cycle is stopped. Annie Grace likens this itch-scratch process to sitting in poison ivy in order to enjoy scratching your bum. Jason Vale compares the deprivation-relief pattern to putting on too-tight boots, so you can enjoy taking them off.

Sober people don't get involved in the cycle whatsoever. Just as ex-smokers have freed themselves from the urge-smoke-urge-smoke wheel.

MYTH
Boozehounds are party-going pleasure-seekers

REALITY
They're likely survivors of childhood trauma

Society pigeonholes heavy drinkers as hedonistic, outgoing personality types. While people do often behave in a belligerent way while smashed, that's the drug at work, not their actual personality. '*In vino veritas*' is nonsense. You would never say that a heroin user is their true self when they're high. People are their true selves when they are drug-free.

Meanwhile, the strongest predictor of whether someone will become addicted to alcohol, is a traumatic childhood. A high number of adverse experiences during childhood makes people seven times more likely to develop an addiction to alcohol in later life, reports a study of 17,000 Americans conducted by Kaiser Permanente.

The booze works as an escape route, at least for a while, says Dr Julia Lewis. 'Alcohol is really good at blocking out memories via a real brain mechanism.' Until it starts to backfire.

It seems that for many, drinking is less a pursuit of pleasure and more of a hunt for pain relief.

MYTH
You're either a normal drinker, or an alcoholic

REALITY
It's a spectrum of dependence

Traditionally, thinking around addiction has been black or white, normal drinker or dependent drinker. But that's all changed. Addiction is now often regarded as a spectrum. 'It isn't an issue of "sensible drinker" and "dependent drinker",' says Dr Julia Lewis. 'People often don't realize that everyone has their own "tipping point" along that spectrum, whereby the dependence will suddenly start running away with them.' Dr Marc Lewis agrees with the spectrum model too. 'It's a good way of putting it. There is no dichotomy; no line in the sand.'

As Jason Vale writes in *Kick the Drink...Easily!*, 'On the whole, people just don't realize they are addicted. In fact, many drinkers have lived and died without ever realising it...what happened with prohibition, when all alcohol was banned? It resulted in organized crime because it soon became clear that people were not choosing to drink, they had to drink. Would the same have happened if they had banned bananas?'

MYTH
Sober people don't have a choice

REALITY
Every ID-carrying adult has a choice

Every now and then, I'll come across somebody, normally a drunk somebody, who is very keen to find out whether I 'had a problem'. Once they've ascertained that I did, they're relieved. Triumphant, even. They'll then say, 'Ahhh, so you didn't have a choice. You *had* to stop drinking.'

This is what I want to say to that person. 'Ummm, of course I had a choice, buddy. Nobody *has* to stop drinking. I had a problem, yes, but now I'm living in the solution. Liver wards are full of people who have been told they will die if they continue to drink, and they continue to drink. Unless we are sent to a dry colony on Mars, all adults with ID have access to alcohol.

'I choose not to drink. So, please don't make me into a victim or a tragic figure, because I'm not one. Please don't pickpocket my greatest achievement to date by saying I didn't choose it. I did. And so does every other sober person out there. They should all be given credit for making that life-enhancing choice. Now, do be a dear and bugger off out of my personal space.'

Of course, I never actually say any of this. I just say, 'Guess so!' Because: what's that saying about not arguing with idiots? That one.

As I type this, there are a bottle of wine and a bottle of Bailey's within a nine-foot radius of me. I live with drinking housemates. I'm here alone. I'm here five days a week alone, because I'm a freelancer. I don't *have* to not drink it. I choose not to drink it.

MYTH
The person is to blame. They have an addictive personality

REALITY
Alcohol is addictive. It is the villain of this piece

As Annie Grace says, 'We protect alcohol by blaming addiction on a person's personality rather than on the addictive nature of alcohol… The concept of addictive personality lets us close our minds to the fact that alcohol is addictive, period.'

She goes on to point out that the personality traits most exhibited by alcoholics, are actually positive things; including openness to experience, extroversion, conscientiousness, agreeableness and neuroticism.

Indeed. Save the final trait, these are all excellent things, no? Also linked are: experience-seeking, decisiveness, impulsiveness and nonconformity. But again, those traits are good things when applied to life in a healthy way.

'Sobriety deserves a medal, not a stigma.'
- ANNIE GRACE, THIS NAKED MIND: CONTROL ALCOHOL: FIND FREEDOM, DISCOVER HAPPINESS & CHANGE YOUR LIFE

SOBER HEROES SPEAK OUT

BRAD PITT
'I was boozing too much. It's just become a problem. And I'm really happy it's been half a year now, which is bittersweet, but I've got my feelings in my fingertips again. I think that's part of the human challenge. You either deny them all of your life or you answer them and evolve.'

FEARNE COTTON
'I found it quite easy to give up [drinking] completely – and now I feel bloody brilliant.'

ZAC EFRON
'What I found [in being sober] is structure…I'm much more comfortable in my own skin. Things are so much easier now.'

DAVINA MCCALL
'You can be quite hedonistic completely sober, you know. Everybody else was absolutely hammered, and I'm leading the conga round this nightclub to mental rave music, and we're all going completely mad, and I'm just as mad as everybody else, but I'm stone-cold sober.'

EWAN MCGREGOR
Got sober aged 30. 'Originally, I was a happy drunk. But later I was miserable because it's a depressant…There comes a point, and it was quite a clear point for me, where things started going downhill with my work and every other aspect of my life.'

BLAKE LIVELY
'I don't drink. I've never tried a drug …It's just something that I genuinely don't have a desire for…I grew up with the mindset that after work you go to dinner and watch a movie. I don't want to go to a club and not wear panties.'

BRADLEY COOPER
Got sober aged 29. 'I don't drink or do drugs at all any more. Being sober helps a great deal.…I was so concerned what you thought of me, how I was coming across, how I would survive the day. I always felt like an outsider. I just lived in my head. I realized I wasn't going to live up to my potential, and that scared the hell out of me. I thought, "Wow, I'm

actually gonna ruin my life; I'm really gonna ruin it." I'd always gotten up at the crack of dawn, and that was out the window. I remember looking at my life, my apartment, my dogs, and I thought, "What's happening?" If I continued it, I was really going to sabotage my whole life.'

'[After quitting] I was doing these movies…and I was sober. And I'm like, "Oh, I'm actually myself. And I don't have to put on this air to be somebody else, and this person still wants to work with me? Oh, what the f*** is that about?" I was rediscovering myself in this workplace, and it was wonderful.'

SIMON PEGG
'I find it easier to keep fit if I don't drink. I have given up for two years and I don't miss it in the slightest.'

LANA DEL REY
'At first it's fine and you think you have a dark side – it's exciting – and then you realize the dark side wins every time if you decide to indulge in it.'

COLIN FARRELL
Quit drinking in 2005. 'There was a lot of partying. I had a good time, but I paid a heavy price. I just wanted to stop. I was done with it, I was tired of it. I wanted to get off the treadmill. Giving up alcohol has put more focus on my career. I'm a lot more appreciative over what I have…I'm really grateful. It's really lovely to be present in my life.'

KIM CATTRALL
'I don't drink or take drugs, so clothes are my only mood enhancer.'

LARA STONE
'The drinking was getting way out of control. I just didn't recognize myself any more. I didn't know what I was doing or where I was. I always had to have some drinks with me in my bag. Just waking up shaking and then having Bloody Marys on your own, first thing in the morning – I started to feel really pathetic about it. So I was like, 'I can't live like this.' It was just this really awful feeling of becoming a totally different person and not being able to control it at all. [Quitting] was the best thing I've done in my entire life. I'm so happy I did that.'

JARED LETO
'I still have plenty of vices, but alcohol isn't one of them.'

STEVIE NICKS
'I learned that I could live my life and still be beautiful and fun and still go to parties and not even have to have a glass of wine.'

MOBY
'I was given a questionnaire, and one of the questions was: how many units of alcohol do you consume in a month? And I realized I was drinking about 60 units a week. I remember lying to my doctor, saying it was somewhere between 30 to 40 and he was even concerned at that. I was having about 300 drinks a month. That made me realize it was maybe time to stop.'

KRISTIN DAVIS
'I drank a lot when I was a teenager and I don't drink any more, because that's when I thought, you know, I'm gonna end up a car wreck…I got into the acting programme, it was very challenging, I was hungover and I wasn't doing so well in my classes. I thought, "Do you know what? It's going to be one or the other. I can't really have both."'

DAMIEN HIRST
'I saw myself recently getting the Turner Prize in 1995 and I was out of my mind drunk, slurring my words. It makes me cringe. When I was drinking I thought I was the greatest dad in the world but looking back…you're selfish without realizing it when you're drinking a lot.'

CHRISTINA RICCI
'I went through a normal kind of late teens, early 20s drinking, but it [sobriety] was a choice I made, because I didn't think it was very good for my life. I don't go out very often. [When I do] I drink Diet Coke and dance.'

ROBERT DOWNEY JR
'I can be comfortable while someone else enjoys a drink. If I'm out at a restaurant and a waiter asks me if I'd like a glass of wine, I tell him, "I'd love to but I have plans for Christmas." And I'm serious.'

MARIAN KEYES
'By the time I was 30 [my drinking] had all come to a terrible head and, after a suicide attempt, I was lucky enough to get into rehab. (Mind

you I didn't feel lucky at the time! I thought my life was over.) However, I've been one of the fortunate ones and I've stayed sober and – more importantly – happy about it, ever since.'

ED SHEERAN

'The reason that I don't drink is, I turn into an idiot. I've inherited my dad's genes, I just tend to tell not funny jokes when I'm drunk.'

KELLY OSBOURNE

'I don't drink at all. Even a glass of wine at dinner would probably mean me going home, getting s**t-faced and then being on drugs and doing something stupid that I have to spend the next three months apologizing for…'

JASON BATEMAN

Quit drinking in 2004 when his wife went on holiday to Mexico without him. 'Booze was what would make me want to stay out all night and do some blow or smoke a joint or whatever, so shutting that off was key.... I asked myself, "Do you want to continue to be great at being in your 20s, or do you want to step up and graduate into adulthood?"… I was just ready to graduate from adolescence and try my hand at being an adult.'

KATE BECKINSALE

Sees being sober as a 'smart move, face-wise'. 'Drinking just doesn't make me feel well. I find wine very depressing. I get into a kind of despair the next day.'

NAOMI CAMPBELL

'I have more energy and I have more fun than when I was drinking and I can hang out really late and get up early in the morning with no hangovers and still smile.'

TOBEY MAGUIRE

'It doesn't seem like I'm made to have a little bit [of alcohol]. It seems to be I'm made to have more than a little bit! I had a lot of fun, but what it did cumulatively to my life was not worth it.'

JENNIFER LOPEZ

'I think that [drinking] ruins your skin.'

BEN AFFLECK

'I want to live life to the fullest and be the best father I can be.'

CALVIN HARRIS

'My live shows are a million times better now. If you drink, you can't even remember if it's a good show or not – and that's probably for the best, because it would have been rubbish because I'd have been drunk and not making any sense.'

MATTHEW PERRY

Has openly said he can't remember around three years of filming *Friends* and was often 'painfully hungover' on the set.

'From an outsider's perspective, it would seem like I had it all. It was actually a very lonely time for me because I was suffering from alcoholism....When you're having a bad day, the best thing you can do is call somebody and ask them how they're doing, and actually pay attention and listen to the answer to get out of your own head.'

JADA PINKETT SMITH

Said in 2005, 'I found myself drinking two bottles of wine on the couch and I said, "Jada, I think we've got a problem here". I had problems with alcohol and I really had to get in contact with the pain, whatever that is, and then I had to get some other tools in how to deal with the pain. From that day on I went cold turkey; I haven't had a drink in eight years.'

Husband Will Smith doesn't drink either.

PAUL WELLER

'When you are in the bubble of drink or drugs you can't see outside of you...the high times and the good times don't balance out all the down times. I don't think I'll go back to it. I feel fitter now. I go to the gym.'

GERARD BUTLER

'I had gone from a 16-year-old who couldn't wait to grasp life to a 22-year-old who didn't care if he died in his sleep...One or two drinks was never enough for me. I was a foot-on-the-floor-all-the-way drinker, so it had to go. I don't miss it. Now it's as if I never had a drink in my life. At one point, I could never have conceived going out and not drinking but, as time goes on, you lose the urge and the insecurity that often makes people drink in the first place.'

DANIEL RADCLIFFE

'I'm a fun, polite person and it turned me into a rude bore....[My life is] a lot better and less chaotic. I just felt like I was chasing chaos and making my life difficult, all the time thinking I was having fun. So it feels very nice to not be putting myself in danger, to be waking up in the mornings and not thinking, "Oh my God, who am I going to hear from? What did I do?" It's a life lived without dread and fear, and it is lovely.'

DEMI LOVATO

'"Sober is Sexy" is my new motto, and it couldn't be more true! All you need to have fun in life is a great attitude and good friends. I've made a commitment to myself to live a happy, healthy life the best way I know how, and I want to spread the message that you don't need to drink or do drugs to have fun.'

TOM HARDY

'I thought I'd have a little bit of a party, and I'd end up high and frightened, in places that scared me. In a blackout I could end up anywhere, I might wake up somewhere the other side of London, or in another country or in bed with someone I didn't know, not knowing how I got there. Bleeding. This was on a daily basis and I was going to work, I didn't want to appear rock 'n' roll, I didn't want anyone to know I was out of control, but I couldn't hide it.'

THE WILLIS SISTERS

Demi Moore and Bruce Willis's three daughters are all sober.

Tallulah wrote about being three years sober: 'I was hoisted from my hole (one so deep I was certain we were nearing the Earth's magma core) on the backs of powerful human beings that I will forever be indebted to, and on that day my life was gifted back to me.'

Rumer said of her six months sober: 'It's not something I planned on but after the long journey of getting here I can honestly say I have never been more proud of myself in my entire life.'

Scout honoured her one year sober by writing: 'One year of being fully present with ma self, no filters, no chemical relaxation, no short cuts. I am meeting the best version of myself every day.'

XI: CHOOSE YOUR OWN SOBER ADVENTURE

PRO-CHOICE RECOVERY

'When you go out into the woods and you look at trees, you see all these different trees. And some of them are bent, and some of them are straight, and some of them are evergreens, and some of them are whatever. And you look at the tree and you allow it. You appreciate it. You see why it is the way it is. You sort of understand that it didn't get enough light, and so it turned that way…The minute you get near humans, you lose all that… That judging mind comes in. And so I practice turning people into trees. Which means appreciating them just the way they are.'
– Ram Dass

If there's one thing I've learned about being sober, it's that what works for me will not necessarily work for someone else. Hitting upon the right mix of tools is like chancing upon the correct combination that opens a safe door. *Cue a satisfying clunk.* The door swings open and beyond it, there's freedom from alcohol.

I know successfully sober people who did ten-plus years of AA, decided it wasn't for them, and swapped it out for yoga and meditation; I know people who mix up Smart Recovery and AA; people in Refuge Recovery; people who do straight AA five times a week and yet have never done the steps or gotten a sponsor; people who rely exclusively on CBT therapy; people who simply read a lot about recovery.

Myself, the combination that led to that lovely clunk was: an addiction counsellor, online recovery groups, the resulting in-real-life recovery friends, reading voraciously, podcasts, meditation and exercise.

Before I found my unique sobriety combination, I had been told that 'AA is the only way'. So, I went to thrice-a-week AA meetings for six months. But, given the choice of a lifetime inside AA, or drinking, I kept choosing drinking. That wasn't AA's fault, it was just my reaction to it. I needed a third door.

It was only once I stopped going to AA and started designing my own sobriety, that my sobriety started sticking. AA helped me get to sober, for sure, but staying in AA was not the right decision *for me*. I went to more than 75 meetings before deciding that.

Why did I leave? I actually wrote 8,000 words for this book about my good and bad experiences there, trying to explain why I left. I decided to leave those words locked in my computer. AA is a different animal for everyone, meetings have an entirely unique vibe, and I don't want to influence your opinion of it. I recommend everyone check out AA and decide for themselves.

Some of the best advice I ever received was: 'Don't try *harder*. Try *different*.' If something's not getting you sober or keeping you sober, try something else. Just as you would try a different therapist, or a different exercise regime, if your current one wasn't giving you results. If you stop doing something and you drink, whoa, hotfoot right back to doing what you were doing before. If you stop doing something and you don't drink, you're fine.

> JUST AS TWO PEOPLE CAN LOOK AT THE SAME PAINTING, WATCH THE SAME FILM OR MEET THE SAME PERSON AND HAVE VASTLY CONTRASTING REACTIONS, RECOVERY METHODS ARE THE SAME. **WE REACT DIFFERENTLY TO THE SAME STIMULUS.** BECAUSE WE ARE DIFFERENT.

Click through combinations of numbers, and see what happens. See what gives you that lovely clunk. Your successful combination will be unique to you. There is no 'right way' or 'only way' to get sober.

CHOOSE YOUR OWN WAY...

'Every person is an individual and a "one size fits all' approach to treatment is not at all effective,' says Dr Julia Lewis, who has worked with over 2,000 dependent drinkers. 'AA may work wonderfully for some people, but it won't work for everyone.'

AA's own magazine, *The Grapevine*, reported on this in May 2001. They wrote that 60 per cent of successful recoveries occur independently, outside of recovery groups, or professional counselling and treatment.

A study by Stanford University found that AA edged it over therapy. After 16 years, 67 per cent of the AA group were abstinent, compared to 56 per cent of the therapy group.

Other studies show different results, as is the nature of the research beast. For instance, in 1992 a massive 42,000-person study found that those who had no treatment (treatment includes therapy, rehab or recovery meetings) had *better* recovery rates than those who had undergone treatment. Three-quarters of the 'no treatment' group were successful, compared to two-thirds of the 'treatment' group.

Meanwhile, Project MATCH, took 1,726 problematic drinkers and set them on three different paths over eight years: 12-step methods, cognitive-behavioural therapy and motivational-enhancement therapy. It was the 'largest scientifically rigorous alcohol treatment trial ever seen' and cost millions. It found that the three different types of treatment rolled in at around the same success rates.

Finally, a huge review (of eight different studies involving 3,417 participants) also found that no treatment shone as more effective, whether it was AA or other treatments.

So, what's the answer? There isn't one. There's only one thing we know for sure; there's no such thing as a magic bullet. There are multiple ways to get sober. And you, dear reader, get to choose.

CHOOSE YOUR OWN TRIBE

The ever-wondrous Anne Lamott says, 'My mind is like a dangerous neighbourhood; I should never go there alone.' Think of that scene, which occurs in most thrillers, where the renegade cop is outside the house where the serial killer lives. 'Wait for back-up!' they're advised. They don't. And it's a disaster. Don't do what renegade movie cops do. Get some back-up buddies.

'Human beings are a social species,' says neuroscientist Alex Korb. 'We need each other to survive and be happy. Feeling disconnected from people gives us distress. If trying to connect with others without drinking brings anxiety, it makes sense to find social support in sober groups instead, until you get used to socializing without alcohol. Social interactions stimulate the dopamine system. We know that when rats are given dopamine, their addictive urges reduce. So, it's a win-win. The more you feel connected to people, the less you will feel like drinking.'

It was a profound shift for me, seeing happily sober people in AA with my own eyes. They existed! They weren't a myth. They were THERE.

But it was when I found a Facebook group called the BFB ('Booze-Free Brigade') that I discovered My People. In the BFB, there was a kaleidoscope of people recovering in different ways.

There are so many ways to find your tribe. There's obviously AA, which is by far the biggest and most widely known, with millions of meetings. Then there's Refuge Recovery (based on Buddhist principles), there's SMART recovery (grounded in secular science and self-empowerment), there's Women For Sobriety (I love their version of the steps), there's Rational Recovery (which is where Addictive Voice Recognition comes from), there's Hello Sunday Morning (aimed at those who want to take a break or cut back), there's Soberistas (a raft of online discussion boards), there's Club Soda (mostly Brits, wanting to 'cut down, stop for a bit, or quit') and more.

The best thing about sober tribes? They're the antithesis of Fakebook or Insta-brag. People drop all of that fakery and are utterly imperfect, real and flawed. Your tribe will celebrate and honour your milestones in a way your regular friends won't. They'll know that clocking up 100 days deserves a unicorn parade, a gown made of glowworm silk or having a star named after you.

CHOOSE NOT TO DRINK

A 2013 Boston College study showed that people who say 'I don't' are more successful than those who say 'I can't'. Which is why I say 'I don't drink' rather than 'I can't drink'.

Choosing not to drink, rather than being forced into it, is a subtle but powerful mental shift. 'When our brain actively chooses something, we release more dopamine than when something is thrust upon us,' says neuroscientist Dr Alex Korb. 'Our brain likes things that we choose a lot more.'

CHOOSE YOUR OWN LABEL

When I heard 'alcoholic' used as a dirty word, as a slur, it drove me further into my addiction, because I was frightened of wearing that label. I cannot emphasize enough how dangerous it is to stigmatize addiction.

Things are changing, thankfully, with the 'recovering out loud' movement. I wear the label of 'recovering alcoholic', because I think that (currently) the answer is to own the label, rather than try to dodge it. When people ask if I am (they whisper it) 'an alcoholic', I say yes, because if I own it with pride, it might change their perception of it.

But, you don't have to do what I do. You can do whatever you like! I know plenty of long-term sober people who don't say they were or are alcoholics. They know they were addicted, but refuse to define themselves by that addiction.

For instance, there's the 'teetotaller' trend, spearheaded by Holly Whitaker of *Home* podcast. She decided that sobriety needed a re-brand; something I vigorously agree with. Cue hordes of women using the word 'teetotaller' rather than 'recovering alcoholic'. She even designed her own 'Tt' periodic-table-style tattoo. It looks like a scrabble tile and is deeply cool. The teetotal tribe comes to Instagram to showcase their 'Tt' tattoos, rather than hiding them.

This shift is being reflected in the press too. The 2017 *Associated Press Stylebook*, which is basically the go-to guide for journalists, now recommends that magazines and newspapers 'avoid words like alcoholic, addict, user and abuser' and 'instead choose phrasing like *he was addicted, people with heroin addiction or he used drugs*'.

The lead author of the *Stylebook* was interviewed by *Slate* magazine as to why he implemented this subtle, but powerful change. He said it was because of a paper he read by President Obama's chief advisor on drugs, Michael Botticelli, named 'Changing the language of addiction'. In it, Botticelli cited a study that found that doctors were slightly more likely to recommend harsher measures for 'substance abusers' as opposed to 'people with substance abuse disorders'. That small shift in focus, from the person, to the problem itself, is huge. After all, we don't describe ex-smokers as 'smokeaholics' for the rest of their lives.

Maybe one day, when society has a new language around addiction, I will use a new label. Who knows.

CHOOSE YOUR OWN TIME-FRAME

I had a conversation with my addiction counsellor when I was around a month sober. I told him that the 'one day at a time' thing felt too short, and cliff-edge tentative ('just make it through today!') for me. He said that different time-frames work for different people. I ended up signing up to Belle's *Tired of Thinking About Drinking* '100-day challenge'. That was right for me. I needed something larger than a day, but smaller than forever.

> NOW, I HAPPILY COMMIT TO FOREVER. BUT YOU DON'T HAVE TO. I KNOW PEOPLE WHO DO IT A DAY AT A TIME, A MONTH AT A TIME OR TELL THEMSELVES THAT IF THERE'S EVER A LOCUST APOCALYPSE, THEY WILL DRINK AGAIN. I LOVE SAYING 'FOREVER', **IT MAKES ME FEEL SAFE, BUT YOU ARE NOT ME, AND I AM NOT YOU, AND YOU CAN DETERMINE YOUR OWN PARAMETERS.**

You can choose to break your run into sobriety into staggered chunks. There's an app called *Sober Time* that chunks it into five minutes, one day, three days, a week, ten days and so on.

But, do me a favour. If you really are sober-curious, then go further than Dry January. Dry January is an amazing idea, a fantastic start and I wholeheartedly applaud the organizers, but a month won't show you what sobriety feels like long-term. Remember what I said about the first 30 days being the hardest bit? Yeah. So, it's like doing the rough bit (say, the start of a run) without waiting for the spoils (the delicious endorphin buzz a mile in).

'A month off is fine,' says Dr Korb, 'but it's not teaching your brain the lesson you want it to learn long-term, which is the creation of new habits. You're only not drinking because it's Dry January. Just as people don't drink at work.' This is why many people find that their intake shoots straight up to what it was before Dry January. The big picture of their drinking remains the same.

Why? A scientific study showed that it takes a minimum of 66 days to bed a new habit in. To create that new pathway in your brain. So, if you want to give sobriety a whirl, I advise at least three months off booze.

CHOOSE TO BE PRO-CHOICE

'We know from research that people with substance-use disorders are likely to have better outcomes when they're offered choices for, and have a say in recovery and treatment approaches,' writes Anne Fletcher, author of the *New York Times* bestseller, *Sober for Good: New Solutions for Drinking Problems – Advice from Those Who have Succeeded.*

Meanwhile, the co-founder of AA himself, Bill Wilson, said, 'Upon therapy for the alcoholic himself, we surely have no monopoly.' And, 'In no circumstances should members feel that Alcoholics Anonymous is the know-all and do-all of alcoholism.' Wise words.

Judgment is corrosive, in whatever direction it goes, whether it be from Refugers towards AAers, or Rational Recoverees towards yogis, or AAers towards Smarters.

The sober world features some *Lord of the Flies*-style in-fighting. You see spiteful rows in the comments section of the (excellent) addiction news website, *The Fix*. It's such a shame. We judge each other, when we could be supporting each other. Time for a ceasefire. We're allies, not foes. 'Helping someone' can sometimes accidentally segue into 'trying to control someone'. It's like Anne Lamott says: 'Help is the sunny side of control…you can't save, fix or rescue any of them, or get anyone sober.'

Matt Haig writes in his spectacular book, *Reasons to Stay Alive*: 'When we are trying to get better, the only truth that matters is what works for us…Hell, if licking wallpaper does it for you, do that… in the absence of universal certainties, we are our own best laboratory.'

If somebody's strategy is to paint themselves blue and walk around town introducing themselves to everybody as 'Sober Smurf', then bully for them. If it works, and helps keep them sober, don't knock it – even if you think it's bonkers. Buy them some blue paint for their birthday. Let's choose to see our similarities, rather than our differences.

'Whatever works' is one of my favourite recovery slogans. I would love to see a sober sphere that is pro-choice. After all, our common goal is sobriety, not matchy-matchy recovery choices.

'You have your way. I have my way. As for the right way, the correct way and the only way, it does not exist.'
– NIETZSCHE

A LETTER TO MY INUIT

I wrote this tribute to my mum on Mother's Day 2016. I shared it on some recovery boards I'm a member of. In response, one of my wisest sober mates, Laura, said, 'She's your Inuit!' She then posted a clip which told the story of the Inuit.

The Inuit proverb is about an explorer in the North Pole, caught in a blinding storm. Freezing to death, he prays to God to save him. God doesn't come. But an Inuit does. And the Inuit carries the explorer back to his camp and saves his life. Heart-glow.

Here's my letter. And her letter back.

Dear Mum,

I wanted to write a tribute to you today, for Mother's Day. I wanted to tell you that you saved my life. Here's why.

1. You never stopped saying how worried you were about my drinking, in the last year of my drinking. Despite my angry responses. Looking back, that was a radical act of love.

2. You attended Al-Anon, the support group for the family and friends of alcoholics, long before I even started attempting to quit. The number one takeaway message you chose sums up how loving you are.

This message was a proverb about when people try to get us to stop drinking, before we're ready. The story goes thus: the wind blew and puffed and raged to try to get the man to take off his coat. And the man kept his coat on, stubbornly. He wrapped it around his body in staunch refusal. But then the sun rose and shone and gently warmed him. And he removed the coat of his own volition.

3. When others were telling you to 'let me hit rock bottom' and feel the wrath of my financial irresponsibility you could see that I had already hit rock bottom, mentally. You could see that I hated myself enough. That I was already suicidal. You paid off my £4,000 of debt (under the understanding that I would of course pay you back, which I have). You took me out to buy beautiful clothes, to replace the shabby drinking uniform I'd started to hide in. You took me on holiday to Malta, my first in years, and didn't even blast me when I secretly (I thought) drank at times during said holiday. You soul-searched and went against all the 'tough-love' advice. You lifted me up rather than let me fall down further. The light you showed me helped me find the impetus to crawl out of the abyss. I couldn't have handled any more darkness.

4. When I was still going to AA you drove me to meetings, often three or four a week. You would sit outside with your tea and your cryptic crossword. You gave up your evenings gladly, without a trace of bitterness. You often fell asleep; I would come back to the car and find you gently snoring, glasses lopsided, newspaper on the floor.

5. Towards the end of my drinking, you weren't scared to get fierce and brutally honest with me. I vividly remember one evening when I was pretending to have a bath. Instead, I sat on the closed toilet, drinking a beer I had hidden. You knew. You shouted through the door that drinking would not be tolerated if I wanted to continue to live at home. I hated it at the time, but you did me an enormous favour. That mix of 90 per cent sun-warming and ten per cent zero-tolerance was the right mix for me.

6. These days, when my self-esteem swan-dives, which is often, you recognize that this is when I am most in drinking peril. You champion me, remind me of my good points, and make sure I always have a safe place to go to. I know I can always, always go home. For as long as I want.

7. It's not all about sprinkling me with fairy dust. You're also the first person to call me on it when I'm acting like a tosser. Equally as loving an act.

I don't actually think I would be here today if it wasn't for you. Seriously. So, THANK YOU Mum.

Catherine

MY MUM'S REPLY

Aww. Is that me?

Well, of course it is, but it all seems slightly strange and out of context. Because we did it together and it was our joint dynamic which made it work. It sounds as if I'm some sort of saint – but I got payback, which came bit by bit by bit. And each bit was huge and enormously worthwhile, despite some slips in between.

Like when you admitted back in 2013 that you had a problem. That was the admission we needed to start this stupendous roller-coaster of a journey together. You got sober and really got to enjoy being sober. You revelled in it. Your sobriety became the freshest, most joyous experience and you lost the fear of telling people about your alcoholism.

You drew your existing friends closer and found wonderful new soulmates all over the world. You started liking and looking after yourself. You started liking and looking after lots of other people. Increasingly, you started appreciating your world with childlike wonder but a wiser perspective. You no longer feared brown envelopes!

I couldn't really begin to help until you owned your problem. In 2013 I was allowed into the ring with you. We could fight this fight together. My fear of your suicide or accidental death began to recede (big biggie that). I could breathe again. Your active enjoyment of the mini sober periods at the beginning allowed me to become quite casual about slips.

You'd seen both sides now; drinking and sober. I knew what your choice would be in the long-term. I knew that your true friends would rally round and bolster this wonderful, new, non-prickly you. I myself could stop walking on eggshells. And, as you relaxed into your fresh new life and became a better and nicer person, I got me a newly buffed and caring daughter.

Your point number six: rightly or wrongly, I now have no more conscious fear of you drinking again. I may be too complacent but that's the way it is. I bolster you up because it's the right thing to do. If you're feeling down it's usually because you've let some misguided person get to you, and make you doubt yourself. Begone, demons! Get on your unicorn again.

But I couldn't have supported you as I did if it hadn't been for your stepfather; lovely Stewart. I've often said that I know being married to him has helped me become a better person. It's that better, stronger me who was able to reach out the way I did because he was constantly behind us both, ready to take up the slack if needs be.

I love to live vicariously and I'm relishing each new experience you have, each new success, each new helping hand you extend towards others. I love it when you're home but I also love it when you're away and happily on your travels. I love not worrying about you – insofar as I'm able!

I hope we've both grown together during your fabulous phoenix phase. You've certainly made me an extremely happy and proud mum. Just tuck me into your heart and keep talking. Stewart and I are wrapped round you wherever you are; and whether you like it or not!

Mum

See? She's my rescuer. And Stewart is too. He has been there every step of the way, sidestepping to-and-fro beneath me with his safety net. I remember saying to him once that as a single person, I feel like I have no one to lean on when the shit hits the fan.

'But you do,' he said. 'You have us. *Lean in*,' he said, emphatically. I mean. What a legend.

I know that I can always, always go back home if things go wrong, and be very happy there too. Very few people have that.

FEEL THE SOBER FEAR
AND DO IT ANYWAY

'Rock bottom became a solid foundation upon which I built my life.'
– J K ROWLING

I'll level with you. Back in 2013, I was not overjoyed about getting sober. Nuh-huh. Not a happy camper, whatsoever. I only chose it because I could see that if I continued to drink, my life was definitely going to spiral out of control. I felt like I was in a damned-if-you-do, damned-if-you-don't spot with drinking. At a conundrum of a crossroads, where either choice was totally undesirable. I took off down the 'sober' road with all of the enthusiasm of a condemned inmate trudging to their cell. 'GREAT.' *Dramatic sigh.* 'My life is going to be lame.'

But, I was gobsmacked to discover that I became happier than I had ever been. Like, not just a little bit happier; a million times happier. Trading in my drinking life for a sober life felt like trading in a wizened spider plant and being given a giant greenhouse crammed with sunflowers. Like giving somebody a toy boat with a broken propeller, and getting a yacht with an on-deck swimming pool. Like going from the fiery hell blast of Mordor and finding myself transported to the elven utopia of Rivendell instead (what up, *Lord of the Rings* fans).

I know that sounds melodramatic, but it's absolutely true. And the reason I've written this book, the reason I've revealed immensely personal things, is that I wish more people could also discover the wonderment of that trade-in. You don't even have to be addicted, like I was, to choose sober. Even threes on the addicted-drinking scale have hangovers of Dementor soul-sucking proportions (hey, *Harry Potter* fans). Even fours do and say stuff they acutely regret. Even fives feel that 'I want wine' scratch once the working day is done, like a cat relentlessly scratching at a door. If there's one iota of your being that suspects that the minuses of boozing might outweigh the pluses, I urge you to give it a whirl.

After decades of autopilot drinking, where's the harm in trying on a sober life for size, if only for a few months? Who knows, you might find that you love it. That you don't want to go back. If you do want to go back to drinking, you won't find any judgment here. I am the last person to judge people for drinking, given I drank my head off for two decades.

The improvement in your life may be less gargantuan than mine. Where you are on the spectrum determines how dramatically your life changes. I was a nine on the scale, or maybe even a ten, so it makes sense that my gains were juggernaut-proportioned. Yours might be more dinky. It might be that you appreciate having six more hours in your weekend, freed up from hungover lie-ins. It might be that you love your whittled-down waist, your fatter bank account and your pin-clear memory of nights out. The flipside of the smaller rewards, is that it will take less effort for you to get sober, I wager. Wherever you are on the spectrum, you have to ticker over back to zero. So, fours have less of a ways to go.

> THE QUESTION TO ASK YOURSELF IS NOT: 'AM I AN ALCOHOLIC?' **SWIVEL THAT FOCUS. THE QUESTION IS: 'WOULD MY LIFE WOULD BE BETTER IF I WAS SOBER?'** IF THE ANSWER IS YES, THEN SHOOT FOR SOBER!

Alas, I need to leave you soon. Which is sad, because I want to write so much more (and will do, on my blog, www.unexpectedjoy.co.uk, check it out yo) But, I only have one book to fill. So, let's wrap things up for now.

Here are the main messages I want to leave you with.

SOBER IS 95 PER CENT EXQUISITE, 5 PER CENT SAVAGE

Hey, it's no walk in the park, quitting booze. I'm not going to lie to you. At times it will be fist-bitingly hard. Particularly in the first few months. Largely because of how pro-drinking our society is (which is a-changing, thankfully). You're trying to overwrite an ingrained habit of what, ten, 20, 30 years? You're re-wiring your brain. So, yes, it's tough.

However, the seesaw ratio of savage/exquisite overwhelmingly tips towards exquisite. So it's worth it. Of course it is. For the moments of heart-exploding elation that you get the longer that you're sober.

IT'S AN END TO THE 'SHOULD I DRINK?' MENTAL SPIN CYCLE

'Should I drink tonight, if so, how much should I drink, what if I drink too much, I've got that thing I need to do tomorrow, OK, so I drink, but not more than two, how do I make sure that happens, maybe I shouldn't drink…'

Aargh. It's madly draining. When you take drinking completely off the table, your mind is freed up to think about much more interesting things. Your life gets bigger as a result. You read more. You have more money. In the past few weeks I have spent a fraction of the money I would have spent in the pub or off-licence on: a Thai massage, going to the Hockney exhibition at Tate Britain, a long weekend in the Lake District, a comedy show in a shipping container at the Brighton festival and a gorgeous orchid from Kew Gardens that has now been nicknamed 'Dead Man Walking' given my propensity for killing plants (update: two months on, DMW is still alive! Maybe sobriety means plants live too?!).

MODERATION IS A MIRAGE

We've already heard about why it's so crazy difficult to achieve and how few of us actually achieve it, and yet it's held up as something we 'should' be able to do. Which results in us self-flagellating when we can't.

I think of moderate drinking as a desert mirage. Every time I tried to leap on it, I always wound up lying on the floor, stunned, dejected and with a mouthful of sand. Let's stop chasing that mirage around.

Once you try extended sobriety, you'll see exactly what I mean. No booze is so much easier than a little bit of booze. Alcohol is incredibly addictive. It's more-ish. It's fiendishly difficult to stop at one or two. So, don't start. Simple.

I always thought it was the third or fourth drink that was the problem; actually, it was the first. Because that always led to a third or fourth. It placed me on the downward escalator into the tunnel. Trying to get off that escalator at the fourth drink was like trying to run back up the escalator, once I was nearly at the bottom. (Speaking of escalators, I once sat down on an escalator while drunk and refused to get back up. My friend Helen filmed it, to show me when I was sober. Mortifying.)

WE GIVE BOOZE TOO MUCH CREDIT

As a society, we tend to drink when we do fun stuff. Skipping out of work on a Friday, going to a gig, eating at a Michelin-starred restaurant, playing *Articulate* with friends, lying on the sofa bingeing on *American Gods*, chilling on a beach in Ibiza.

We then assume that the drink was the fun-creator, the party-starter, the joy-giver. We Instagram the pretty cocktail, the tumbler of whiskey, the flight of wines, and award it centre stage of The Fun.

Here's the thing: all of those things are fun, because they are...fun. The booze just so happened to be there. They will still be fun if it's not in your hand. I promise you. They'll be more fun, long-term, once you've got your sober sea legs.

And guess what, as we've mentioned on page 91, alcohol numbs your taste buds. So it's not imperative to your dining experience. (Another clever marketing strategy by the drinks industry that has absolutely no basis in actual fact.) The best drink to have to enhance a mind-bendingly delicious meal? Water.

DRINKING IS A THIRD LIMB

As much as we try to separate alcohol from other drugs by saying 'alcohol and drugs' (which makes no actual sense: it's like saying 'foxgloves and flowers' or 'BMWs and cars'), alcohol is a *drug*. We already know it kills 24 people a day in the UK, that it's a carcinogen that can directly cause eight different cancers and that it is actively *bad for you*, even in the smallest amounts. Even moderate drinking shrinks your brain.

When you're sober, you are just drug-free. That's all. It's liberation, not deprivation. We are not *meant* to drink, despite what the world tries to tell us. We're meant to eat, exercise, shag, sleep, love people, stroke animals and drink things that hydrate us rather than dehydrate us. As we've already discussed on page 172 our bodies *hate* us drinking.

Our natural, intended state is drug-free. We're only losing something we never actually needed in the first place, but were told we did, and grew to rely on. Turns out we're much more aerodynamic, efficient and graceful without the extra appendage. Run! Twirl! Enjoy how much better you feel without it.

SOBER WILL BECOME YOUR NEW NORMAL

It will take a while, obviously. It won't happen overnight. Four days used to take a Herculean effort for me, but I'm now over four *years* sober and it feels practically effortless.

The first 30 days are the hardest, but then you're on a roll, you're flying, and it gets easier and easier. If you just keep saying 'no ta' to the first drink, none of the others will follow. It's that simple.

As we learned on page 169, the more you flex the 'not-buying-booze' muscle, the more steely and Popeye-impressive it becomes. Remember what we found out about it taking 66 days (see page 243) before a new habit is formed. It's all about the reps, people.

FROM DISENCHANTMENT TO ENCHANTMENT

I still write a gratitude list most nights. It means I'm constantly seeking out and noting those moments of beauty even on the dreariest days. I'm now a gratitude-hunting lighthouse rather than a slight-seeking missile.

My default state when I was drinking was: disenchantment. Nothing was ever good enough. I was always thinking, 'If only X would happen, or Y would profess undying love, or I would get Z amount of money, I would finally be happy.'

I thought my disenchanted default kept me reaching, striving, bettering my life. But the problem was, each time X, Y or Z came off, I would instantly 'tick' and take those for granted. Then swivel to find a new XYZ to point towards.

Gratitude isn't about giving up on the attempt to better your life. It's about stopping to smell the roses you already have gathered around you. Making a note of how enchanting *they* are. While also continuing to plant and tend new ones.

WEATHER FORECAST: BLUE SKIES

As you know, I lived in the drunk, hungover, dry day, drunk, repeat cycle. Mentally, it felt like living inside a thunderstorm, with the occasional bright spot of an hour or so, normally my first hour drinking, when my psychological craving (and later physical) was finally sated. I lived for 'happy hour'. But then the skies darkened once more, because I always chased the night until the very, very end.

In addiction the thunderstorm turned into a tornado. I was constantly trying to cling to things that were being ripped from my grasp: money, the respect of my colleagues, a potential promotion, a boyfriend, good relations with friends and family. Finding I'd been transported somewhere I didn't recognize. (That tornado also took approximately five phones, thirteen cardigans, a passport, some Habitat book-ends and a birthday cake.)

Now, I live with blue skies most of the time. I have the odd terrible day where the clouds gather and I swear like a sailor and punch pillows. But those are only maybe one in 30 now. And the clouds are marshmallow-esque, cute and quick to skitter off; rather than growling, immovable thunderbanks containing spine-shuddering lightning bolts.

My head-weather is now made by Pixar, rather than Wes Craven.

NO MORE BLACKOUT SLEUTHING

I no longer have to be a sleuth and detective to piece together horrifying gaps in my memory. What did I do? Where did I go? How did I end up here? Why is there no money left in my bank account? Where is my phone? Where is my hat? Whose is this pink sombrero? Why has my boyfriend sent me a text saying, 'It's over'? It was a fresh hell to contend with, most weekend mornings. I now remember *everything*. (Well, apart from what I came upstairs for.)

A HANGOVER-FREE LIFE

Hangovers are the body's way of telling us 'please don't do that to me again'. They are withdrawal from an addictive substance. Which is why Bloody Marys soften a hangover. They're *withdrawal*. And as we heard on page 172, they can last up to 72 hours.

Imagine never having a hangover again? You'll find that it's super-easy to make it to the gym (100 per cent Classpass attendance can be yours) and a total doddle to swerve fast food (you just don't crave trans-fat when you feel glowy-healthy). You'll hardly ever, ever dodge a diary commitment.

Remember how my mates used to use 'I got Cathed' (see page 31) as shorthand for a seventh-circle-of-hell hangover? Now they use it as shorthand for having done a ferocious spinning class and eating their body weight afterwards. I'll take it.

PREDICTABLY HAPPY

Some sober people talk of missing the off-the-hook thrills and ooh-what-will-happen drama of drinking.

What?! I don't, at *all*. Finally being able to predict my own behaviour is one of the best things about being sober. I know I will do my work, I know I will be able to find my way home without assistance, I know my card won't be refused because of a £40 round of shots I forgot, I know I'll look after myself, I know I'll wake up where I intend to wake up. In my own house, in my own bed; or in someone's bed who I chose to sleep with. That never, ever gets old. It's deliciously humdrum.

NOBODY REGRETS GETTING SOBER

In the sober community, when somebody shows up who got sober in their 20s, the universal reaction is 'I'm so jealous! I wish I'd done it back then!' Once you're sober, you see that you wasted so many years drinking your well-being away. I used to hate watching my birthdays roll by, because I knew I was squandering my life. Mostly in *Be At One*. Addiction is unfulfilled potential. When people ask me, 'Do you ever miss drinking?' I can honestly say that no, I don't. At all.

If they invented a moderation pill which made it achievable for me to have one or two drinks and then STOP, I would *not take it*. I don't need that any more, why would I go backwards?

If you're shooting for sustained sobriety and finding that you keep failing, don't give up. Never give up. As Einstein said, 'You never fail until you stop trying.' Do you think the Wright Brothers invented the plane on the very first go? Nope. They had many, many failed attempts first.

It's like playing a computer game. Yes, you have to go back to the start when you slip. But that doesn't erase what you learned about the game. You learned some valuable lessons, that you can now apply to get further on your next attempt.

THE DREAD PIT

Hope is by far the biggest gift being sober has given me. An unnamed dread sat in the pit of my stomach, when I was still drinking. It was subdued somewhat when I poured wine on it. But when I awoke the next morning, the dread was bigger. Blacker. Thirstier. When I thought about the future, all I felt was dread. Dread that I wouldn't be able to wrangle the wild horse of my drinking, dread that I would continue letting my loved ones down, dread that I was destined to stay stuck in this work-shy, promiscuous, shonky rut.

It took a few months of sobriety for the dread to depart, but eventually it was replaced by a tiny spark, then a flame, then a blaze of hope for the future. As I got to know my Actual Self, the person I was when sober, the real me, I grew more and more hopeful. As long as I don't drink, I know everything will be OK. Even when it's not OK. Because I am a decent, thoughtful, hard-working person when I don't drink.

I feel hope every day without fail. Some days it's a little hope buzz that shows up to say hello, other days it's a whole-body-bliss euphoria.

COURAGEOUS, NOT A COP-OUT

It's traditionally been seen as 'weak' to order a soft drink in a pub. But the truth is, it takes serious balls to go against the grain. (Or serious vagina, as Betty White of *The Golden Girls* would say. 'Why do people say "grow some balls?" Balls are weak and sensitive. If you wanna be tough, grow a vagina. Those things can take a pounding.')

You're swimming against the tide, rather than letting the current pull you downstream. Being sober takes effort, courage and indeed, vagina, even if you were only a two on the addictive spectrum.

And if you've fought your way back from addictive drinking, if you were a seven or up; you're one of the iron people who've been forged in the fire. You have learned to override the urgent 'drink, drink, drink' pathway in your brain. The sober community is packed with people blessed with grit, humour, empathy and self-awareness.

In Japan, they repair broken ceramic bowls with gold lacquer and consider it 'more beautiful for having been broken'. That, to me, sums up the people I have met who are in recovery.

WE ARE THE LUCKIEST

#wearetheluckiest is a hashtag that is gathering pace in sober circles, thanks to Laura McKowen of *Home* podcast. For centuries, being sober has been seen as a cross to bear, a stone in your shoe, a burden to carry, and I've even seen it likened to tinnitus. But, it doesn't *feel like that*.

It actually feels like freedom, relief and indeed, like 'we are the luckiest'. Why? I think a huge part of it has to do with the contrast of a heavy-drinking life versus a sober life. People who can easily stick to one or two drinks at the Christmas party, do not find themselves overjoyed that the morning after a sober Christmas party doesn't come with a side order of intense shame. People who have never had grim mornings where they feel sick on a train? They don't sit on a train, as I did this morning, and grin because they feel good. People who have never felt twinges of failure as they put out a wind-chime-clanking recycling bag, do not appreciate the peace that comes with putting out a recycling bag that doesn't make them feel guilty.

The further down you sank into the abyss of addictive drinking, the more you appreciate the view on your ascent out. And once you've clawed your way out, you feel more than a little invincible. 'If I got sober, when it felt impossible, what else can I do?'

ALCOHOL IS LIKE A CHALK HORSE ON A HILLSIDE

You have to put some distance between you and drinking before you see it clearly. It's like those hill figures in the British countryside. When you're next to one, all you can see is the white of the chalk: you're too close to see what it *is*. It's only once you're airborne or at a distance that 'ohhhh', the horse appears. Similarly, you can only see the full picture of alcohol, once it's a silhouette in the distance.

I've travelled from being distraught that I couldn't drink any more, from wistfully glancing over my shoulder, to finally seeing drinking as a total waste of time, to being elated that I never have to drink again, and charging ahead into my sober future. The longer you're sober and the better you feel, both physically and mentally, the more you will think 'I deserve *not* to drink' rather than 'I deserve a drink'.

HORROR MOVIE SET

For the sevens, eights and nines out there, and maybe even the fives and sixes, getting sober will feel like an inverted horror film.

You start out in a house replete with creepy lighting, weird noises, and a pervasive sense of doom. You keep sabotaging yourself (perhaps by running upstairs and hiding in the wardrobe, which is like, the most obvious place). You're scared and you don't know how to get out of this predicament.

When you get sober, you're on the same film set, but the glower has switched to a glow. The furniture is the same, but the lighting is rosy, there's a smell of baking, and birds are tweeting in the garden. You're no longer afraid of your own shadow. You were being stalked by a monster; now you're about to go eat some apple pie in the garden. It's bloody lovely.

Don't choose happy *hour*. You deserve bigger than that.

Choose a happy-ever-after instead.

WAKING UP INTO THE DREAM

5 AUGUST 2017

Last night I dreamt I was back in the cell at Brixton police station. When I was drinking, I always woke up into the nightmare. Now, I wake up into the dream.

Back in 2013, when I was only a couple of months sober, I wrote a list of 'Goals for 2014'. It was astronomically unrealistic. Buying a flat (how I was going to save at least 20K in one year, I don't know), getting a dog, learning a second language, writing a book, climbing Everest, yadda yadda. I showed it to my mum. She snorted (kindly), told me I was over-reaching, and crossed it all out, apart from two things; 'stay sober' and the humblest goal of 'get a new wardrobe'.

She took me shopping a lot in 2014. She bought me a lot of clothes. And I did stay sober. But the point was, she knew that if I stayed sober, everything would work out.

Those moonshot goals haven't materialized, yet. But, what I actually have is way better. Clearly, I've now written the book. I'm a full-time nanny to my housemate's gorgeous Wheaten Terrier, Barney, who is currently lying with his legs wide open, snoring his head off. I'm renting a room in the most beautiful house I've ever seen with my own eyes, with a bunch of friends I love.

I'm nowhere near owning my own place, but I do now own flat-pack furniture ('See that bed? I bought it!' I tell my friends, while they pretend to be impressed). I don't have a penny of debt. I'm single and genuinely happy about it, much as I would love to meet The Guy. He'll come along, eventually. I have solid-as-a-rock working relationships, fantastic friendships and am closer to my family than ever before. All of this happened because I'm sober. I'm happier than I ever, ever was while drinking, even when I was drinking somewhat 'moderately'.

I'm back in London now. I'm over-writing the shame memory map with wholesome memories, just as you might cover and re-invent a bad tattoo. There's a particular bus stop on Oxford Street, for the night bus to Hackney, that used to make me shudder. I stood there night after godforsaken night in my 20s with a Happy Meal (sound the irony klaxon), blind drunk and blinking back tears of puzzled despair. 'Why have I done this again. It's 2am! Again. I need to work tomorrow.'

I can walk past that bus stop now and I don't feel a thing: I don't live there any more.

I recently went to a comedy night. I asked the barman for a tonic. I didn't watch him make it, because I was watching the show. I took a long slurp and immediately felt weird. Dizzy, hot, heart racing, panicky. He'd given me a vodka tonic. I must have only had a fifth of a shot, but I felt it. And I hated it.

I took the drink straight back to the bar, got them to change it, and waited for the discombobulated feeling to depart. Ugh. It took an hour for me to feel normal again.

That mis-pour absolutely confirmed: nope, not for me. I don't need, or want, that feeling any more.

POSTSCRIPT

Something big happened a week ago. My dad died. From lung cancer, aged just 65. It happened quickly, within a month of him being diagnosed with pneumonia, but my brother and I were lucky enough to have the chance to say goodbye in the Philippines, where my dad had retired.

On our final night in the Philippines, my brother and I headed out into the neon-lit, seedy, snaking main street of Angeles city. We played pool, drank lemonade, talked about Dad and were in bed by midnight.

Five years ago, my MO would have been to get off my face, lose my brother, probably get mugged, somehow find my way back and then be absolutely hanging for my last day with my father. He would have smelled the booze on my breath as I said goodbye. None of that happened.

Dad was a complicated, challenging and remarkable man. He was fiercely intelligent, intimidating, sarcastic and formidable. Woe betide the fool, or the disobedient, or the entitled, around Dad. Having him as a father was, at times, difficult. But he was also an open-minded hippy, a baby-talking softie with animals, a tickle monster with kids, devil-may-care playful, always up for a go-faster adventure, totally proud and 'out' about his sobriety and intensely committed to helping others quit booze.

I sometimes joked that I loved and feared Dad in equal measure. He found it hard to show love, having experienced a less-than-loving childhood himself, but in his final days, those walls fell away and revealed his interior. He held our hands, cried, looked us straight in the eye, mouthed that he loved us, and my brother and I really, really believed it. We got to tell him the same, before he slipped away. What a gift.

Grief is up-down unpredictable, as you may have the misfortune of knowing. One minute I feel fine, but then something will remind me of Dad – a snatch of an Elvis Costello song, a book by John le Carré, the word 'gobshite', a black Labrador bounding past – and there'll be a sudden flood of toddler tears. Because I don't use alcohol to numb my sadness, there's no escape from it, no doorway to duck into, no umbrella to dive under. It soaks me to the skin. Then the dark skies brighten once more. Grief forecast: fine, then floods. It feels much like the monsoon season of the Philippines, which was thundering through the skies above Dad's hospital when he died.

I remember that I used to say, when asked if I would ever drink again. 'Well, obviously I have no intention of doing so, but perhaps something catastrophic will de-rail me...like the death of a parent.' But, it hasn't even occurred to me to drink on this sorrow. It's not in my repertoire of reactions any more. I know drinking would not be self-soothing; it would be self-sabotage.

Dad was 23 years sober when he died. One of my absolute favourite memories of him was when I was 24. He was ten years sober then, while I was growing increasingly reliant on booze. He'd figured out that I thought dancing was impossible without alcohol, so one afternoon, he whacked on 'Sultans of Swing' by Dire Straits and started dancing around the living room. There he was, the Chief Executive who was often on the Northern Irish news being all gruff and businessy, shaking his arse at me like a showgirl.

'See!' he shouted, over the music. 'You CAN dance sober. If I can, you can.' I cringed, held my hands up as a shield, refused to let him pull me to my feet and yelled, 'Noooo, stop!' but I secretly thought he was the coolest person ever.

My dad was just one of hundreds of sober people who helped me see that there was a different way to live. Who emphatically told me, 'Don't stay there – it's better over here.' They were right. It is better.

And, he was right. You absolutely can dance sober.

If I can, you can.

Want more? Go to www.unexpectedjoy.co.uk or follow @unexpectedjoyof on Instagram.

SOURCES

INTRODUCTION
'Sober' definition, synonyms and antonyms, *Oxford English Dictionary*, en.oxforddictionaries.com

67% want to cut back on drinking, five million did Dry January this year. Walker, Rob, (2017), 'Forget the hangover, under-25s turn to mindful drinking', the *Guardian*, www.theguardian.com

43% of women want to drink less, 84% of men want to drink less. McVeigh, Tracy (2015), '"Women on the wagon" club together to cut back on drinking', the *Guardian*, www.theguardian.com

A fifth of Brits now teetotal, a quarter of women teetotal, 43% haven't drunk in the past week. *Adult Drinking Habits in Great Britain 2005–2016 survey*, Office for National Statistics, www.ons.gov.uk

30 TOOLS FOR THE FIRST 30 DAYS
White matter study. 2013, 'Exercise may prevent alcohol from damaging the brain'

Running creates new neurons. Dahl, Melissa, 'How Neuroscientists Explain the Mind-Clearing Magic of Running', *New York Magazine*, www.nymag.com.

Caroly, H.C., et al., (2013), 'Aerobic exercise moderates the effect of heavy alcohol consumption on white matter damage', *Alcoholism: Clinical and Experimental Research*, Vol.37, No.9,1508–15

10 minutes of exercise reduces alcohol cravings. Sampuran, Ussher, M., et al. (2004), 'Acute effect of a brief bout of exercise on alcohol urges', *Addiction*, Vol.99, No.12,1542–7

Writing heals wounds, and means fewer doctor visits. Vedhara, Kavita, et al. (2017), 'The effects of expressive writing before or after punch biopsy on wound healing', *Brain, Behaviour and Immunity*, Vol.61, 217–27

Pennebaker, J.W., Beall, S.,K. (1986), 'Confronting a traumatic event: toward an understanding of inhibition and disease', *Journal of Abnormal Psychology*, Vol.95, No.3, 274–81

Missouri music study. Ferguson, Yuna, L., Sheldon, Kennon, M. (2013), 'Trying to be happier really can work: Two experimental studies', *Journal of Positive Psychology*, Vol.8, No.1, 22–33

65% success rate addictive voice recognition. Trimpey, Jack (1996), *Rational Recovery: The New Cure for Substance Addiction*, Pocket Books

ADDICTIVE VOICE RECOGNITION
Jack Trimpey quote. *Rational Recovery*, www.rational.org

HELLO, SOCIALLY AWKWARD TEEN
Brain blood flow introvert. Johnson, D.L., Wiebe, J.S., Gold, S.M., Andreasen, N.C., Hichwa, R.D., Watkins, G.L., Boles, Ponto, L.L. (1999), 'Cerebral blood flow and personality: a positron emission tomography study', *American Journal of Psychiatry*, Vol.156, No.2, 252–7

Human faces extroverts/introverts. Fishman, Inna, Ng, Rowena, Bellugi, Ursula (2011), 'Do extraverts process social stimuli differently from introverts?', *Journal of Cognitive Neuroscience*, Vol.2, No.2, 67–73

WATERFALLS AND TREES BECKON
Stress recovery during exposure to natural and urban environments. Ulrich, R.S., Simons, R.F., Losito, B.D., Fiorito, E., Miles, M.A., Zelson, M. (1991), 'Stress recovery during exposure to natural and urban environments', *Journal of Environmental Psychology*, Vol.11, 201–30

View through a window may influence recovery from surgery. Ulrich, R.S. (1984), 'View through a window may influence recovery from surgery', *Science, New Series*, Vol.224, No.4647, 420–1

Barton, Jo, Pretty, Jules (2010), 'What is the

Best Dose of Nature and Green Exercise for Improving Mental Health? A Multi-Study Analysis', *Environmental Science and Technology*, Vol.44, 3947–55

Aspinall, Peter, Mavros, Panagiotis, Coyne, Richard, Roe, Jennifer (2013), 'The urban brain: analysing outdoor physical activity with mobile EEG', *British Journal of Sports Medicine*, Vol.49, 272–6

A GRATITUDE ADJUSTMENT
Gratitude – 92 per cent are happier. Ryan, M., J., (2009), *Attitudes of Gratitude, 10th Anniversary Edition: How to Give and Receive Joy Every Day of Your Life*

Sleep improved by gratitude. Wood, A.M., Joseph, S., Lloyd, J., Atkins, S. (2009), 'Gratitude influences sleep through the mechanism of pre-sleep cognitions', *Journal of Psychosomatic Research*, Vol.66, No.1, 43–8

Eight different studies of depression. Lambert, N.M., Fincham, F.D., Stillman, T.F. (2012), 'Gratitude and depressive symptoms: the role of positive reframing and positive emotion', *Cognition and Emotion Journal*, Vol.24, No.4, 615–33

Gratitude lessens anxiety. Vernon, L.L., Dillon, J.M., Steiner, A.R. (2009), 'Proactive coping, gratitude, and posttraumatic stress disorder in college women', *Anxiety, Stress and Coping Journal*, Vol.22, No.1, 117–27

Cardiac health improved by gratitude. Dubois, C., M., Beach, S.R., Kashdan, T.B., Nyer, M.B., Park, E.R. (2012), 'Positive psychological attributes and cardiac outcomes: associations, mechanisms, and interventions', *Journal of Psychosomatic Research*, Vol.53, No.4, 303–18

Memory improved by gratitude. Ramírez, E., Ortega, A.E., Chamorro, A., Colmenoro, J.M. (2014), 'A program of positive intervention in the elderly: memories, gratitude and forgiveness', *Journal of Aging & Mental Health*, Vol.18, No.4, 463–70

Lawyer study. Aspinwall, L. G., Brown, T. R., Tabery, J. (2012), 'The double-edged sword: Does biomechanism increase or decrease judges' sentencing of psychopaths?' *Science, AAAS*, Vol.337 846–9

I GIVE UP MY FAVOURITE BLOODSPORT
Coffee study. Aronson, E., Willerman, B., Floyd, J. (1966), 'The effect of a pratfall on increasing interpersonal attractiveness', *Psychonomic Science*, Vol.4, 227–8

TELLING PEOPLE
Contemplation of suicide 120 times more likely. Pompili, M., Serafini, G., Innamorati, M., Dominici, G., Gerracuti, S., Kotzalidis, G.D., Serra, G., Girardi, P., Janiri, L., Tatarelli, R., Sher, L., Lester, D. (2010), 'Suicidal behaviour and alcohol abuse', *International Journal of Environmental Research and Public Health*

THE BRAIN BOUNCES BACK
Brain pathways paper. 'Addiction changes the brain's communication pathways', *Mental Help*, www.mentalhelp.net

Exercise flushes adrenaline and cortisol. 'Exercising to relax', *Harvard Health Publications*, www.health.harvard.edu

PHYSICAL WINS OF QUITTING
Cheeks flush when drinking. 'Alcohol and health', *Family Doctor*, www.familydoctor.com

Vogue quote. Kim, Monica (2016), 'Why Giving Up Alcohol Could Transform Your Skin', *Vogue*, www.vogue.com

Hair loss can be caused by drinking. 'Hair loss and drinking', *Belgravia Centre*, www.belgraviacentre.com

Snickers bar and half a stone. Smith, Rebecca, 'Average wine drinker puts on half a stone of fat a year', the *Telegraph*.

REM sleep affected by drinking. Chan, J. K. M., Trinder, J., Colrain, I. M. and Nicholas, C. L. (2015), 'The Acute Effects of Alcohol on Sleep Electroencephalogram Power Spectra in Late Adolescence', *Alcoholism: Clinical and Experimental Research Journal*, Vol.39, No.2, 291–9

Dehydration can cause anxiety. 'Anxiety symptoms: 8 surprising triggers', *Medbroadcast*, www.medbroadcast.com

SOBER DATING
OkCupid online dating profiles research cited in Ansari, Aziz, *Modern Romance: An Investigation* (Penguin, 2015)

Anne Lamott quote. Lamott, Anne, (2017),'12 truths I learned from life and writing', *Ted*, www.ted.com

VANILLA SEX
Wilson G.T., Lawson D.M. (1976), 'Effects of alcohol on sexual arousal in women', *Journal of Abnormal Psychology*, Vol.85, No.5, 489–97

Wilson G.T., Lawson D.M. (1978), 'Expectancies, alcohol, and sexual arousal in women', *Journal of Abnormal Psychology*, Vol.87, No.3, 358–67

Malatesta V. J., Pollack R.H., Crotty T.D., Peacock L.J. (1982), 'Acute alcohol-intoxication and female orgasmic response', *Journal of Sex Research*, Vol.18, 1–17.

UNPLUGGING FROM THE ALCOHOL MATRIX
Source 80–95% films/TV portray drinking in a positive light. Koordeman, R., Anschutz, D. J., Engels, R. C. M. E., (2014), 'The Effect of Positive and Negative Movie Alcohol Portrayals on Transportation and Attitude Toward the Movie', *Alcoholism: Clinical & Experimental Research*, Vol.7, No.4, 1392–431

Sarah Hepola quote. Hepola, Sarah (2016), 'Ask a former drunk: How do I keep my sobriety from being the thing that defines me?' *Jezebel*, www.jezebel.com

French Instagram hoax. 'Like my addiction', *Addict Aide*, www.addictaide.fr

HMRC shows that people buy double what they admit drinking. 'Teetotaller numbers rise in UK with one in five adults not drinking', the *Guardian*, www.theguardian.co.uk

43% of women want to drink less, 84% of men want to drink less, one in six health developing problems, 437K wound up in hospital. McVeigh, Tracy (2015), '"Women on the wagon" club together to cut back on drinking', the *Guardian*, www.theguardian.com

A quarter of women want to quit drinking altogether. 'Club Soda survey', *Club Soda*, www.joinclubsoda.co.uk

Alcohol worse than crack or heroin. Nutt, David, J., King, Leslie, A., Phillips, Lawrence, D., 'Drug harms in the UK: a multicriteria decision analysis', the *Lancet*, Vol.367, No.9752, 1558–65

Professor David Nutt asked to resign. Tran, Mark (2009), 'Government drug adviser David Nutt sacked', the *Guardian*, www.theguardian.com

2015 report shows alcohol tax profits in England more than double costs. Snowdon, Christopher (2015), 'Alcohol and the public purse; do drinkers pay their way?' *Institute of Economic Affairs Discussion Paper*, No.63

63% of regular and occasional drinkers would not be happy alcohol-free. Hachette UK online survey

Drinking international number one killer. 'Global Status Report on alcohol and health 2011', *World Health Organisation*, www.who.int

Alcohol deaths 2014. 'Alcohol Related Deaths in the United Kingdom: Registered in 2014', *Office for National Statistics*, www.ons.gov.uk

90% of drinkers think alcohol is fine. Hachette UK online survey

Couples who drink together stay together. Birditt, Kira S. et al., 'Drinking Patterns Among Older Couples: Longitudinal Associations With Negative Marital Quality', *The Journals of Gerontology*, Series B, gbw073

Alcohol linked to eight cancers, you're five times more likely to die from alcohol than car accident. 'What is a safe level of alcohol to drink?' the *Irish Catholic*, www.irishcatholic.ie

Heavy drinking causes life span to be shortened 10–12 years. 'Alcohol Use Disorder Report from A.D.A.M', the *New York Times Health Guide*, www.nytimes.com

No level of alcohol safe. 'UK Chief Medical Officer's Alcohol Guidelines Review 2016', *Department of Health*, www.gov.uk

Alcohol a carcinogen – half of people don't know this. 'Alcohol Behaviour and Attitudes 2014 survey', *Alcohol Health Alliance*, www.ahauk.org

Boston University study. Nelson, David E. et al. (2013), 'Alcohol-Attributable Cancer Deaths and Years of Potential Life Lost in the United States', *American Journal of Public Health* Vol.103, No.4, 641–8

Brain shrinkage even in moderate drinkers. Topiwala, Anya, et al. (2017), 'Moderate alcohol consumption as risk factor for adverse brain outcomes and cognitive decline', *British Medical Journal*, Vol.357, j2353

Drinking less important to teens. Birdwell, Jonathan, Wybron, Ian (2015), 'Character and Moderation: encouraging the next generation of responsible drinker', *Demos*, www.demos.co.uk

Teetotallers Britain 2015 ONS figures. 'Adult Drinking Habits in Great Britain 2013', *Office for National Statistics*, www.ons.gov.uk

Half of young people drank in the past week. 'Adult drinking habits in Great Britain: 2005–2016', *Office for National Statistics*, www.ons.gov.uk

Drug use on decline. 'Statistics on drug misuse: England, 2016 report', *NHS Digital*, www.content.digital.nhs.uk

Coffee shops increased by 12%. 'Project Café UK', *World Coffee Portal*, www.worldcoffeeportal.com

Half of UK's nightclubs closed. Connolly, Jim (2015), 'UK nightclubs closing at "alarming rate", industry figures suggest', *BBC*, www.bbc.co.uk

MINDFULNESS STOPS ME FROM GOING INSANE

Naming emotions helps. Lieberman, Matthew D., Eisenberger, Naomi I., Crockett, Molly J., Tom, Sabrina M., Pfeifer, Jennifer H., Way, Baldwin M. (2007), 'Putting Feelings Into Words', *Psychological Science*, Vol.18, No.5, 421–8

FBI hostage negotiaters, plus more studies on naming emotions. McMains, Michael, J., Mullins, Wayman, C. (2010), *Crisis Negotiations: Managing Critical Incidents and Hostage Situations in Law Enforcement and Corrections*, ed.4

Stanford – trying not to feel something doesn't work. Gross, James, J. (1997), 'Hiding Feelings: The Acute Effects of Inhibiting Negative and Positive Emotion', *Journal of Abnormal Psychology*, Vol.106 No.1 95–103

Polar bears study. Wegner, Daniel, M., Schneider, David, J. (2003), 'The White Bear Story', *Psychological Inquiry*, Vol.14, 326–9

Doorways cause you to forget. Radvansky, Gabriel A., Krawietz, Sabine A., Tamplin, Andrea K. (2011), 'Walking through doorways causes forgetting: Further explorations', *Quarterly Journal of Experimental Psychology*, Vol.64, No.8

THE MYTH VS THE REALITY OF BIG DRINKERS

Graduates twice as likely to drink hazardously. Sassi, F. (2015), *Tackling Harmful Alcohol Use: Economics and Public Health Policy*

People twice as likely to binge drink when earn over £40K. 'Adult Drinking Habits in Great Britain: 2005–2016', *Office for National Statistics*, www.ons.gov.uk

A quarter of rock stars die of alcohol/drugs. Bellis M. A., Hennell T., Lushey C., et al., (2007), 'Elvis to Eminem: quantifying the price of fame through early mortality of European and North American rock and pop stars', *Journal of Epidemiology & Community Health*, Vol.61, 896–901

Doctors twice as likely to be alcoholics. Dr Craig, Jim, *Doctors as patients*, www.castlecraig.co.uk

Drinkers have higher IQs. White, J. W., Gale, C. R., Batty, G. D. (2012), 'Intelligence quotient in childhood and the risk of illegal drug use in middle-age: the 1958 National Child Development Survey', *Annals of Epidemiology Journal*, Vol.22, No.9, 654–7

Childhood trauma leads to addiction. Felitti V.J., Anda, R.F., et al (1998), 'Relationship of childhood abuse and household dysfunction to many of the leading causes of death in adults. The Adverse Childhood Experiences (ACE) Study', *American Journal of Preventive Medicine*, Vol.14, No.4

Source addictive personality. Littlefield, A. and Sher, K. (2010), 'The multiple, distinct ways that personality contributes to alcohol use disorders', *Journal of Social and Personality Psychology Compass*, Vol.4, No.9, 767–82

CHOOSE YOUR OWN SOBER ADVENTURE

Anne Lamott quotes. Lamott, Anne (2017), '12 truths I learned from life and writing', *Ted*, www.ted.com

60% of recoveries The Grapevine. The Grapevine (2001). Cited in Neal, McKenzie, Richard (2008), *The path to addiction...and other troubles we were born to know*

Stanford University 16-year study. Moos, H. Rudolph, Moos, Bernice, S. (2006), 'Participation in Treatment and Alcoholics Anonymous: A 16-Year Follow-Up of Initially Untreated Individuals', *Journal of Clinical Psychology*, Vol.62, No.6, 735–50

Source 42K people study. 'Alcohol Consumption and Problems in the General Population: Findings from the 1992 National Longitudinal Alcohol Epidemiologic survey' (2002), *NIH Publication* No.02–4997

Project MATCH. Ashton, Mike (1999), 'Project Match: unseen colossus', *Drug and alcohol findings library*

Project MATCH same success rates. 'NIAAA Reports Project MATCH Main Findings' (1997), *Journal of Studies on Alcohol*, www.niaaa.nih.gov

I don't, rather than I can't study. Patrick, Vanessa M., Hagtvedt, Henrik, '"I don't" versus "I can't": When empowered refusal motivates goal-directed behavior,' *Journal*

of Consumer Research, Vol.39, No.2, 371–81

Halvorson, Heidi, Grant, Ph.D, 'The Amazing Power of "I don't" (rather than "I can't")', *Huffington Post*, www.huffingtonpost.com

Slate magazine and the Associated Press. Associated Press (2017), *The Associated Press Stylebook 2017: and Briefing on Media Law, Basic Books*, cited in Siegel, Zachary (2017), 'Journalists, Stop Using Words Like Addict and Drug Abuser', *Slate* magazine, www.slate.com

66 days to form a new habit. Lally, P., van Jaarsveld, C. H. M., Potts, H. W. W. and Wardle, J. (2010), 'How are habits formed: Modelling habit formation in the real world', *The European Journal of Social Psychology*, Vol.40, 998–1009

Rosenthal 1978 345 studies. Rosenthal, R., Rubin, D. (1978), 'Issues in summarizing the first 345 studies of interpersonal expectancy effects', *Journal of Behavioral and Brain Sciences*, Vol.1, No.3, 410–15

Cochrane review. Ferri, M., Amato, L., Davoli, M. (2006), 'Alcoholics Anonymous and other 12-step programmes for alcohol dependence', *Cochrane Database of Systematic Reviews*

INDEX

ACKNOWLEDGEMENTS

There are four whip-smart, wise, funny and inspirational women without whom this book never would have happened.

Firstly, my mum, who has saved me from more perilous snowstorms than I can ever count. My 'accountability coach' Kate Faithfull-Williams, who read every word, cheered me on, dispensed clever feedback and provided me with the fake deadlines I needed to keep chugging along. Thirdly, my incredible agent, Rachel Mills of Furniss Lawton, who I now never want to be without. And finally, my sunshine-warm, instantly likeable publisher, Stephanie Jackson, who ardently believed in this book – and me – from the very start.

They say 'it takes a village' to get sober. Indeed, hundreds of people helped me; hoisting me up on their shoulders whenever I wanted to give up. My GGAC sisters, who provided me with a soft place to fall and honest velvet-gloved guidance. The BFB, *Home*, The Mellowship: I have so much love for these groups. Jen and Mark: eternal gratitude that I have you by my side. Holly, Laurie, Bridget, Jen and Jess: my sober tribe, who I know would rush to my aid at 2am if I ever needed them to.

I owe a bottomless debt to my beloved family and friends, who loved me when I didn't love myself, and who stuck by me when I was an absolute bloody nightmare. The Grays, the Clarkes, the Smallwoods, the Bradys, the McGinns, and many more besides. Alice, the Purser-Barriffs, Helen, Laura McAdam, Kate Colliver, Gemma, Laura Sibley, Matt and Piumi, Iain and Emily, Andreina and anyone I've forgotten; thanks for making it through the dark years to meet Cath 2.0. Who is, hopefully, a lot less of an ordeal.

It definitely takes a village to make a book too. I'd like to thank the marvellous team at Aster, who have been a constant joy to work with: Pauline, Karen, Ashley, Yasia, Sabrina, Nicky and many more. The Aster team have made this process the most rewarding of my working life thus far.

All of you have, and will continue to, feature in my gratitude lists.